HOW TO MARKET
LEGAL SERVICES

Robert W. Denney

VNR VAN NOSTRAND REINHOLD COMPANY

Library of Congress Catalog Card Number: 84-5255
ISBN: 0-442-21980-6

Manufactured in the United States of America

Published by Van Nostrand Reinhold Company Inc.
135 West 50th Street
New York, New York 10020

Van Nostrand Reinhold Company Limited
Molly Millars Lane
Wokingham, Berkshire RG11 2PY, England

Van Nostrand Reinhold
480 Latrobe Street
Melbourne, Victoria 3000, Australia

Macmillan of Canada
Division of Gage Publishing Limited
164 Commander Boulevard
Agincourt, Ontario M1S 3C7, Canada

15 14 13 12 11 10 9 8 7 6 5 4 3 2 1

Library of Congress Cataloging in Publication Data

Denney, Robert W.
  How to market legal services.

  Includes index.
  1. Practice of law—United States. I. Title.
KF300.D46 1984   349.73'068   84-5255
ISBN 0-442-21980-6   347.30068

To all the attorneys everywhere who are confronted with so much change in the profession—I hope this book helps.

Preface

This book is designed, quite unabashedly, to be the most comprehensive and authoritative reference work on the new, complex, and often misunderstood subject of marketing legal services.

It is intended for use by the sole practitioner, the specialty or "boutique" firm, the large general practice firm, or the growing category of large national and multinational firms. It covers the subject from both a management point of view—the development and implementation of an organized marketing plan—and from the individual attorney's point of view—the development of his or her own personal marketing skills.

I have tried to provide a conceptual explanation of the entire marketing process as it applies to a law firm as well as the specific steps needed to develop and implement a marketing plan on any scale for any size firm.

I sincerely hope that this book will provide the reader not only with a complete treatment of a new and rapidly developing field, but also with a simplified, down-to-earth approach to a subject that interests many attorneys, disturbs others, but is of vital importance to all.

Robert W. Denney

Contents

PART I
OVERVIEW

Marketing for Lawyers

The private practice of law used to be a whale of a lot easier and a lot less complex than it is today.

In the so-called "good old days" a young lawyer graduated from law school and either hung out his own shingle or joined a law firm. If he joined a law firm, he (there were very few "shes" in the legal profession in those days) began the long but generally secure process of working his way up in the firm toward the eventual goal of partner. He did this by working on increasingly complex client matters that were given to him by one of the partners in the firm. He rarely met clients in his early days as an associate, because the partners handled the contacts with clients. He never had to worry about obtaining new clients, because the clients were just always there or were brought in by the efforts of more senior partners who had earned the designation of "rainmakers." Eventually the young lawyer was admitted to that great inner sanctum of partnership. Soon he began taking over clients that had been handled by older partners who were now retiring. He still didn't have to worry about obtaining new business because that just flowed in automatically as the result of doing "quality legal work" (whatever that meant) for clients who then referred other clients to the firm. Clients rarely if ever challenged the fees they were charged. The partners and the firm as a whole maintained a low profile to the general public, although they might have been active in the community or in professional groups.

Then all hell broke loose.

In 1977, in one of those cases the legal profession likes to refer to as "landmark" (*Bates* v. *Osteen*), the Supreme Court handed down a decision that lawyers could not be prohibited from advertising. Suddenly the entire profession, from the American Bar Association down to the sole practitioner in the middle of the farm belt, had to deal with a whole new set of ground rules. Dire forecasts were made as to what would happen to fees, law firms' profits, and, perhaps most important of all, the quality of law that would henceforth be practiced.

The legal profession just wasn't the same anymore. The practice of law, which previously had been both an honorable and an orderly profession, started to become more and more confusing; some people even called it "chaotic." The Supreme Court, the pinnacle of the legal profession in the United States, was being accused of ruining the profession.

THE ICEBERG COMETH

In the light of both prior and subsequent events, however, the Bates case was merely the tip of the iceberg that had been affecting the practice of law before then and has continued to do so since. While the vast majority of lawyers still do not advertise, the Bates case did give them the option. At the same time, it opened up a whole new area in the practice of law which has come to be called "marketing." We'll come back to that in a minute. First, let's look at some other parts of the iceberg.

One of the other factors affecting the legal profession is the current oversupply of lawyers, referred to as a "glut" by some people. In 1968 there were 130,000 lawyers in the United States. By 1981 there were more than 600,000 lawyers, and unless something happens to change the trend, it is projected that by 1986 there will be 750,000 lawyers in the United States. Several years ago at an investiture in Minneapolis, the presiding judge stated, "There are now more lawyers than lakes in Minnesota." And there are 10,000 lakes in Minnesota! Despite tighter standards, law schools are still turning out more lawyers than can be absorbed by both corporate and private practice. The amount of legal work has grown dramatically, but it has not kept pace with the growth in the number of lawyers. In other words—the competition for legal work has become intense.

Several other factors have also been affecting the way in which law is practiced today. In 1978 three new legal publications made their debuts—*The American Lawyer, The National Law Journal,* and *The Legal Times.* But these were not scholarly journals devoted to the discussion of legal issues and interpretations of the law. They addressed the *business* of practicing law. They even reported in journalistic fashion what was going on in the profession and in particular law firms. They did—and still do—discuss out in the open subjects that lawyers would never have discussed or wished to read in public even ten years ago. They treat events and trends in the legal profession as newsworthy.

Now there is another publication out of Atlanta, *Attorneys Marketing Report,* which is devoted entirely to business development activities of lawyers and law firms. It is safe to say that, prior to 1977, there would not have been a market for this newsletter.

Finally, the growth of in-house legal departments has had an increasing effect on law firms in recent years. First of all, these departments, which are frequently the equivalent of law firms in themselves, have taken over the handling of many functions, from routine work to litigation, that previously had been turned over to an outside law firm. Furthermore, companies have grown more selective in giving business to outside counsel. A firm tends to get the nod these days on the basis of knowledge about a particular matter, not because of traditional ties with the company. Moreover, most corporations (even smaller ones) use several law firms, whereas years ago they tended to give all their legal business to one firm. These developments have resulted in a reduction of work going to outside firms.

MARKETING IS A RESULT, NOT A CAUSE

The Bates case, the oversupply of lawyers, the new journalistic approach to the profession, and the increase and expansion of in-house legal departments have been the major parts of the iceberg that has changed the way law is practiced today in the United States.

And, because these have all tended to dramatically increase competition within the profession, they have led to the need for lawyers and law firms to market their services. This is an extremely important point for the great numbers of lawyers who still oppose the concept of marketing to understand. *It is not marketing which has caused change in the legal profession. It is the changes in the legal profession which have caused the need for marketing.* Furthermore, the impact of these changes—and the subsequent impact of marketing—will be felt for a very long time. They will also require lawyers to learn a whole new set of skills.

New practices, new policies, and even new terminology are becoming part of the practice of law. "Public relations," "market research," "market share," "positioning," "targeting," and "marketing strategies" are just some of the terms that have moved from the giant consumer products companies into the partners' meetings of law firms. Most lawyers are not sure what these terms mean, let alone what they have to do with the practice of law. A few firms have even created a position they call Director or Coordinator of Marketing and, in many cases, have filled that position with a nonlawyer!

What is rapidly happening in the profession was succinctly expressed by the managing partner of one of the country's largest and most prestigious law firms: "While many lawyers still do not realize it, it isn't a question of whether to market or not. It is only a question of how to do it effectively."

NOT REALLY NEW

The strange thing is that, while the *concept* of marketing is new to the legal profession, the *purpose* of marketing is not. Firms have always had the need to (1) retain their good clients, (2) obtain new clients, and (3) promote the firm's image or reputation. These functions, while not specifically defined, were generally carried out by a small group of partners who were the "rainmakers" for the firm who brought in new business on a regular and seemingly effortless basis. They generally maintained an appropriate visibility in the community. Not surprisingly, the founders of the firms usually had this ability, because, if they hadn't marketed their practice at the beginning, they wouldn't have had any clients to serve. Later additions to firms and the next generation of partners, however, mistakenly assumed that the firms developed solely by the founding partners "doing quality work" without any marketing except for, at worst, some occasional rainmaking.

What has happened to most of the old-line firms in recent years is that the founding partners have retired or died. They are no longer around, "filling the pipeline" with new business for the other lawyers to handle. The current generation of senior and middle-level partners in many firms has never had to generate new business—their clients have generally been passed on to them—and they don't know how to obtain new business either. This has provided the opportunity for new firms, and a new generation of founding partners, to open practices and acquire clients from some of the established firms. What it all adds up to is that there are more lawyers and more firms competing with each other for the available legal business. Furthermore, the partners in the leadership positions of many of the firms do not know how to market their services competitively because they have never had to in their ten, twenty, or thirty years of practicing law.

There is a misconception that marketing is just for large firms. Quite the contrary. The need to market exists for *every* firm. Furthermore, the principles and techniques of marketing are essentially the same for the sole practitioner, the small specialty firm, the large general practice firm, and the very large national or multinational firm. Naturally, the larger the firm, the more opportunities there are and the bigger and more complex the marketing program must be. But the need, and the ability, to market exists for every size practice.

A DEFINITION OF MARKETING

For the most part, only people who have been involved in marketing have a clear understanding of what it encompasses. (Perhaps marketing professionals would prefer to keept it that way!) Most of the rest of the world, and particularly lawyers, think that marketing is just one-dimensional, that it is solely a cost center. But marketing is not just a brochure; it is not just public relations or selling or advertising. It is a coordinated effort that, when applied to law firms, has some very specific aspects. Therefore it is important at the onset to have a clear understanding of what we are talking about when we refer to marketing. The following definition, which I have evolved over a period of time, seems to capture everything involved.

Marketing of legal services is the effective execution of all the activities involved in profitably increasing the level of net business by serving the needs and wants of clients.

There is more to this definition than meets the eye or the mind at first, so we must take it apart and analyze it.

In addition to a whole new series of purely marketing functions, marketing also includes nearly every activity a law firm performs. It is not just lunch with a prospective client or accepting a referral from another lawyer. It also includes telephone procedures, certain office routines, and even the way bills are rendered. Practically everything a law firm does can be looked at with a marketing as well as an operational perspective.

Marketing must be *profitable;* it does not exist for its own sake or to perpetuate the existence of a Business Development Committee. Marketing does not mean, for example, that a firm should spend $150,000 a year to increase its net billings $80,000. To be profitable, therefore, marketing must be productive and the marketing program must be so planned that its productivity can be measured.

Marketing is concerned with increasing the level of *net* business, not just obtaining new business. It focuses as much on current clients, client retention, and client development (i.e., "cross-selling") as it does on obtaining new clients.

Finally, marketing begins with the needs and wants of clients as *they* perceive them, not the lawyer.

This is probably the hardest point for all professionals, not just lawyers, to grasp. It is what the *client* thinks or perceives that is important in terms of marketing, not what the lawyer or the firm thinks—or feels they know. No matter how high you feel the quality of your work is or how well you feel you serve your clients, if they don't think so, then you are going to have problems in retaining clients as well as in making the practice grow.

It is also important to understand what we mean by growth. We are not talking about growth that is obtained by just raising fees or hourly rates. That is not marketing, although some amount of sales ability is sometimes needed when you present your bill to the client at the end of a case or matter! What we mean by growth is growing in quality of work, services to clients, billable hours, and client base. Profitable, healthy growth must include all of these.

Finally, we should understand what is meant by "quality work" in a marketing context. Many lawyers define quality work in a technical sense, i.e., work that meets various legal and firm standards. But clients define quality work in a different light. To clients it is work that is timely, understandable, and, most important of all, accomplishes their objectives. Many lawyers still think quality work is drawing up a legally precise agreement of sale or preparing a comprehensive brief. To the client, however, the lawyer did quality work if the sale went through as the client wanted it or if the client won the case. It is often that simple.

Therefore, lawyers must keep both definitions of quality work in mind—theirs and the client's—and work diligently to live up to both.

EVERYONE MUST GET INTO THE ACT

One of the pleasant aspects of marketing in law firms is that there are so many things to be done that every lawyer can find something he or she can enjoy doing as part of the marketing effort. And one of the most sobering aspects is that the job is so complicated and so important that everyone *must* participate. Rainmaking isn't enough anymore; business development in a law firm today requires broad-based, firm-wide effort.

For all the reasons discussed above and others, competition in the legal profession has become so fierce—unless you're the only practitioner for a hundred miles—and clients have become so sophisticated and demanding that no single person or small group of rainmakers can do an adequate marketing job for the entire firm. Just like a major piece of litigation, it takes teamwork. Everyone must get into the act, and fortunately everyone can. There is so much involved in legal marketing that even the most insecure lawyer can find something satisfying to do.

And therein lies one of the secrets of successful marketing for a law firm.

Each lawyer must enjoy what he is doing as part of the marketing program. A shy introvert probably won't enjoy making a presentation to the house counsel and top management of a major corporation—and will probably make a mess of it. A person who dislikes classical music would probably hate being told he must join the board of the local symphony orchestra. And the person who regards golf as a waste of time would probably resist being asked to join a country club in order to make contacts.

But the beauty in marketing legal services is that a firm doesn't have to push square pegs into round holes. Such a broad range of activities can aid the marketing program that, with a little thought and effort, people will find things in their "comfort zone" that they enjoy doing and will therefore do well. There is a personal bonus in this too: the lawyer broadens his or her horizon at the same time as the firm is helped to grow.

There is something else that every lawyer should appreciate about marketing. *Marketing is a process,* a process very similar to what is involved in the practice of law. It begins with a period of research or discovery. This is followed by a period of planning or organization. Finally, you must persuade the client or prospect of the correctness of using you and your firm. The process is much the same; only the application is different.

One final but important point about marketing in the legal profession: there is a big difference between marketing consumer products and marketing legal services. The law is a profession, not a trade or a business. Many marketing techniques that work well for a business may not be appropriate for a law firm. Marketing a general practice law firm is not the same as marketing a line of frozen foods; marketing one's skills in a specialty area of the law is not the same as introducing a new laundry detergent. The principles are the same, but the techniques, and the applications of these techniques, are totally different. Therefore, the development of a marketing plan for a law firm calls for not only a thorough understanding of the marketing process, but also the experience and judgment to know what is appropriate when applying that process to the legal profession.

The New Self-Image of the Lawyer Today

The many changes that have occurred in the legal profession since the late 1970s have not only affected the practice of law and how it is to be marketed, but they have also affected the individual attorney. Until all this turmoil began, most lawyers had a pretty clear self-image, or at least a pretty clear idea of the image they were expected to present to the outside world.

Now, as a result of these changes as well as heightened public interest in the profession and how it operates, many lawyers are groping for their own personal viewpoint regarding these changes and how to adjust to them. In other words, they are trying to develop a new self-image in the midst of all this chaos.

After nearly eight years of working with law firms on marketing programs, I believe that lawyers today see themselves in basically one of five ways.

1. *The Dedicated Lawyer.* This is the contemporary version of the "old-time" lawyer who believed that if you just did quality work

(in the professional sense) the practice would grow. He or she is much the same as the old "green eyeshade accountant." The dedicated lawyer was not (and is not today) opposed to promoting the practice, but has just never thought of it, or never thought it was really necessary. There are several lawyers of this type in almost every firm.

2. *The Anti-Marketing Attorney.* This is the Dedicated Lawyer who also carries a gun, loaded for all those people such as other lawyers and marketing consultants who believe that you must market your practice in order to make it grow. This type of lawyer considers marketing unprofessional and probably unethical as well. He or she is outspoken and at times almost violent in opposition to any organized effort that involves the expenditure of time or money to promote the practice. There are still generally a number of attorneys of this type in every firm of any size.

3. *The Anxious But Insecure Attorney.* This attorney is similar to the Dedicated Lawyer except that he or she realizes that times and the profession have changed and that something should probably be done in the way of marketing the practice. However, because this type of attorney does not know what is entailed or what should be done, he or she is insecure about it. Therefore, such a person anxiously ponders the subject, and even agrees that something should be done about it, but never actually does anything about it. Most firms have a number of attorneys that fall into this category.

4. *The Modern-Day Rainmaker.* If the Anti-Marketing Attorney is one extreme of the spectrum, this is the other. He—and I say "he" because I have never met a woman lawyer of this type—is more salesman than lawyer. In some firms he may hardly produce any billable hours at all. He concentrates almost exclusively on "bringing in new business" (sometimes of dubious quality or ripe with conflicts) and then criticizes the rest of the lawyers because they cannot do the work for all these wonderful new clients he has obtained. There is another version of this basic type—the lawyer who is so busy promoting himself that he never finds time to serve his clients and doesn't promote the firm either. It is generally only in the larger firms that this type of lawyer is found and, fortunately, not too often.

5. *The Modern Lawyer.* This term probably best describes the emerging type of lawyer today. This lawyer appreciates the fact that there are three essential ingredients for success in the practice of law today—professional, marketing, and management. He or she attempts to understand what is required in each of these areas, and tries to develop personal skills in the areas they feel best suited for while developing an appreciation for those in the firm who possess skills or interest in other areas. Modern Lawyers are secure in their self-image because they know what the ground rules of the profession are today and where they are most comfortable. There are a growing number of this type of lawyer in most firms today.

My experience has been that, once the partners and associates in a firm understand what marketing legal services is really all about, they develop either a greater appreciation of or at least a tolerance for the subject. This is not to say that every lawyer in the firm is going to embrace the marketing effort; there will usually be a few (generally from the ranks of the senior partners) who just cannot accept the whole idea. But most of the lawyers are more ready for an intelligent and effective marketing program than they would like to admit. They know, or at least feel, what is happening in the profession today. And, as the marketing program develops, they find their own personal comfort zone. In other words, their self-image changes in the direction of the Modern Lawyer.

The Need to Plan for Growth

When some members of a firm begin pressing to develop an organized marketing program, others in the firm—usually the Dedicated Lawyers and the Anti-Marketing Attorney—will begin to raise objections to the whole effort. If the firm's billable hours have been declining, or even remaining flat, these objections are not going to stand up very well. But if the firm has been growing in billable hours and even adding lawyers, these objections may sound legitimate. "We are already too busy and can't handle the work we have, so why should we spend time and money planning for more growth?'' Therefore, quite often the first marketing job that must be done is *within* the firm—to market the need for an organized marketing program.

There are quite a few reasons why a firm must have an organized plan for growth. Regardless of how well a firm might be doing at the time, when these reasons are raised and addressed, the opposition to developing a plan usually fades away or, at the least, becomes so minor that the project can start. Some of the reasons for a growth plan are:

1. To survive. Peter Drucker has a well-developed theory that the first objective of any business entity is survival. Periods of growth have a way of stopping almost as quickly and mysteriously as they started. Then a firm is left with a lot of problems and expenses that actually threaten its ability to survive and continue in business.
2. To develop the ability to handle larger and more complex matters, which are usually the more profitable.
3. To keep up with inflation—the continually rising costs of staying in business.
4. To provide resources for the development of new services and new areas of the law which a firm will require in order to keep up with changes in the profession and the needs of its clients.
5. To be able to serve more clients, thereby broadening the client base and lessening the dependence on a few clients.
6. To increase partner income.
7. To provide security for retired partners.
8. To provide room and opportunity for the younger lawyers in the firm. These people are the future of the firm. They will leave if the picture becomes static and there is little opportunity for them to move up in the firm.
9. To replace clients lost by attrition.
10. To enable a firm to continually upgrade its client list. A firm that is static, or even shrinking, is naturally hesitant to subtract less desirable clients from its list.
11. To provide continuing professional challenges and greater recognition for the members of the firm, i.e., the ego factor.
12. To enable a firm to direct and control its future, as much as possible.

13. To provide an appealing environment for recruiting capable new lawyers.
14. Competition is doing it.

One of the biggest dangers of unplanned growth is that a firm is constantly playing catch-up. It continually finds itself short of people, or at least qualified people. It finds itself desperately short of office space. It often finds itself short of the financial resources needed to take advantage of new opportunities or requirements. It hasn't developed its people to assume greater responsibilities. The quality of its work declines. It suddenly finds itself locked into situations—certain clients, mergers it has made, or new offices it has opened—that aren't really right and that prevent it from pursuing new and more attractive opportunities.

Gradually, or perhaps suddenly, the sweet smell of success that arose from unplanned or take-it-for-granted growth develops an aroma of frustration or even the odor of disaster. If growth has been occurring without a firm's doing much about it, the firm had better learn how to manage this growth and also how to continue it. If not, the day will suddenly come when the partners will find the practice heading in the other direction.

Two other points should be made about growth. The first is that we are not talking about growth just for the sake of growing. We are talking about *quality* growth with quality clients who pay their bills on time (or reasonably close) and who are good references on which to build a solid, growing practice. Second, we are not talking about growing just by raising fees. Many firms look no further than their rising level of fee income and never face the fact that their billable hours—the real measure of production and "sales"—are not increasing.

In other words, the type of growth we are talking about is a growth in quality of work (by both definitions), services to clients, quality of clients, and client base.

What Clients and Prospects
Want From Their Legal Counsel

If it is really true—and it is—that marketing must start with the needs and wants of clients as they, not the lawyer, perceive them, then it becomes necessary to first understand what clients and prospects want from their legal counsel.

The answer is "many things." A partial list would include the following:

1. Help in solving problems, or, to put it another way, getting them out of trouble. Lawyers often lose sight of the basic reason why their clients retain them. This is one of them. It's one of the simple, down-to-earth reasons why most people, companies, and organizations need and use a lawyer. Don't lose sight of it and don't ignore it.

2. Help in preventing problems, or, to put this another way, keeping them out of trouble. This is an area where some lawyers shine and others, unfortunately, shine too brightly. When a client asks his or her lawyer to draw up an agreement of sale, prepare a contract, or review a proposed transaction, they are really saying, "I want to do this, but will you make sure that I do it without having any problems in the future?" Some lawyers understand this. Others take the position that it is their role to think of every little thing that could possibly go wrong, raise all these problems—and by doing so, they often prevent the sale, transaction, or deal from going through. Yes, there are times when the client really wants the lawyer's opinion on whether or not to take a contemplated course of action. But there are many more times when all the client is saying is, "Just keep me out of trouble." Something else that you should not lose sight of and not ignore.

3. Money—ways to save it, keep it, or make it.

4. Background or even expertise in the particular matter. You may be an outstanding corporate lawyer, but if your client asks you about handling his divorce, what he's really asking is, "Do you have the necessary expertise to handle my divorce?" If you have the required skills, tell the client you do. If not, find a

lawyer who does. Don't bluff clients or prospects: when it comes to working with lawyers, clients want to feel that their lawyer knows the type of matter or area of the law.

5. Background or even expertise in the client's industry or field. This is high on many clients' lists. In fact, the larger the client or prospect, the more important this can be. At the very least, clients feel more comfortable with a lawyer who seems to understand, if not really know, their type of business. At the other end of the scale, they don't want to pay fees to educate the lawyer in their particular field if it is necessary that the lawyer understand it in order to serve the client. Therefore, the more a lawyer knows about the field the client or prospect works in, the better chance the lawyer has to obtain or retain the client.

6. Attention. This is very important to everyone, both lawyers and clients. In fact, the right amount of attention or showing that you really care about the client can overcome shortfalls in some of the other areas. We all tend to be more tolerant and understanding of those people who seem to care about us, even if they don't always succeed in accomplishing what we want.

7. Availability. Many a client has switched to another lawyer because the previous lawyer was not available enough to the client in person, by phone or even by letter when needed.

8. New ideas. This generally applies to a client's financial or business matters but it can apply to other matters as well. Everyone needs fresh, new ideas on how to do what they are doing. Sometimes people are not aware of this until another person gives them some new ideas. Nevertheless, consciously or unconsciously, clients are often looking for new ideas from their attorney.

9. Timeliness. This is really more than a desire of the client; it is *expected* as part of the lawyer's service. Of course the lawyer must be timely with services performed *on behalf of* the client such as filing a brief, taking depositions, etc. But I am talking about being timely *with* the client as well. If a client asks you to review a contract by a certain date, for example, make sure you get back to your client by that date—or say you can't when asked.

10. Confidence or peace of mind. A client must have confidence in

the lawyer and what the lawyer is doing. Even more, a client wants the peace of mind that comes from knowing that the lawyer is competent and equal to the tasks that must be faced on his or her behalf. When a client starts to worry about the ability of the lawyer, the lawyer won't have that client too much longer.

11. The big name or recognized expert. Some clients, quite frankly, want a "name" attorney or law firm and are willing to pay for that. They feel it will bring prestige to them or, in the case of litigation, intimidate the other side. This could mean a national firm instead of a local firm, or a well-known local firm instead of a firm that few people have heard of. It could also mean the highly regarded sole practitioner instead of the one no one talks about.

12. Being kept informed. Many lawyers fail to realize that, even though they are busy handling a matter for a client, the client may not know what they are doing if the client isn't involved. In these cases, the client generally begins to think that the lawyer might not be doing anything. So keep your client informed, somehow, of what is going on. On the other hand, most clients don't really want copies of every letter, memo, brief, and response you send or receive (some few do, of course; they want to play lawyer right along with you). So find a way to keep the client informed, particularly when the client won't otherwise know what you are doing.

13. Follow-up. Most business people, and many others as well, are almost fanatical about this, particularly with their lawyer or accountant. If you say to a client, "I will handle that" or "I'll get back to you on that," you had better follow up or eventually you won't have a client to follow up to. Furthermore, the oft-used excuse "I have been too busy" isn't acceptable to clients. If the lawyer is too busy to follow up for the client, then the client interprets that, probably quite correctly, to mean "You're not an important enough client to me."

14. General business counsel. Many clients look to their attorneys as a source of general business counsel. If you have a talent for providing it, go ahead. Some lawyers are terrible at it, some are excellent.

15. Personal counsel. Because their lawyer may often know more

about their personal affairs than anyone else (including spouse or doctor), clients often turn to the lawyer for advice on personal matters. "Should I stop my daughter from seeing this man?" "Which house should I buy?" "Do you know of a place where my son could get a job?" Even if you are not an expert social psychologist, be ready to become a good listener with some of your clients. That's what they want—and are willing to pay for.

16. Value. Surprisingly, most clients do not necessarily want the lowest possible legal fees. If they did, they would have gone to a legal clinic rather than a law firm. What they *do* want is *value*—the feeling that they received at least what they were billed for and generally much more. It's no secret that many people today feel that lawyers overcharge for their services. It's also true that what constitutes value in one client's mind will often, under the same fee and set of circumstances, not constitute value in another client's mind. But the ultimate point is the same: clients like to feel they received even more than they paid for. If you concentrate on serving the client and accomplishing what the client really wants (assuming, of course, that you can), your clients will feel they are receiving value.

17. The right chemistry. Clients and prospects have to feel that they can work with the lawyer and, if appropriate, that the people in their company or organization can work with the lawyer and other people in the firm. *This does not mean that your client must like you.* In fact, in certain types of matters (such as major litigation or an acrimonious divorce), the client or prospect may even be looking for a lawyer they don't personally like but who they feel will be intimidating to the opposition. Sometimes, however, the Anxious But Insecure Attorney will go overboard in an effort to be liked by the client or prospect. This is wrong. There are more cases than many lawyers realize where a prospective client might like a particular lawyer personally but wouldn't want that lawyer or that lawyer's firm representing them. Chemistry, respect, specific expertise, and all the other reasons discussed above generally rate ahead of the client's wanting to like the lawyer.

Not every client wants all of the things listed above. However, every client or prospect is looking for some of these things in his or her relationship with a lawyer. The particular wants and their priorities will vary with each client, but the first two (get out of trouble and keep out of trouble) and the last (the right chemistry) will exist in almost every case.

The Steps in Developing a Marketing Plan

Planning is an essential part of the corporate world today. It seems as if every company, no matter what its size, has some sort of plan. There is the Strategic Plan, the Tactical Plan, the Financial Plan, the Contingency Plan, and somewhere there may even be the Plan on How to Plan.

Some of this is probably overdone; some companies seem to spend more time planning than doing. Nevertheless, the concept of planning is well accepted and is certainly not foreign to anyone who has ever had to prepare a case for trial. However, planning in a business sense involves more than the orderly arrangement of a succession of tasks. It also involves an analysis of the situation, the setting of objectives, the steps to achieve the objectives, and the monitoring process to determine if the plan is on track.

When lawyers, as well as most other nonmarketing people, think of a marketing plan they probably conjure up an image of some elaborate and dramatic presentation overflowing with suggested ads, colorful charts, and an occasional page of written material bursting with adjectives. But a marketing plan is really a very substantive document that has been developed by following a simple but disciplined process. The end result is a product that shows what the drafters of the plan expect to accomplish, the basis for their reasoning, and how they will accomplish it.

In a corporation the marketing plan is really the blueprint of how a company is using its resources in order to grow. It differs from the operations plan, for example, which is the blueprint of how a company executes the business it is in. The marketing plan has been essential to consumer products companies for many years and to most industrial companies more recently. Now, in just the past few years, law firms have started preparing and implementing marketing plans.

The marketing plan for a law firm may take several forms. For a large national or regional firm it may literally be a volume of hundreds of pages. For the smaller firm it may take the form of a report. For the sole practitioner it may simply be several pages of handwritten notes. The form of the marketing plan is not nearly as important as the substance and the thought that goes into its preparation. There is a sequential process that must be followed in order to achieve a quality product. To short-circuit this, or mix up the sequence, or not to follow the process at all will result in costly errors and perhaps disaster. And it certainly won't be professional.

No matter how large or small the firm, the process is the same. The steps must be taken in sequence, with each one completed before the next one is begun. These are the steps:

- Strategic Marketing Analysis and Report
- Strategic Marketing Plan—three to five years
    Firm (office) Strategic Objectives
    Strategic Marketing Objectives
    Basic Policies—"Rules of the Road"
    Basic Marketing Strategies
    Positioning Statement
- Tactical Marketing Plan—one year
    Specific objectives
    Action steps to achieve
    Dates to complete
    Person(s) responsible
    Budget—time and money
- Approval by firm (office) management group
- Approval by partners
- Presentation to rest of firm (office)
- Begin implementation

At this point the *plan* should have become a *program*. The following are necessary to make the marketing program effective:

- Monitor implementation, evaluate results, and fine-tune.
- Provide training in personal marketing skills as need develops.
- Review Strategic Plan and develop following year's Tactical Plan—annually.

In the next three sections we will "unbundle" this list and discuss each step.

The Strategic Analysis

The Strategic Analysis is a study of the past, present, and estimated future factors, both internal and external, that affect the firm and its practice. It is the important first step in preparing a marketing plan. Some of the information will consist of hard data and some of it will be qualitative. Larger firms will probably have most or all of the hard data already available; smaller firms may have to develop much of it. Either way, this is the information which becomes a data base for similar information in the future, so it is not just a one-time exercise.

There are three major sections to the Strategic Analysis: (1) internal factors—data, information, and assumptions generated from a review of the firm's operations; (2) external factors—data, information, and assumptions drawn from or based on conditions outside the firm; and (3) the potential opportunities for growth—ways in which the firm could direct and manage its future growth. These become fairly self-evident after completion of the first two sections.

In the course of working with law firms of all sizes to develop their marketing plans, our firm has developed a Strategic Analysis Check List which we have found to be an excellent guide in completing this important first step. The list follows below. In working with this list, it is extremely important to keep one thing in mind. Many firms, as stated, may not have all this data and information. Many of them can develop it in a reasonable time without too much cost. Where this cannot be done, or where it would take too long, the firm should make the best educated estimate it can. A "best guess," objectively arrived at, is better than omitting a peice of data altogether.

Many items on the list are obvious; however, I will elaborate on some of them.

Strategic Analysis Check List

I. Internal Factors
   A. Personnel and Organization

      1. List of partners and associates by department; also administrative people
      2. Profile of each lawyer and associate
      3. Skills index of the lawyers
      4. Committees and members
      5. Organization chart
      6. Practice area resumes

B. Fees and Hours
      1. Total fees and billable hours—last three years
      2. Total fees and billable hours each department—last three years
      3. Fees by client, from largest to smallest, in total and by department or area of the law—last three years
      4. Total fees and number of clients by industry—last three years
      5. Total fees and number of clients by geographic area—last three years
      6. Number of partners and associates in each office and total fees for each office—last three years
      7. Each partner's and associate's billable hours—last three years
      8. Hourly rates of each attorney

C. Client Data
      1. Total number of clients
      2. Client list—most recent
      3. New-client report format
      4. New-matter report format
      5. New clients each year—last two years
      6. Number of new clients brought in by each partner each year (i.e., origination)—last two years
      7. Any significant clients lost in the last two years and the reason

D. Marketing
      1. Current firm, department, and individual marketing activities, including:
         a. Seminars (titles, sponsors)
         b. Newsletters (copies)
         c. Articles, talks
         d. Brochures (copies)
         e. Advertising
         f. Use of P.R. firm
         g. Other
      2. Who are considered the successful rainmakers?
      3. Who are the important outside sources of new business?
      4. Target prospects and services they could use
      5. If there is a formal client relations program, brief description and who is responsible
      6. New areas of the law identified for possible development
      7. Industries identified for development or further penetration
      8. Minutes of Practice Development Committee meetings

E. General
      1. Written history of the firm
      2. Assessment of the mid-term future (3–5 years) of major clients' operations and possible impact on firm

   3. Assessment of the firm with regard to the following:
      a. People—quantity, quality, characteristics
      b. Professional capabilities
      c. Facilities
      d. Financial resources
   4. Strategic (5 year) and tactical (1 year) objectives and plans
   5. Locations of any new offices the firm is considering opening
   6. Any firms identified as possible merger candidates—why?
   7. Is there a mailing list? If so, how is it segregated?
   8. Recruiting material
II. External Factors
   A. Opinions and perceptions of the firm
      1. Clients' opinions
      2. Third parties' perceptions
   B. Firms considered as competition
      1. Name
      2. Size
      3. Location
      4. Image/reputation
      5. Nature of practice
      6. Major clients
      7. Fee structure
      8. Strengths and weaknesses
   C. Economic and social environment in the market area(s)
   D. Leading industries, businesses, and organizations in the market area(s)
III. Opportunities for Growth
   A. Current
      1. Clients
      2. Areas of the law or services
      3. Industries
      4. Market area(s)
   B. New
      1. Clients
      2. Areas of the law or services
      3. Industries
      4. Market area(s)

PERSONNEL AND ORGANIZATION

The profiles of each partner and associate are discussed in the Lawyer Profiles section, together with a sample of the profile form. The skills index is a listing of the specific areas of the law that each lawyer is qualified to practice. For example:

J.F. Dougherty—Estate Planning, Family Business,
Federal Taxation

D.G. Osborne—Corporate, Mergers and Acquisitions,
Securities, Finance
H.K. Sklaar—Administrative Law

Of course the list could start with the fields of practice and then name the partners engaged in each field. I prefer starting with the lawyer's name because this places more emphasis on quality control. If the firm lists areas of the law in which a particular lawyer is considered qualified, the firm should have a procedure to review the lawyer's competence in these areas. This can best be done by the department head or chairman.

Practice area resumes are write-ups on the firm's experience and qualifications in specific practice areas such as insurance defense, environmental, taxation etc.

FEES AND HOURS

Section I-B calls for information that every law firm of any size should record. Surprisingly many firms do not. The fees by client, in descending order from largest to smallest, are extremely important to have on an annual basis. Many firms are not aware of who their largest clients are or just how much of the firm's total fees come from these clients. Although a computer is probably required to record this information accurately, it is also extremely important to know which departments serve the clients and the fees generated. For example:

CLIENT	TOTAL FEES	CORPORATE	LITIGATION	LABOR	TAX	ESTATES
ABC Co.	$95,700	$95,700	—	—	—	—
XYC Co.	$83,500	$26,400	$41,000	$ 6,100	$8,900	$ 1,100
HQ Hospital	$81,000	—	—	$72,000	$9,000	—
John Jones	$52,000	—	$36,400	—	—	$15,600

This type of report quickly reveals the clients for which the firm is providing a variety of services as well as the clients that use the firm for only one or a few services. These latter clients are vulnerable for loss because other law firms may be providing other services and therefore have direct contact with these clients. They are, at the same time, potentials for cross-selling of other firm services. In the example above, XYZ Co. is a much more "solid" client than ABC Co.

although ABC's total fees are greater. If it is impossible to record the fees by department or area of the law for each client, the report should at least show which departments are providing services to the client. A simple "X" in the appropriate columns would reveal this.

In order to record total fees and number of clients by industry, the originating or responsible attorney must note on the client's record the industry. Large accounting firms use the SIC code for this purpose. I believe this is too unwieldy and complicated for even the largest law firm. We have developed a much simpler industry classification code which is shown at the end of this section.

The geographic location of a client is simple to determine by answering the question: Where is the location that the law firm deals with? For example, if an Arizona law firm does defense work for a Hartford-based insurance company but works with the regional office in Arizona, this would be considered an Arizona-based client. On the other hand, if the same firm was handling real estate development work in the United States for a German company, this would be considered a foreign client. Five basic geographic categories seem to be sufficient for most firms: local (within two hours' drive from the firm's office), balance of the state, region, balance of U.S., and foreign. Of course further refinements and breakdowns can be made within each category.

CLIENT DATA

Section I-C again calls for information that every firm should have, yet a surprising number of firms do not. Total number of clients means the number of active clients who were billed for work in the most recent year. Some firms can give a total number of clients in the file but cannot distinguish between active (billed this year) and inactive (no billings this year). Some firms can give a count of the total number of matters handled in a year but do not know how many clients were involved.

Practically every firm has some form of new-matter report in order to get the billing information into the system, but most firms do not have a new-client report form. The importance of this, as well as an example of the information that should be recorded, are discussed in the section titled The Client Profile. When it comes to documenting any "significant clients" lost and the reasons, most firms will quickly answer "none." Over a period of a year or two, however, this is just not realistic and the question should be pursued. Every firm is going to lose a few clients now and then. The important thing is to learn why. Many times it is beyond the firm's control, such as a conflict arising between clients, but other times there may have been problems that the firm could have solved and thereby retained the client.

Under Section I-D-1, about current marketing activities, the usual response is "very little" or a quick recap of the activities that everyone is very much aware of, such as a firm brochure. Here, however, it is important to dig deeper. There is usually more marketing activity going on in a firm, however informal or unrecorded it may be, than most people are aware of. To properly answer this question usually requires checking with the department heads and even individual lawyers.

The answer to I-D-2, the rainmakers, should reflect the general impressions of the Business Development or Strategic Planning Group, whoever is preparing this information. These impressions or reputations will be checked against hard data or at least impressions that can be gained from other sources.

The important outside sources of new business should start with categories such as bank loan officers, public accountants, other law firms, etc., and then list specific people or firms in each category.

GENERAL

The proper answer to I-E-2 generally requires that either one person or a small group of people who have a good overview of the total client list prepare a brief written analysis. For example, if a large percentage of the firm's client base is in the health care, hi-tech, and financial services fields, the general outlook for these clients, and therefore the firm, should be favorable. If, on the other hand, the firm has a strong client base composed of buggy whip manufacturers, underfinanced companies, and 85-year-old businessmen, the outlook for the firm's future is not too cheerful; it may not have many clients left in two or three years.

Many people may be surprised at the question regarding a mailing list. They shouldn't be. It is surprising—and disturbing—how many large firms (let alone small ones) cannot do a mailing because they do not have an accurate mailing list or, in some cases, any list at all. The segregation question means can mailings be done to clients only, one category of clients, nonclients, other lawyers, etc.

CLIENT AND THIRD-PARTY INTERVIEWS

Under External Factors, Section II, one of the most important pieces of information is to determine client opinions and third-party perceptions of the firm and its work. Clients and third parties will always see a firm in a different light than it sees itself, but, in terms of marketing, it is how *they* perceive the firm that is important. How do you obtain these client and nonclient opinions? The best way is to retain an outside objective source—such as a marketing consultant!—to interview them. Select a representative cross section of the client list to cover large and small clients, from different geographic locations, being served by one and several departments, and representing different responsible attorneys. If the firm wishes to do this itself, then several partners should follow the same criteria and ask these clients and nonclients to critique the firm and its services. The process is pretty much the same as the Client Review Program, which is covered in a later section. Don't guess for this part of the analysis; conduct these interviews or, better still, have someone outside the firm conduct them.

It is important to give some extra thought to II-B, firms considered as competition. This will, of course, often vary with the practice area, but it will often include firms that, on first thought, were not considered competition. The client and third-party interviews will be an excellent source to determine what other firms are being used and what are people's opinions of these firms versus your own.

Plenty of studies are usually available on the economic and social environment in the market area; it is just a question of which study you want to use (or believe). If the firm has offices in several cities, a study should be made or obtained for each area in which the firm has an office. The same holds true for compiling a list of the leading industries, businesses, and organizations in each market area.

After the above information, both quantitative and qualitative, has been assembled, prepare a Strategic Analysis Marketing Report. This will amount to a hard look at where the firm stands today in a marketing sense. To be perfectly honest, you will also have looked at the firm from some other viewpoints as well—practice management, quality of resources, even quality of practice. As you complete this part of the report, you will see various opportunities for growth, both current and new. This will have taken a lot of work, but you and the firm will have learned a lot.

You will also have taken the first big step in developing a marketing plan.

Industry Classifications

Code

M	Manufacturing
OG	Oil and Gas
D	Mining, Drilling, and Miscellaneous Energy
R	Consumer Wholesale and Retail
E	Estates and Trusts (Individuals)
T	Tax-Exempt Organizations
HC	Health Care
RE	Real Estate Development and Investment
C	Construction and Fabrication
TR	Transportation
CM	Communications
B	Financial Institutions
I	Insurance
IV	Investment
P	Professional
CO	Conglomerates
A	Agribusiness
G	Government Bodies
U	Utilities
O	Other

The Strategic Marketing Plan

Up to now the work involved has been fairly easy. Now comes the hard part. It requires the firm to think about itself and its future and to come to a consensus, if not some conclusions.

The Strategic Marketing Plan is a look ahead at where the firm wants to be in three or five years and the marketing strategies that it will employ in order to get there. It includes:

- The firm (or office) strategic objectives
- Strategic marketing objectives
- Basic policies to be followed
- Basic marketing strategies
- The Positioning Statement

While the typical corporate strategic plan is usually done on a five-year or even ten-year basis, it is my experience that law firms should not attempt to plan more than three years ahead. The entire process is too new for them, and the different characteristics of a professional practice seem to make a longer time frame impractical anyway.

FIRM STRATEGIC OBJECTIVES

A successful marketing plan must emanate from sound marketing objectives. These in turn must be based on well-developed strategic objectives for the firm. Most law firms have not yet initiated any formal strategic planning (although increasing numbers are beginning to). Therefore they have not developed any strategic objectives. While this creates a major obstacle to the marketing planning process, a firm cannot delay the development of a marketing plan until some unknown time in the future when it has completed its overall strategic planning.

Therefore, in order to proceed with the development of a marketing plan, it is generally necessary for the marketing group to assume certain firm strategic objectives for the subsequent three years. Here are some examples:

1. To provide a continuing environment for the attorneys to attain the highest level of capability in the practice of law.
2. To become the largest law firm in the state.
3. To increase partner income at least 12% each year.
4. To achieve gross fees of at least $50 million based on a minimum of 620,000 billable hours at an average rate of $80 per hour.

Note that two of these objectives are somewhat general while the others are quite specific. Both types of objectives are appropriate, but it is important to be as quantitative as possible wherever possible. This makes tracking and evaluation of the program far easier.

STRATEGIC MARKETING OBJECTIVES

Once you have established, or at least assumed, the firm's long-range objectives, you can then establish some long-range marketing objectives. Here are some examples of strategic marketing objectives that could follow from the firm's strategic objectives shown above:

1. To achieve a minimum of 400,000 billable hours from our downtown office, 150,000 billable hours from our suburban office, and at least 70,000 billable hours from a new downstate office.
2. To broaden our client base to a minimum of 3,100 active clients.
3. To provide services from at least two areas of the law to one-third of our clients.
4. To raise the general awareness of the firm in our state.

Notice that these objectives are quite specific for the most part. This is important. You can't measure the results of a program that has vague or mushy objectives. For example, "To be recognized as the outstanding firm in our city" sounds like a wonderful objective, but how would you measure it? On the other hand, "To have four of the ten largest companies in our city as clients for at least one practice area" can be measured—and it just might be attainable too! Certain lawyers will oppose attempting to establish specific, quantified objectives. Don't give in. With a little thought and effort, most objectives can be quantitative.

POLICIES

The next step is to decide what basic policies or "rules of the road" should be established and followed during the strategic planning period. Again you may meet some resistance on this point, but don't give in. This is the time, when you are thinking ahead, to establish certain basic policies. They will save the firm a lot of time—potentially billable time!—during the next few years and will probably prevent some wrong decisions as well.

Here are some examples:

1. Additional offices will be opened if they meet certain criteria.
2. The firm will only enter into new practice areas in which it can achieve a superior level of professional competence and can practice profitably.
3. Lateral entries at the partner level will be considered in order to provide the firm with expertise in a specific area of the law.
4. Conscientious and effective business development time is considered as valuable to the firm as billable time.

STRATEGIES

The next step is to define the basic marketing strategies the firm will follow during the strategic planning period. Is it going to place first priority on expanding services to current clients or on expanding the client base? Is it going to stress personal involvement in community activities by every partner and senior associate? Is it going to count on external growth, such as mergers, for a significant part of its growth? Is it going to emphasize external marketing communications such as public relations or even advertising?

A firm can't do everything; therefore it is important to determine at this point what basic strategies are suitable for each firm. There is no single "best" strategy. It is a case of selecting the appropriate strategies that the particular firm will be comfortable with and can execute.

THE POSITIONING STATEMENT

A firm can't market effectively until it has decided what messages it wants to communicate through its marketing effort. Therefore the next step is to develop a Positioning Statement. This is an internal marketing document that positions the firm vis-à-vis other law firms in the market area and defines the features and qualities about the firm that are to be emphasized in the marketing program. The Positioning Statement is not a mere exercise in semantics. It is very important. It becomes the basic script for all the marketing activities.

The Positioning Statement for a law firm can consist of five or six points, rarely more. Here are some examples:

1. We are one of the largest law firms in the state.
2. We provide a full range of legal services through teams of lawyers who specialize in all major areas of civil practice.
3. We are a young and dynamic firm; the average age of our partners is 37.
4. We are extremely progressive in making maximum use of the latest equipment and technology in order to serve our clients in the most modern and cost-efficient manner.
5. We are considered extremely aggressive in litigation.

This may seem like a nearly impossible step to accomplish. It really isn't, because by the time you have reached this step, a number of the points about your firm and your competition will have become apparent.

Once the Positioning Statement is established and agreed upon, the Strategic Marketing Plan is done, and the development of the balance of the plan, the Tactical Marketing Plan, will become considerably easier. A description of the firm is practically completed. Certain specific marketing activities become obvious. And, most important, all of the marketing efforts will spread and reinforce the same message about the firm. Two of the secrets of successful marketing are *clarity* and *reinforcement*. A well-constructed Strategic Plan, including the Positioning Statement, provides the basis for both.

The Tactical Marketing Plan

Once the Strategic Marketing Plan is completed, the next step is the development of the Tactical Marketing Plan. "Tactical" is one of those corporate buzz words and really means "short-term." In the case of strategic planning, it is generally used to mean a one-year time frame. The Tactical Marketing Plan will be much easier to develop if the firm, or more likely the marketing or business development group, has done a good job in its Strategic Analysis and in preparing the Strategic Marketing Plan.

The importance of following this sequence, and the reason the Tactical Marketing Plan should be relatively easy to develop, are best understood if you compare the process to that of planning a vacation trip.

The Strategic Analysis is equivalent to studying the various places you would like to travel to. The Strategic Marketing Plan is equivalent to selecting one or several places to visit, deciding how long you will be gone, the overall budget, and the means of travel. The Tactical Marketing Plan is the same as planning how far you will travel each day and where you will stay each night. It is far easier to plan a trip if you first determine where you are going and how long you will allow to get there. Then you work your way back to your starting point and work out each detail. The tactical plan is the same for a vacation and for marketing—with one exception. At the end of a trip, you usually return to your starting point. At the end of a tactical marketing plan, you should never be back where you started! You should have arrived at a level of accomplishment which becomes a new starting point to reach the next level.

THE TACTICAL OBJECTIVES

The first step in developing the Tactical Marketing Plan is to plan the tactical objectives or, in other words, the specific things that will be accomplished in the next year. These should relate to or work toward the strategic objectives. For example, if one of the strategic objectives is to provide services from at least two practice areas to at least one-third of the clients (by the end of the strategic planning period), the tactical objectives for the first year might include the following:

1. Develop and implement a formal Client Review Program (discussed in detail in a later section).
2. Determine which clients have need for additional services the firm offers
3. Develop and distribute a brochure on the firm's capabilities to all clients and interested third parties.
4. Develop and publish quarterly newsletters from at least two departments.

When beginning a formal, organized marketing program, a law firm is wise to keep it as simple as possible. It is far better to undertake and accomplish a limited number of objectives than to develop an overly ambitious and complex program and fail to accomplish most of it. For this reason, when our firm is working with a law firm on developing its first marketing plan, we generally recommend that the firm set no more than six or seven objectives for the first year. Some firms, with large resources and a very strong commitment to marketing, can undertake more. Others, with either very limited resources or, probably more significant, an uncertain commitment to marketing, should not attempt even that many. In addition to practical business reasons, there is an important psychological reason for not trying to do too much at the outset. A lot of inertia must initially be overcome when launching a marketing program. Some people will be opposed to it and others will be skeptical. Therefore, it is important to achieve an early record of success and accomplishment. A firm that sets five objectives for the first year and accomplishes all of them develops a great sense of enthusiasm and confidence; it is ready to do more the next year. A firm that sets ten objectives and only achieves five has batted only .500, and, regardless of what it has accomplished, the level of enthusiasm and confidence about marketing is not as high.

The Tactical Marketing Plan basically consists of the objectives and the specific action steps that will be taken to accomplish each of the objectives. All tactical marketing plans follow the same format, whether for a giant corporation or a small law firm. They include the objective, the action steps, the completion date, who is responsible, and, if appropriate, the budget. Here is an example:

To establish and implement an organized program for client development that will result in one-third of our clients using at least two of our services.

A. Establish and implement a formal client review program for all major clients and key clients.
   1. Designate clients to be classified as "major" and "key." Major clients are defined as those with significant fees and/or significant matters; key clients are defined as those with significant potential for additional fees either through growth of their own operations or their ability to refer new business. Marketing Committee responsible. Complete by March 1st.
   2. Select partners to conduct Client Reviews in accordance with the procedure outlined in Appendix XII. Copies of reports to department head chairmen and Marketing Committee. See Appendix for format. Select partners by April 1st. Complete reviews by June 15.
B. Identify opportunities for cross-selling of other services in order to further "wed" the client to the firm.
   1. Discuss these needs with client to obtain further background and stimulate interest.
   2. Review with appropriate lawyers what would be involved.
   3. Arrange for introduction of appropriate client executives to appropriate lawyers.
C. Initiate other activities relative to client retention and development.
   1. Arrange early contact with new executives when changes in management occur.
   2. Watch for clients that may be tender offer targets or potential sellers.
   3. Identify clients that may be potential buyers or changing their business objectives and offer assistance.
   4. Keep abreast of client employment of other law firms.
   5. Visit with major and key clients frequently by phone, in their offices, or socially.
   6. Expand contacts throughout client organization, particularly with present and future decision makers; involve younger lawyers as soon and as intensively as possible.
   7. Invite clients to speak to our lawyers about their organizations.
   8. Maintain frequent contact with client's bankers and accountants.
   9. Develop a Client Profile for each major and key client.

Sample in Appendix XIII. Develop effective system whereby client lists could be kept current and used for announcements and other information retrieval use.

10. Review each major or key client at least annually with client responsible lawyer to determine if attention is being paid to above points.

In the course of working with a great number of law firms in recent years, I am frequently asked if we don't often take out of our files a plan we have previously done for one firm and present it to another. The answer is "no." I can honestly say that we have never duplicated a marketing plan despite the number of firms we have worked with. The reason for this is important for all firms to appreciate when they are developing their first plan.

EACH FIRM'S PLAN IS DIFFERENT

Each firm will have a distinct and different plan because each firm faces different circumstances and is a collection of different individuals with different personalities and professional skills, different clients, different objectives, and different resources. One firm cannot adopt another firm's exact plan, no matter how similar the firms may be and no matter how successful the first firm's plan may have been.

In other words, don't copy another firm's plan.

The final step in the preparation of the marketing plan is to describe the process that will be followed in monitoring it as well as to establish definite periods for review. The normal review periods are at mid-year and year-end; time must be allowed for things to happen. On the other hand, monitoring should be an ongoing process. It must be the responsibility of one person in a small firm and of the business development or marketing group in a larger firm. Ultimately, it also is the responsibility of department heads, the heads of the various offices, and, of course, the firm's governing body. Some of the activities or plans should be monitored monthly, others less often. Every activity should be monitored at least twice a year. The well-prepared marketing plan will spell most of this out.

There it is—the step-by-step process to follow in developing a marketing plan. If you follow it, you have an excellent chance of developing a sound plan which can be understood and implemented and which should be successful. On the other hand, if you don't follow this process, the chances are that the lawyers involved will waste time and money and wind up accomplishing little or nothing.

This is as good a place as any to emphasize one other very important point. When they have finally developed their first marketing plan, the lawyers in most law firms mistakenly think that it is the marketing group (or whatever the committee is called) who will do all the marketing for the firm. *This is wrong!* It is the responsibility of every partner and associate to do the marketing. The marketing group's responsibility is to plan, initiate, monitor, budget, and get everyone involved in doing what he or she does best. Of course, the marketing group will also be doing a lot of the marketing, but the rest of the firm cannot sit back and expect this group to do it all.

Conflicts

It may seem strange to address the matter of conflicts in a book on marketing. However, client conflicts can and do occur periodically in any law practice. Indeed, if the marketing plan is successful, the firm will probably grow at a more rapid rate—and there will be more opportunities for conflicts to arise!

The real points about conflicts and marketing are these: First of all, even the most marketing-oriented attorneys realize that there will be times when the firm cannot accept a new client or handle another matter for a current client because of an actual or potential conflict. This is important to remember. Marketing does not mean that the firm will overlook conflicts just to grow.

Second, there are certain steps in a good marketing program which can detect potential conflicts early in the game and can save the firm a lot of embarrassment later on. Target prospecting, which is discussed later, requires learning as much as possible about a potential client. This often uncovers potential conflicts and either leads to their resolution beforehand or saves the firm time, effort, and money that would ultimately be wasted because it could not represent that client if it obtained it. The Client Profile, discussed in more detail later in this book, is another means of verifying that a conflict does not exist, although that is not the main purpose of the profile.

A few firms that we have worked with had already established what they called, more or less, a "New Business and Conflicts Committee." While their emphasis was more on preventing conflicts— although at times they created conflicts which didn't really exist—than it was on marketing, this title did reflect the reality that a thorough and careful marketing system is one of the best means of also avoiding conflict situations.

Lawyer Profiles

The biggest asset of any law firm is its people. The marketing of legal services is a people-oriented process. Therefore, the strategic analysis necessary to prepare the marketing plan must begin with the people in the firm.

The first step is to "take inventory" of the people who will be primarily involved in implementing the marketing plan. This naturally means all of the partners and should include all the associates as well. When working with firms in any profession, we start with a personal profile. This is both a personal and professional inventory of the background, skills, interests, and attitudes of a person. The profile form which we have developed follows. It begins with personal background on the individual—where they live, family, education, etc.—then goes into their professional background. It then addresses outside nonprofessional activities and interests and concludes with several questions about clients, prospects, and personal strengths.

What can you learn from these profiles and how do they help in the marketing program?

First, let's discuss an individual profile. The address does more than just tell you where a person lives; it also indicates the logical geographic area of any activities they might be currently or eventually involved in within their communities. You would not, for example, encourage someone who lives 20 miles east of town to become active in something 30 miles west of town. The same principle applies with the person's family. Spouses often have careers or interests of their own that could indirectly aid the firm's marketing efforts. Furthermore, a couple that does not have any children would not normally be interested in family-style activities such as Little League, Brownies, or a swimming club oriented to families and children. On the other hand, a person who is already active in various professional organizations might not be too interested in community involvement. When it comes to personal interests, a low-handicap golfer would not be a likely prospect to join a tennis club, or a sports buff might not be enthused about the local symphony orchestra.

The question about favorite clients can be very revealing. Most professionals enjoy working with certain types of clients—large companies or small entrepreneurs; professional groups or retail stores; individuals or corporations; challenging clients or undemanding clients. The answers to this question will tell you a lot, particularly if you find out why they selected the clients they did.

The question about key prospects gives you some clue to what thinking, if any, the person has done about obtaining new clients for the firm and who they think would be appropriate. Quite often this question will not be answered. That could mean that the person has never given the subject much thought. On the other hand, if it is answered, this provides the basis for developing a target prospect list (discussed later in this book).

The question about personal strengths will often not be answered, at least initially. It may take some discussion or evaluation. But when it is answered, it is usually done with a great deal of thought and gives you some additional guidance in how and where a person could be effective in the firm's marketing program.

Several items on the profile also serve to provide information about the overall marketing activity that has actually been going on in the firm. It is our experience, after more than ten years of working with professional firms of all kinds, that more marketing is always being done than the firm is aware of. It may be the work of a very few people; it may not be organized (and probably isn't); some of it may be inefficient and some may duplicate other efforts. But there are always things which individual people are doing to market themselves or the firm that are not generally known and are not picked up in the marketing section of the Strategic Analysis.

For example, the questions on professional activities, published writings, and trade association memberships often uncover specific activities that either have already been effective or, if properly coordinated with others, can be effective in the future.

Besides the specific answers provided on the profile, the overview is important. A form with just about every section filled in shows a person who is energetic, inquisitive, and involved in other things besides just the practice of law. These are often the more effective people in certain parts of the marketing effort. Remember, however, that partners will usually have more to report than associates. A form that has mostly blank spaces could reveal a number of things. It could indicate a person who is interested in nothing but doing the work and going home. Or it could indicate someone who has just never given any thought to what else they might do besides accumulate 2,500 billable hours a year.

We find that the best technique for developing the profiles is to have them completed and turned in to the person responsible for marketing. Then, with the form as a guide, that person should "interview" each partner and associate to learn more about them as a person, not just as a practicing lawyer. If conducted after the profile has been completed, this type of interview should not take more than half an hour and usually takes less.

After the profiles have been completed, they should be spread, as shown at the end of this section. Use one column for each line on the form. When you look at several pages that contain, for example, all the partners in the firm, you will quickly learn a lot about the firm—who is active, who does what, where they belong, what they are interested in, etc. In other words, you will have a profile of the firm developed from a people standpoint.

It is a good idea to assemble lists of the various categories—professional organizations, country clubs, lunch clubs, etc.—to find out just which members of the firm are involved in what specific activities. This will be very revealing. We will come back to this subject and how to effectively use this information later in the book.

Of course this type of information, as well as much of the other information called for on the Strategic Analysis Check List, is ideal for entry into a computer. Then it becomes not just a static reference but a living biography of each person that can be referred to, reviewed, and periodically updated.

As stated earlier, this is the place to start your internal analysis of the firm. And be prepared for surprises. You will see your firm, and the people in it, in a different light than you ever did before. And it will provide you with valuable information with which to assemble and implement many parts of your marketing plan.

PROFILE

Name _____ Birth Date _____

Dept or Area of Practice _____

Address _____

Spouse's Name _____

Spouse's Occupation _____

Spouse's Organization
& Club Memberships _____

Children's Names and Ages _____

Undergraduate Education _____

Law School _____

Current College Activities _____

Prior Employment_____

Special Expertise _____

Published Writings _____

Professional Activities _____

_____

Business/Trade Association_____
Memberships

_____

Country Club Memberships _____

Lunch Club Memberships _____

Charitable, Community & _____
Civic Activities

_____

Pro Bono Activities _____

Other Memberships or
Activities _____

Interests & Hobbies _____

Favorite Clients _____

Key Prospects_____

Personal Strengths_____

Lawyer Profiles

PARTNER	ADDRESS	CLUBS AND ORGANIZATIONS	INTERESTS AND HOBBIES
Ronald Katz (Edna) (Paul, Michelle)	183 Mermaid Lane Germantown	Park Hills Golf Club United Way—Chairman Urban Club Chamber of Commerce—Board	Golf Music (plays violin) Energy problems
Steven Parker (Wendy)	2557 Greenwood Avenue Bridgetown	Rowing Club	Rowing Travel
Ann Duffy (Frank) (Peter)	924 Lanstate Road West City	Art Alliance West City Civic Association	Art (paints) Music Neighborhood affairs

PART II
MARKETING ACTIVITIES

Client Retention:
The Client Review Program

I stated earlier that "Each firm will have a distinct and different plan" and that "one firm cannot adopt another firm's exact plan." This is true. However, it does not mean that each part of a firm's marketing plan will be totally different from another firm's plan. Furthermore, there is one marketing activity that we recommend in every marketing plan for every firm we consult with. It is a formal Client Review Program.

Since marketing should start with your current clients, it is vital to know how they feel about your firm and your work. It is also necessary to recognize that they will have a different opinion of the firm than the firm thinks they have. Clients always perceive a firm differently from the way in which it perceives itself, and also differently from the way the firm thinks its clients perceive it. The only way to determine what your clients think is to go and ask them. This is the essence of the Client Review Program.

A QUALITY CONTROL PROGRAM

The idea of going to clients and asking them how they feel about the firm and the work it has been doing for them is quite upsetting to certain lawyers. Some feel that clients are not qualified to judge their work. Others feel that it is degrading to ask clients. Still other feel that it is an open invitation for the client to dream up all kinds of criticism, most of it minor, and dwell on the negative aspects of the relationship.

When the client review program is properly conducted, none of these things happen. In fact, the results and the benefits are amazing to many lawyers (but not to anyone who has a real understanding of what marketing is all about). Some of the most common results are these:

1. The clients will be impressed that the firm is really interested in how its clients feel they are being served. Just the fact that you

take the time to ask them what they think is a tremendous "sales pitch" of its own.

2. After conducting a number of these reviews and analyzing the results, you will learn a lot about how your firm is perceived by its clients. There will be patterns—some good, some bad. This will provide you with two valuable pieces of information— favorable points about the firm that you want to market to the world and less favorable points that should be corrected.

3. You will often uncover little misunderstandings which, if not detected, could build up over time into an unhappy client which a competitor can take away from you.

4. You will occasionally be able to keep a client you were on the brink of losing.

It all adds up to a quality control program of client relations. It goes a long way toward building and keeping loyal clients and providing the firm with important information to use in obtaining new clients.

HOW TO CONDUCT A CLIENT REVIEW

The client review is best done by a partner who is not the responsible attorney. It is always easier for a client to discuss this subject with someone other than the person he or she deals with on a regular basis. Therefore, if there are two or more partners in the firm, they should interview each other's clients. This also prevents the interviewing partner from getting involved in minor details about the client's work, because he or she is not aware of all the details. He or she can also, where necessary, explain some things with more credibility and objectivity (in the client's mind) than the person who was handling them.

The proper way to set up this type of interview is for the responsible attorney to contact the client first, explaining that the firm has this procedure with all its important clients and that Partner X will be calling the client to set up a short meeting. The responsible attorney should encourage the client to be open and frank in discussing things with the interviewing partner. If the interview is set up in this manner, the client will not feel that one partner is "spying" on the other; the client will also be much more honest in his or her comments, both favorable and unfavorable.

Admittedly, to have a partner interview another partner's clients requires a great degree of "team spirit" within the firm. The interview is not a chance to criticize another partner. In fact, it generally results in partners' learning many favorable things that make them more appreciative of their fellow lawyers. However, particularly the first time around, it is sometimes difficult for the partners to agree to this. Some will be very reluctant to have another partner talk to their own clients. Actually, of course, the clients should be regarded as the firm's clients, not any particular partner's clients. In these cases, it is far better for the responsible or billing lawyer to interview his or her own clients than not to do the interview at all.

The atmosphere for conducting the client review is important. It should be conducted in a little more relaxed setting than a normal meeting with the client. That does not mean that a couple of drinks in a noisy bar is the right setting. That is too relaxed! In fact, it isn't really a business setting. Lunch is a good opportunity, or a cup of coffee before the normal business day starts. An additional twenty or thirty minutes after a meeting on the client's matters is also a good time. Always advise the client in advance of the purpose of the meeting. It emphasizes the importance to you and also permits him or her to give the subject some thought or research.

HOW NOT TO CONDUCT A CLIENT REVIEW

An effective client review can rarely be conducted on the phone. If the client is located a great distance from the firm, it may be necessary for the responsible lawyer to conduct the interview himself or herself when meeting with the client in the normal course of working with that client. This is better than for someone else who does not know the client to try to conduct the interview over the phone.

Never conduct a Client Review Program by mail. When firms try this tactic the results are always bad. The replies are always less accurate than those obtained in person. Even more important, a mail survey turns many clients off because of its impersonal nature. So never conduct the Client Review Program any way but in person (or, if absolutely unavoidable, on the phone). It is better not to do the client review at all than to do it by mail!

The client review should be held at the highest possible level in the client's organization. If most of the firm's contact is with house counsel or the chief financial officer, it is still best to try to include the president in this meeting. Remember that one of the benefits of this program is the impact it has on the client. Therefore, you want to deliver this impact as far up in the client's organization as you can.

HOW TO SELECT THE CLIENTS

A firm can't conduct a client review with every client. If it tried to do so, the partners would spend all their time doing client interviews and nothing else. Therefore, it is necessary to select those clients that are most important to the firm. We have developed two classifications of these clients:

Major: The largest-fee clients. These generally constitute no more than 10 percent of the client list. They are the clients who, if they were lost, would have a major economic impact on the firm.

Key: The smaller-fee client who is very important to the firm for one of two reasons. It may be a client whose operation could grow much bigger or for whom the firm could do much more work. Or it may be a client who will always be small-fee but can be very important in recommending other, larger clients to the firm.

There is no rigid format for conducting a client interview. Each person should conduct it in a manner that is comfortable to him or her. The most important question, however, is the last one: "May we use you as a reference?" (Obviously this question is not asked if the tone of the meeting has been negative.) If the client agrees, you can count on the honesty and sincerity of what he or she said. If the client refused, one of two situations could exist. There are some people who just do not want their name used as a reference, even if they are delighted with the work the firm has done for them. Most of the time, however, a "no" will indicate that the client has some reason which he or she has not yet divulged. Therefore, if the client says no to this last question, it is very important that the inteviewer dig further to find out the reason.

STRATEGIC ANALYSIS CLIENT INTERVIEW

In the earlier section on strategic analysis, I stated that "One of the most important of the external factors is to determine client and third-party opinions of your firm and your work." This initial market research is conducted in the same manner as the client review discussed here. However, the selection of clients to be interviewed for strategic analysis is slightly different from the selection of major and key clients in an ongoing program. In strategic analysis it is important to select a representative cross section of your clients, large and small, from different geographic locations, from different industries being served by one department or several, and representing clients served by each of the partners. This may very well give you a different list of clients to interview than if you follow the "major" and "key" designations. When you are preparing the strategic analysis of your firm, the important thing is to obtain a representative sampling of your entire client list. If properly balanced, this can consist of from 1 to 2 percent of the list. On the other hand, when you are conducting the client review program as a regular part of your firm's operations, the important thing is to obtain a reading from the clients who are most important to your present and future practice.

Naturally, when you are interviewing third parties as part of the strategic analysis, you do not ask the same questions as you would a client. In these interviews it is important to determine what the third party thinks and hears about your firm. The third parties should be people who have some contact with, or knowledge of, the firm. Bank officials, particularly loan and trust officers, accountants, insurance agents, and other prominent people are generally good third parties to include in this research.

Remember that the most objective and productive client and third-party interviews that are conducted as part of the strategic analysis will generally be those done by a competent and experienced outside party.

A REGULAR PART OF OPERATIONS

Once the partners have conducted the first round of client interviews, any fear and hesitation vanishes. In fact, they are generally so pleased with both the clients' reactions and what has been learned about the firm that they want to make these reviews a regular part of the firm's operations. And that is just what they should be. The Client Review Program is not just a one-shot process. It should be an ongoing part of every firm's operations. It should generally be conducted once a year with retainer clients or at the close of a matter or case.

The Client Review Program is the single most important marketing activity any firm can undertake, and every firm should do it. An outside consultant cannot conduct the Client Review Program for the firm. At this point the lawyers must do the interviewing themselves.

Over the years of our consulting with law firms we have developed a Client Review Program format that has proven quite effective. Here it is:

Client Review Program

There are two important purposes of the Client Review Program:

1. Initially—as an essential step in the Strategic Analysis to determine client perceptions of the firm. The same basic idea should be followed in interviews with sources or intermediaries to determine some nonclient perceptions of the firm.
2. Subsequently—as a regular Quality Control of relations with important clients as well as to monitor any changes in how the firm is perceived by its clients.

Two categories of clients should be covered, both in the initial research and subsequently as a regular operating procedure.

1. Major clients—largest fee income.
2. Key clients—smaller fee income but important as sources or referrals.

For the initial research, a representative cross section of clients should be selected to cover:

- general counsel services
- specialty services only
- size of fee income
- size of client's operation
- industry

- geographic location
- longevity

The sole purpose of the meeting with the client is to obtain feedback on the firm's service of the client's matters. *Do not try to sell additional services* to the client. Ask. Listen.

If possible, the Client Review should be conducted by a Partner other than the one that is in direct charge of the client's matters.

Desired contact—highest possible level. If there is house counsel, try to also include CEO or other member of client senior management.

Recommended procedure:

1. Responsible partner advise client of purpose of meeting. It need not be long—20–30 minutes. Should be in a more relaxed setting, i.e., over lunch, before business day starts (generally *not* over cocktails). If another partner will be conducting the interview, identify that person to the client.
2. Each person should do his or her own style. The points to cover are:
    a. Client's opinion of our firm and services.
    b. Client's opinion of members of the firm with whom they have had contact.
    c. Does client feel we have been prompt? Kept him informed? Have followed up?
    d. Have we helped the client in other areas besides the particular areas we are working in?
    e. Does the client feel we have let them down?
    f. Would the client recommend us to other people if asked? May we use the client's name as a reference?
3. Do brief written report afterwards with distribution to appropriate parties.
4. Do summary overview after reviews are completed.

SUMMARY CHECK LIST FOR CLIENT INTERVIEWS

Explain that:
1. The firm has a program designed to ensure that we are providing the best possible service to our clients.

2. We value the client's opinion.
3. He or she will be asked a few specific questions.
4. The interview will be approximately one-half hour.
5. The interview will be conducted by a partner who is generally familiar with the client's matters.
6. The purpose is to afford the client the opportunity to make frank comments, both good and bad.
7. The interview may be over lunch or breakfast.

The Client Profile

It is amazing, and also tragic, how little many lawyers (and also many accountants) really know about their clients.

Whenever I make that statement in the course of conducting a seminar for lawyers, it generally brings rebuttals from the attendees until we discuss the subject. After a few minutes they wind up agreeing with the statement, but, more important, they are then much more interested in how to correct the situation.

The lawyers who are often the most knowledgeable about their clients are the sole practitioners. This is probably because these lawyers realize that they must provide that extra measure of interest and personal attention in order to retain their clients and develop their practice. Whatever the reason, many lawyers fail to learn everything they should about their clients—whether the client is a major corporation, a nonprofit organization, or an individual.

The lawyer will (or should) know everything about the client that relates to the matter the lawyer is working on. That is, after all, the lawyer's business. However, the lawyer will too often know little or nothing else about the client. Here are a few examples from our experience with law firms.

Client A is in the plastics business. The general counsel knows all about the client's legal and corporate matters but little or nothing about other factors. For example, what kind of plastics does the company manufacture or distribute? Who are its customers (other manufacturers, wholesalers, retail stores, etc.)? Who are its main competitors? How does the company stand in its industry? What are the company's strategic plans?

Client B is a surgeon who wants a will prepared. The lawyer knows everything about the surgeon's estate and what he would like done with it. But he fails to learn that the surgeon is a nationally recognized figure in his field; is on the board of two major hospitals (one of which is a target prospect of the law firm!), and is also a very close friend of another target prospect of the firm.

Impossible? No. It happens far too often. Ridiculous? Yes. It should never happen. There are at least three good reasons why every lawyer should know more about his or her clients than just what affects the particular matter they are working on.

1. To understand the client better and therefore make that client feel important.
2. To develop the perspective necessary to give the client good advice.
3. To detect opportunities for additional business either with that client or with other people or operations the client has contact with.

The best way to develop this process of learning everything pertinent about your clients is to have some form of client profile on all major and key clients (as defined in the section on the Client Review Program) and on all new clients when they are obtained.

(Note: See the later section on Target Prospects. Much of the information included in the Client Profile can be developed in the course of tracking a target prospect.)

A suggested format for the Client Profile follows. There is no set or perfect form; I am including our format only as a means of stimulating each firm to give the matter some thought and to develop a form that is appropriate for them. This is a piece of client information that can be computerized easily and should be recalled for periodic review and update.

Date Prepared _____

Date Reviewed _____

Responsible Attorney_____

CLIENT PROFILE

_____

Name_____ SIC or Industry Code _____

Address _____ Phone_____

_____ No. of employees _____

Other locations_____

_____

Subsidiaries _____

Description of business _____

_____

Sales volume last year _____ Anticipated billing next 12 mos. _____

Union(s) _____ F.Y. _____

No. of shareholders _____ Public (exchange)_____

Private _____

On file: Current annual report _____

Latest 10K _____

Proxy statements _____

Accounting firm _____ Bank_____

Other law firms_____

Investment advisors _____

Other questions to be answered:

1. Our current services to client.
2. Other services we could perform; opportunities for cross-selling within the firm.
3. New areas where client has needs and in which the firm could develop expertise.
4. Key contacts; position; personal and family information.

Notes:

Seminars

Seminars—giving them, sponsoring them, or participating in them—can be an effective marketing tool if they are the right thing for your firm to do and if they are executed properly.

What would make seminars the right marketing tool for your firm to use? First of all, you must have one or preferably several people who enjoy giving a seminar and are reasonably good at it. If you don't have this skill in-house, you still have the option of sponsoring seminars with nonfirm speakers on the agenda, but that defeats one of the most important objectives of giving a seminar. What's that? To expose, publicize, and promote your firm's expertise on a particular subject. You can only achieve that when it is your people who are addressing the attendees and presenting the material. Of course, you can achieve some public relations benefits by sponsoring a talk or program that features recognized authorities who are not members of your firm. But I categorize that under the topic of public relations and address it later on. When I refer to seminars, I mean programs that feature, at least in part, speakers who are members of your firm.

Another requirement is that your speakers have something worthwhile to say. You must be demanding about this. If the people who attend one of your seminars come away with the feeling that they didn't learn anything, you have done your firm more harm than if you hadn't held the program in the first place. Now, don't construe this to mean that the speakers must be the reigning authorities on their particular subjects. But they must know their subjects in some depth and be able to express themselves before a group of people in simple, informative, and interesting terms. Often you may find that some of the associates are as good as or even better than the partners at this. Don't be reluctant to give them the opportunity.

To have an effective seminar, you must match the audience and the subject. Either can come first. For example: if, through your strategic analysis, you have discovered that medical clinics are a significant part of your practice, give some thought as to what topics would be of interest to this audience. The same holds true for general contractors or bank loan officers. This is the technique of picking your target audience and then selecting a topic that should appeal to that audience.

On the other hand, there is nothing wrong with identifying a topic or two and then determining what groups, if any, the topic would appeal to. Toxic waste disposal has been a "hot" topic the past few years; it would be of interest to both manufacturing or processing companies and also to regulatory or civic groups. Patent matters are generally of interest to high-tech companies. Programs dealing with personnel, human resources, and labor problems are generally of interest to a broad range of audiences.

The point is this: the subject of the seminar must be targeted to the audience or vice versa.

DEFINE THE PURPOSE

After you have determined that you have some qualified speakers and at least one worthwhile subject, you still should not rush into giving a seminar until you have determined what you are trying to accomplish. What is the purpose of the seminar? Are you trying to alert your clients to some new developments or changes in the law that they should be aware of? Changes in the tax law often give rise to this kind of seminar. Are you trying to impress a particular group or industry with your expertise in their field and therefore develop potential new clients? A well-organized program directed to general contractors, nursing homes, or real estate developers, whether they are clients or not, could serve this purpose. A program directed to house counsels on how to control legal costs could be more effective than a lot of entertainment in selling them on using your firm when they must turn to outside counsel.

Defining the purpose of the seminar—providing information to clients, introducing a new practice area, developing leads, or educating third parties—usually answers the question of whether or not you should give the seminar in the first place and, if so, how you should go about giving it.

You may discover at this point that you have the speakers, the subject matter, and a targeted audience, but you don't feel you can attract the audience you want. In these cases consider joint-venturing a seminar with someone else—an accounting firm, a bank, a brokerage house, or the like. Perhaps they can provide the audience you need, or the promotional support you cannot provide, or even some additional speakers. Don't let pride of authorship stand in the way of having a co-sponsor in your seminar. It is better to be co-sponsor of a program that is successful than be the sole sponsor of a program that bombs. Besides, a co-sponsor can lend additional credibility and prestige to your sponsorship and can probably attract people that your firm could not attract on its own.

Even if a particular seminar is the right thing for your firm to do, it can still fizzle if you don't execute it properly. At the end of this section is a check list of important things to keep in mind when planning a seminar. It does not tell "Everything you need to know before planning and giving a seminar." Our firm has prepared a more comprehensive guide on the subject for use by our clients. But this check list does cover the major things that a firm should consider in order to carry it off effectively.

One other important point is so obvious that it doesn't appear on any check list. Since it takes a lot of time and effort to prepare a good seminar, even a brief two-hour one, make every effort to develop one that can be repeated. An effective "road show" that can be given over and over repays its development cost many times over, even if it is only moderately successful. A program that you can give only once may have to win an Academy Award to justify the cost of developing it.

Seminars Checklist

1. Select seminar coordinator.
2. What is the purpose of the seminar—public relations, develop leads, sell new services, or provide additional information to clients?
3. Subject.
4. Invitation list—only clients or include others?
5. Sponsor—third party?
6. Where to hold—firm's offices, sponsor's offices, or outside?
7. Speakers—all from the firm or some outside?
8. Agenda.
9. Date, length, and time of day; avoid holidays and busy periods for attendees.
10. Charge for attendance? If so, how much?
11. Include lunch, cocktails, dinner?
12. Announcement—should be received at least three weeks before seminar.
13. How to promote—direct mail, written invitation, other?
14. Registration—by mail, phone, or both?
15. Advance materials—send confirmation of registration and any materials to be read in advance.
16. Conference materials—charts, illustrations, workbooks, worksheets, etc.
17. Visual aids.
18. Name cards and tent cards for attendees.
19. Participant evaluation sheet of seminar.

Writing for Publications

Writing articles for outside publication, as distinguished from writing for a firm newsletter or bulletin, has been an effective lawyer's marketing activity for a long time. The problem is that it may be the wrong activity for many firms. Like most of the activities discussed here in Part II, it all depends on the situation.

To begin with, let's discuss the firm's marketing objectives. If one of the objectives, either strategic (long-range) or tactical (short-range), is to develop a strong professional image or reputation, then writing for publication should definitely be considered one of the marketing tactics. It can be one of the most effective ways to embellish the firm's legal reputation and expertise.

On the other hand, if this is not one of the objectives, then placing a lot of emphasis on writing may be a waste of time and resources. The main objective that writing can accomplish is to improve or spread the firm's professional reputation. It can also result in referrals from other law firms. Generally, this applies in a specific area of law (such as tax) or in a specific industry. There is little else that writing can do. In a small community, over an extended period of time, writing in the general press may raise the recognition level of a firm or a particular lawyer. But this is a slow pay-out and in most cases is not worth the time and effort just to accomplish this objective. There are far more cost-effective ways to accomplish this than writing; see subsequent sections on Talks and Speeches, Community Activities, and Social Clubs.

CAN ANYBODY WRITE?

Even if the firm does wish to enhance its public image, writing may still not be an appropriate method. The standard of writing must be at least reasonably good in order to be effective, and in many firms there really aren't many lawyers who can write a decent article in clear, basic English that would be of interest to anyone other than another lawyer. In these cases the effort put into writing would be wasted, because either the material would not get published or, worse, if it was published, the poor quality of the writing would hurt rather than help the firm's image.

So the next thing to check is the writing ability of the people in the firm, particularly those people who say they would like to do some writing. You can't afford to let poor writers waste their time (and the firm's) producing unpublishable work. In a medium-size firm, the chances are that you can find several lawyers who are adequate writers. They don't have to be amateur Hemingways, but they must be able to write clearly and logically so that the potential audience can understand them.

If none of the partners or senior associates meet these requirements, don't give up. Look at your younger associates. Perhaps one of them has the ability to turn out good copy if given the technical material. He or she could ghostwrite for a lawyer who has the professional experience or reputation but does not have the time or skill to put it down on paper. If this is not possible, but if the firm still feels that it is important to have some writing published under the name of one or several of its attorneys, consider hiring a professional writer to ghostwrite articles.

EDITING AND REVIEW

In most cases someone in the firm should review written material from a technical viewpoint before it is released to the outside world. Even if, for example, the labor department knows everything there is to know about some obscure section of the latest law, the department head or some other qualified lawyer should look over the material to make sure the expert isn't advocating violating the law. If an associate has written something, an appropriate partner should review it.

You can, of course, relax this requirement for specific lawyers when you are confident that their professional presentation will always be well-documented and correct. But you should establish a quality control process for outside writing. A piece that is professionally incorrect is just as damaging to the firm as a piece that is badly written.

Before going any further on the subject of writing, I'd like to summarize the points made above because they apply to most of the marketing activities discussed in this Part II of the book.

The selection of a particular activity or tactic to be included in the marketing plan depends on several factors:

1. Does it fit into the marketing objectives?
2. Does the firm possess the ability to perform or execute it effectively?

3. Is the activity executed in accordance with the firm's ethical and professional standards?

Now let's return to the particular subject of this section.

TYPES OF ARTICLES OR BOOKS

Generally speaking, there are two types of articles or books a lawyer can write: professional and general. Which type you write depends on the target audience and the intended publication.

Professional articles are obviously articles intended for other professionals, generally lawyers, and will therefore be published in professional journals of some kind. They are more technical in nature. They are not intended to be read or understood by the general public. They can be very effective in raising the author's professional image—and also his or her ego.

General articles are those primarily intended for audiences outside the profession. They should usually be directed toward a specific audience such as house counsels, mortgage bankers, or a specific industry such as retailing, general contracting, or nursing homes. Articles could, of course, be directed toward the general public; for example, an article giving tips on how to prepare a will could be written for a local newspaper.

HOW TO GET INTO PRINT

It surprises many attorneys to hear that most publications—professional, trade, or general; monthly, weekly, or daily—are always looking for material. That does not mean that they will necessarily be interested in your brilliant article on incorporation for bee keepers or the OSHA requirements for an art gallery. But it does mean that they have pages they must fill with material of interest to their readers. Sometimes they have too much for a particular issue and other times they are scratching around.

If you have a subject that you know is "hot" or of interest to a specific audience, then go ahead and write the article first. After writing it, contact the editor or managing editor of the appropriate magazine, journal, etc., and tell him or her that you have this marvelous piece all ready to go. On the other hand, if you have targeted a particular publication that you want to appear in, it is better to first prepare a list of possible subjects, then contact the editor to discuss them before writing the article. The editor may have already run something on these subjects, or might not be interested. But after talking with you, he or she may think of some other subject for you to tackle, and you will not have wasted time preparing an article you can't place.

REPRINTS

It is usually important to obtain and distribute reprints of articles after they are published, especially articles in nonlegal publications. The readership of the particular publication is only a small part of the audience you want to reach. Wide exposure of an article via reprints makes the author more of an authority to more of an audience. Reprints can certainly be displayed in the firm's reception area. Often you will want to mail them to clients and other interested parties. You may also want copies available for an "information kit" on your firm.

It takes a lot of work to prepare even one article, so try to get as much mileage as you can out of each one. Obtaining and distributing reprints is the best way to increase your "reputation mileage" as much as possible.

BOOKS

Some of the above principles apply to the writing of books as well. It is generally best to have at least a tentative agreement with a publisher before spending the extensive amount of time required to write a book. Of course, the lawyer need not write an entire book. He or she can co-author a book with someone else, or can write one or several chapters in a book on a broad subject.

When a book is published, there is ample opportunity to have some of the chapters reprinted or adapted in periodicals, journals, etc. This gives more mileage and publicity to the book—and will probably sell additional copies as well!

Talks and Speeches

On the surface you might think that the same ground rules that apply to writing also apply to speaking. Well, some do and some do not.

A speaking program will fit into the marketing objectives of almost any law firm because effective speaking can accomplish a number of things. It can enhance the firm's and the lawyer's professional image; increase recognition; penetrate groups that might otherwise be closed to the speaker; and bring about face-to-face contacts. They also produce opportunities to be invited onto other platforms. In other words, the giving of talks and speeches is a very flexible and versatile marketing activity.

But if it is important to have people who can write before you launch into a writing program, it is even more important that your potential speakers can speak effectively before encouraging them to "hit the banquet circuit."

EFFECTIVE SPEAKING

Good public speaking, to an audience of five or five thousand, starts with a couple of basics. First, the speaker must be reasonably knowledgeable about his or her subject. Second, the topic must be of some interest to the audience. No matter how much you may know about the subject, the chances are that the neighborhood garden club is not interested in personal injury defense for tractor manufacturers. Third, the speaker must be able to express himself or herself in front of an audience. That may seem obvious, but the painful truth is that many knowledgeable people are just not able to face an audience. So a firm had better determine this before encouraging its people to get out and speak. When you have written an article that puts people to sleep, you may never know it; but when you give a talk that puts people to sleep, they do it right in front of you. It hurts the firm, and the lawyers, to have ineffective speakers.

It is also important, just as in writing, for the firm to have some quality control on what its people are saying. It is impossible, of course, to screen every talk before it is given, but someone in the firm, such as the department head, should approve what is said if there is any chance of controversy or misunderstanding. The more important the audience, the more important is this review.

TYPES OF TALKS

Just as there are two types of articles, there are two types of talks, professional and general, depending upon the audience. Speeches or the presentation of papers to legal or professional groups can enhance a lawyer's professional reputation—and perhaps his or her speaking ability. They can also lead to referrals. General talks also can have great marketing impact because they are delivered to clients, potential clients, or potential referrals of new business. It is important to give everyone some kind of guidelines as to what types of speaking engagements they should seek or accept. These may relate to the firm's objectives, target industries and businesses, or just the general nature of the practice. Some well-intentioned lawyers will speak to the Cub Scout den mothers or the Little League coaches' meeting without ever stopping to think whether the audience might contain any potential clients or could help bring the firm business.

Some people can be very effective speakers without writing more than a bare outline; some can even speak extempore. Others either cannot or will not speak unless every word is written out and edited first. This latter type, by the way, are often the most boring speakers because they tend to read, rather than deliver, their talks. Nevertheless, both types of talks, extempore or written, can be effective. If someone requires a completely written text before he or she is comfortable delivering it, perhaps you can find a speechwriter either within the firm or outside. Remember this word of caution, however: It is harder to find good speechwriters than it is to find good ghostwriters.

HOW TO OBTAIN SPEAKING OPPORTUNITIES

Plenty of groups are looking for qualified speakers. Sometimes they are more interested in a particular speaker, and sometimes in a particular topic. Some lawyers develop several talks on different topics and give them over and over, as long as the topics are current and interesting. This way their original preparation time can be leveraged into many additional talks. These lawyers also become identified with these topics and become somewhat recognized as authorities. In these cases the subject matter is perhaps less important than the particular speaker. On the other hand, a group might be interested in someone to speak on the subject of toxic waste disposal, or the tax advantages of a professional corporation. The particular speaker is then less important than the subject.

In other cases the speaker develops a following, perhaps regardless of the area of law or subject, because he or she has a reputation for being informative, interesting, dramatic, or even humorous. Then the speaker becomes more important than the subject. Generally, however, the subject of the talk is more important.

Various types of groups should be considered as possible audiences. The professional organizations are obvious; groups of lawyers can include excellent referral possibilities. Every community has business groups such as Kiwanis, Rotary, Chamber of Commerce, etc. However, I feel that specialized audiences are generally more productive for marketing purposes. The local or national chapters of trade groups are excellent audiences, particularly if the firm has targeted certain industries for further development. Specific professional groups such as doctors can also be important. A general talk to a general audience is not as effective a marketing tool as a specific talk to a specific target audience.

If an attorney has become active in a group, it provides a better opportunity to appear before the group as a speaker. For other groups, locate the person responsible for programs and discuss with him or her what topics that might be of interest to the members. Customize each talk for the particular audience, even if it is from a basic script. This indicates the speaker's knowledge of the audience and also enhances the impact the speaker makes.

Some firms, once they get the momentum going, even develop a mini "speakers bureau." Someone in the firm gathers the information on which lawyers are qualified to speak on which topics and then contacts various groups to offer a speaker on whatever topic is agreed upon. Once the word begins to spread that a particular lawyer or a firm can deliver some interesting talks on worthwhile subjects, speaking opportunities will flow in. In fact, the problem could become one of being selective and turning down some audiences that have less marketing potential.

SHOULD COPIES BE AVAILABLE?

There are two schools of thought on whether copies or at least outlines of talks should be distributed to the audience. The first school says never hand out anything to a nonprofessional group except your business card. The other school says always have some kind of handout and always have the firm name, address, and phone number on it. I tend to favor the latter school. Of course a lawyer isn't going to give away any secrets, least of all in writing. But personally I feel that a speaker enhances his or her credibility when they distribute some kind of material. It also makes it easier for the members of the audience to contact the speaker afterward.

If the talk is on a sensitive or complicated subject, then verbatim copies definitely should be distributed—after the talk. The only exception would be if there is going to be press coverage; copies of the talk should be given to the press before it is delivered.

Frequently there are people in a firm who could become effective speakers with a little professional help. Since there are plenty of speech coaches, presentation consultants, and the like available today, many firms are finding it a worthwhile investment to make some of this training available to their people. Ability is the most important quality a speaker must have; knowledge of the material is second.

The bottom line in developing speaking as an effective marketing activity is this: the speakers must be interesting and must have something worthwhile to say. It takes both to successfully implement this marketing tactic.

Membership in Professional Groups

Now to spend a few words on a subject that is every sensitive to most professionals, not just attorneys: membership in professional groups.

Being active in such groups is extremely important in terms of developing a reputation within the profession, improving one's professional knowledge, making professional contacts, and even doing some recruiting from other firms. But is this important to the marketing program? It is my opinion that in most professions it has little to do with marketing—except in the legal profession.

Remember that the term "marketing" comes from the word "market," which basically means a place where business is carried on. To a professional, this means a place where clients and prospects are to be found. In the case of law, however, there is another important market: referrals. While clients and prospects (except for some house counsel) are not normally members of bar groups, attorneys who could possibly refer business are. This simple fact, added to whatever professional recognition comes with being a member of a particular group, makes membership in bar groups a worthwhile marketing activity—if the lawyer uses it for this purpose.

In terms of marketing, it does relatively little for a lawyer to be just a member of a bar association, whether the ABA or the state or local association. As with certain other activities (see later sections), the lawyer must be visible. He or she must be active, either in a leadership role or in one or more special sections that "showcase" their expertise in a particular area of law. Just joining a bar or professional group to add it to a resume is, in terms of marketing, a complete waste of time and money. That isn't marketing; in fact, it is sometimes an excuse for not doing any real marketing. There are some lawyers who hide within bar group membership in order to avoid being called upon in the firm to participate in any other membership in professional groups as a marketing activity; they are using it as a marketing excuse.

In adition to membership in bar or legal groups, lawyer membership in certain other professional groups can have some marketing benefit. Some accounting groups fall in this category. The same concept holds, to a somewhat lesser degree, for architecture and engineering. On the other hand, involvement in medical groups should be classified primarily as being as much a marketing tactic as it is a professional activity.

Community Activities

There is nothing new about the idea of lawyers and accountants becoming involved in community activities for the purpose of developing business. So why bother to discuss the subject? There are several reasons—and the first one has nothing to do with practice development.

Even in this day and age, many lawyers make a serious mistake. It probably starts when they enter the law; then, as time goes on and their habits are formed, they continue the mistake. What is it? They concentrate almost entirely on succeeding in their profession to the exclusion of developing any outside interests, hobbies, or skills. This might even include their families. As a result they quickly or eventually become narrow, dull, and unexciting people who, while they might be real stars in their profession, are absolutely lost when they leave their offices. These are often the same people who suffer what is currently termed "burnout" sometime in their careers.

I fully realize the pressures that a lawyer faces, particularly one just entering the profession. Billable hours, continuing legal education, billable hours, managing a practice, billable hours, business development, and billable hours—just to name a few. And there is really no way to avoid all this, particularly for the young associate. It's part of learning the profession and, as the old-timers like to say, "paying your dues."

COMMUNITY ACTIVITIES HELP DEVELOP THE PERSON

But that still does not mean that the only thing a person should do is practice law. Everyone needs some outside interests, whether or not they are related to obtaining new business. Spending a few hours a week or a month doing something that is not related to practicing law, *and* which a person enjoys, will make him or her a more complete person as well as a better attorney.

This is the first reason for this section and several others that discuss involvement in outside, nonprofessional activities. I firmly believe that every lawyer should do at least one thing outside the professional field: play golf, collect coins, race stock cars, coach kids' sports, take up needlepoint (one famous pro-football tackle did), or do anything that he or she enjoys doing. It should be done for its own sake and because it's enjoyable; if it isn't, it should be dropped and something else should be done in its place.

The second reason for this section and several others is to discuss how to do certain things effectively in order to advance the firm's marketing program. Involvement in community activities can help lawyers obtain a lot of new business if they have the interest and if they know how to do it effectively. Some lawyers, as discussed above, do not have the interest. You can't force people to do things, no matter what the personal benefit would be. You can only create an atmosphere that encourages a situation. However, for those people who either want to, or at least are willing to, get involved in community activities, you can follow some definite guidelines that will make the experience more enjoyable for the person—and also beneficial to the firm.

HOW TO IMPLEMENT

The place to start is with the individual and his or her interests, which leads us back to the lawyer profiles discussed earlier. The profile will give you some good clues as to the person's interests and the type of outside activity he or she would enjoy.

The next area to address is more complex but equally important. You need to prepare a list of the community activities that could be important for the firm to have people involved in; that is, activities that could lead to business opportunities because current clients, prospective clients, or good sources of leads are involved in them. This requires some qualitative analysis. For example, suppose your office is located in a suburban community twenty miles from a major city and your practice consists largely of businesses, organizations, and individuals in that community. Your list of important activities should first cover those in your community—the local chamber, school board, Little League, Brownie troop, etc.—before you consider anything in the city, such as its chamber of commerce, charity drives, etc. Remember that the guiding principle in designating target activities is that clients, prospects, or sources be involved in them.

After you have prepared this list of target activities, go back to the profiles and make another list of the activities your people are currently involved in. Compare your two lists. You will find that some lawyers in the firm are active in these target activities and some are active in other things. You will also find, possibly to your surprise, that no one from the firm is involved in certain important areas.

MATCHING UP

Now you must start the delicate process of examining the profiles and the un-covered activities and matching people up with appropriate activities. This is the key step. You must match people's personal interests with the firm's goals. People must have an interest in, and an aptitude for, the area you want them to become involved in. If they do not, they will resent the firm for pushing them and will be ineffective or may even do damage to the firm's image. If, after careful examination and effort, you can't cover every activity with an appropriate person, then leave that area un-covered for the time being until you have the right person. To repeat—you can't force square pegs into round holes. It is far better to have your people doing what they enjoy, even if it means not having the firm represented in certain key areas, than to force someone to try to do what they don't want to do.

If, on the other hand, your "match game" is well executed, you will have an enthusiastic group of lawyers and some effective marketing effort underway as well.

A simple example of how to analyze community activities and potentially target your people is in the Community Activities Analysis table at the end of this section.

GETTING STARTED

Many people would be delighted to get involved in something in their community, particularly if they know it can help their professional careers as well as broaden their lives and interests, but they often don't know how to go about it. Several years ago one of our clients in Philadelphia found this true with a number of its people. The client's director of business development and I prepared some guidelines on how to select and become involved in various organizations in the city. The seven points proved of such help in that case that our firm has continued to use these guidelines (with that client's permission, of course) with many other clients. Those guidelines are listed here.

GUIDELINES FOR SELECTION
AND INVOLVEMENT IN CHARITABLE,
CIVIC, EDUCATIONAL,
AND CULTURAL ORGANIZATIONS

1. Find something you enjoy doing and/or whose results are important to you.
2. Find out who belongs or is involved.

3. Ask your contact about the group and how you can help.
4. In most organizations you can help in a variety of ways by giving sheer volume of time (volunteer worker); giving money (large amounts); or giving your own skilled time.
5. Some of the larger institutions have many avenues of potential involvement. For example, the University of Pennsylvania has many activities not limited just to alumni, such as:
   • Botanical Gardens
   • Annenberg Center
   • Institute of Contemporary Art
   • University Museum
   • University Hospital
6. It will be harder to be important or to work with important people at the larger, more prestigious organizations. However, they offer more choice, more flexibility, and generally more contacts and community visibility.
7. Whatever you select, work at it; give your time; work at rising to a position of importance—don't just be a "joiner." You'll find that you have learned a lot, met some interesting people, and vastly improved your own and the firm's business opportunities.

Every community has different levels of activities, based on the business and social status of the people who are involved in them. This is more true in cities than in rural areas, but the principle applies in most communities. There are some blue-chip activities that involve company CEOs, bank presidents, social leaders, etc., and are therefore appropriate only for the managing partner or some senior partner to be active in. Then there is a group of "important" activities where the next level of executives and other people mingle. This level is appropriate for most of the partners in a firm and perhaps a senior associate. There are always many activities, including very large ones, where people can become involved regardless of their business level or age. In some communities there are also certain types of activities that attract young people who become involved for a period of years and then graduate on to other areas.

Philadelphia is one of several cities in which we have researched this subject for clients and have prepared a comprehensive analysis. The list of Philadelphia cultural organizations is a good example of this hierarchy principle.

Cultural Organizations

Blue Chip
  Philadelphia Museum of Art
  Academy of Music
  Philadelphia Orchestra Association
  Pennsylvania Ballet
Important
  Pennsylvania Academy of Fine Arts
  Orpheus Club (men's glee club)
  Curtis Institute of Music
  Historical Society of Pennsylvania
  Pennsylvania Horticultural Society
Open to All
  Franklin Institute
  Free Library of Philadelphia
  Academy of Natural Sciences
  Friends of Independence National Historic Park
  Maritime Museum
For Younger Members
  Print Club—1614 Latimer Street
  Plays & Players (acting)
  Savoy Opera Co. (Gilbert & Sullivan)

So there you have it, "all you need to know to succeed in the community activities game." Is this a "must" marketing strategy for every firm? No, but like most of the strategies discussed in this book, it is something to consider. It works, but only if it is executed correctly and if it is right for your firm.

Community Activities Analysis

ACTIVITY	CURRENTLY INVOLVED	POTENTIAL
Chamber of Commerce	Carter Smith	Anderson
JC's	Palmer Parker Reichelberger	
Development Authority		Gilkerson

(Continued)

Community Activities Analysis (*Continued*)

ACTIVITY	CURRENTLY INVOLVED	POTENTIAL
Downtown Redevelopment Authority		Miller
Symphony Orchestra	Newman	
Opera Guild		Bartolini
United Way	Carter Johnson Wright	
Catholic Charities	Kelly	Henderson
Allied Jewish Appeal	Katz	Mandell
Metropolitan		Carter
St. Mary's Hospital		Kelly

Social Clubs

A strategy that is frequently used to develop business is membership in clubs, specifically social clubs—luncheon, golf, tennis, swimming, etc.—as opposed to professional clubs. Once again you address the subject by listing the clubs in your area whose memberships match up relatively well with your firm's client list or whose members include a high percentage of likely prospects. This list may or may not include the so-called prestigious clubs in the area; that depends largely on the firm's client list and target prospect list. The guiding principle is "What clubs do the firm's clients or likely prospects belong to?" If a significant group of clients and prospects belong to various prestigious clubs, then it is necessary to target this kind of club. If your clients and prospects are members of other clubs, don't overshoot the mark and target the so-called prestigious ones. *The real purpose of the club game is to socialize in areas where you could meet prospective clients.* It is not to feed the partners' egos (although that can be involved).

The next step, of course, is back to the profiles of the lawyers to learn which clubs, if any, they belong to. Then you prepare the same type of analysis you did for the community activities. An example is shown here:

Downtown Clubs

CLUB	MEMBER	POSSIBLE
Urban	Katz	Duffy
Union	—	Parker
University	Greenbaum Davison Gorman Palmer	
Vesper	—	Katz Davison Borzell

Country Clubs

CLUB	MEMBER	POSSIBLE
Park Hills Golf Club	Katz	Greenbaum
Mountain View	Davison	—
Old Warson	—	Rogers Gorman
Greenwood	—	Stevens Rogers
Bellevue Tennis Club	—	Palmer

MATCHING UP

Matching the right people with the right clubs becomes even more important here than in some other strategies. Some rules of thumb are obvious; a single person shouldn't be targeted for a family-type swimming club, or someone who can't stand golf shouldn't be encouraged to join a club that is mainly for golfers. But you also have to include some other considerations. Look at your lawyer's spouse and children. What type of club would they enjoy? Take geography into account also; no matter how ideal the "fit" might seem, a person probably won't want to drive twenty miles to a club if there are similar clubs closer to home. Finally, you should consider social styles, perhaps nationality, and even the department the person is in.

Another important point: spread your people around. Try not to let them all join the same clubs. If there are three downtown clubs you feel the firm should be represented in, avoid having everyone in one club and no one in the other two clubs.

Each club has certain membership characteristics that you must analyze and consider. The same warning that applies in community activities applies to clubs—probably even more so: No matter how important a particular club may be in your marketing strategy, if you don't have an appropriate person for that club, leave it un-covered until you do have the right person.

SHOULD THE FIRM PAY?

Whenever I address the strategy of club membership in one of my seminars or in consulting with a client firm, the question invariably comes up, "Should the firm pay for its people to join clubs?" Needless to say, this is a delicate subject both economically and personally.

There is no right or wrong answer. However, after being involved in professional-firm marketing for over ten years (about as long as the field has existed), I have developed a viewpoint: If the firm can afford the cost, I favor the concept of the firm paying the initiation fees and a proportionate share of dues and entertainment costs.

I have two reasons for favoring this policy. The first is purely a marketing one. Membership in the right club can help bring additional business to a firm if the people involved enjoy clubs and if they know how to meet people in the clubs. True, many people do not enjoy belonging to a club, or many firms are comprised of people who do not really care for clubs. In these cases the strategy won't work. But for people and firms who are suited to this concept and who enjoy it, club memberships can pay off effectively in developing business. This idea may turn off a lot of people, but the fact of life still exists that personal contact is one of the most effective ways to market a firm and an individual—assuming, of course, that the firm or the lawyer has a reputation for doing quality work.

The second reason I favor this policy is a management one. The one who holds the purse strings has the final say. If the firm is paying some or all of the costs of joining and using a club, it can exert a far stronger hand in directing where it would like its people to be members. Once again this is a delicate situation, but if the correct principles are followed in executing this strategy (as discussed earlier), the policy works out quite well. I know. I have seen it work in many firms.

SOME CONDITIONS

Now for the ground rules. I recommend paying for membership if a particular club is either on the firm's list of "target" clubs or if it is approved by the executive committee or its equivalent. There may be some discussion when a partner wants to join a club in which a number of other partners are already members and the firm would prefer that he or she join a different club in which the firm has no members. But if you have analyzed your people and the clubs properly, these occasional problems can be resolved without too much friction.

Suppose that a partner insists on joining a club that the firm (i.e., the executive committee or even the marketing committee) does not feel will help the firm's marketing effort; what then? The practical answer is that the firm finally approves the partner's request if all efforts at persuasion have failed. The burden of proof is then on the partner to show that this affiliation is helping the firm's marketing effort. If it isn't, the costs of this membership are considered the partner's personal expense rather than a marketing expense of the firm. Some lawyers may say this approach will never work in their firms. But the fact is, more and more firms are adopting this hard-nosed business approach—which is the way many law firms handled the subject a long time ago.

IS IT WORTH IT?

This leads to the final question: How do you evaluate whether a particular club or the entire club game is worth the expense? After a period of time you can track the contacts a person is making through a club and the results of those contacts in terms of keeping or obtaining business. It isn't an exact science by any means, but a reasonably accurate conclusion can be reached.

You will note that I have referred to partners in this section. If the firm is going to pay the cost of club memberships, I firmly believe this policy should be limited to partners only. To extend this to the senior associate level, no matter how important it may be in a few cases, eventually leads to a lot of problems that could have been avoided.

And besides, partnership in the firm should have some special benefits—even if they include the obligation to play some productive "customer golf."

Target Influential People

It is a simple fact of life that in every organization, whatever its size, there are certain people who can be classified as influential. This is as often a result of the positions they hold as it is of their own abilities. Regardless of the reason, they are accepted as influential people whose words or opinions on many subjects are given great weight.

The president of the largest bank in town is more often than not an influential person. The mayor of the city might be. Outstanding lawyers and accountants often attain this stature. High-visibility CEOs are generally regarded as influential. Sometimes the president of the local university falls into this category. The list will vary in any community or industry, but I'm certain the reader understands the principle.

It can be a great help to a law firm's marketing efforts if the firm is recognized and even "endorsed" by one of these influential people. To have such a person say, "Such-and-such a firm? I've heard of them (or I know them). They are quite good," can do as much or more to bring a firm new business as a front-page interview with one of the partners in the local paper. This type of recommendation can happen, and to a great degree it can be caused by the firm.

It is another curious fact of life that if an individual concentrates on meeting and developing a relationship with someone, more often than not it will happen. This is as true in New York, Chicago, or Brussels as it is in Nashua, New Hampshire, Grand Island, Nebraska, or Macon, Georgia. Admittedly it takes a little luck, but it also takes some work and being alert. For some strange reason, if you set out to meet someone, learn about that person, and keep alert for opportunities (or occasionally make one), you wind up meeting that person.

RESEARCH THE PEOPLE

So another marketing strategy to consider is that of developing a list of target influential people for the lawyers in the firm to research and

The Influentials

NAME	POSITION	BOARDS (OTHER THAN OWN)	CLUBS AND ACTIVITIES	ADDRESS	PERSONAL HISTORY
John T. Johnson	President and CEO, International Bridge Company	First National Bank ITT General Motors	Greenwood CC Bellevue TC Art Museum C of C, Board	1200 Old Golf Road, Greenwood (564–1234)	1920, Johnstown, PA Yale, 1944 MBA, Harvard, 1949
Robert D. Goldman	Chairman and CEO, Goldman Brothers	UNA Corporation Guaranteed Life Insurance Company	Brandeis U, Trustee Symphony Orchestra	Grays Lane, Strafford (813–4280)	1928, Chicago, IL Northwestern, 1950 Stanford Law, 1953

track toward meeting. You may find that suddenly your next door neighbor works for the person in question, or your sister is married to that person's best friend, or you find yourself sitting next to him or her at a meeting. How it happens, I don't know; I can only tell you that it happens often enough to make the effort worthwhile.

The process of tracking such people is very simple and is similar to what I recommended in the section on lawyer profiles. Begin accumulating information on the person—where he or she lives, spouse, family, memberships, activities, interests, schools attended, etc. Then lay out the information in tabular form as you did with the lawyers' profiles; an example is given below. Circulate these spread sheets to the partners and possibly the associates and keep following up with further information as it is obtained. Perhaps you will soon uncover a mutual acquaintance who can arrange an introduction, or, as mentioned above, you may suddenly find yourself in that person's company.

An important point to remember in designating influential people is that they need not necessarily be prospective clients. The important point is that you want them to eventually meet someone from the firm and to be impressed with that lawyer and the firm.

What type of relationship should you strive for with such people? It need not be a close one, although of course this might develop. The guideline I give my clients is this: If you called that person, would he or she recognize your name or that of your firm and take the call? That is the minimum. Anything above that is a plus.

Clients' Stockholders and Boards of Directors

This marketing strategy requires some discussion, either because it is sometimes overlooked or because it can lead to problems.

Let's take the matter of client stockholders first.

Many of a law firm's clients are businesses that have more than just one or two stockholders who are also involved in management. (Naturally I am referring to closely held companies.) Quite often the general counsel or the law firm will look at these stockholders as a faceless group rather than as individuals. It is almost as if they had the title "stockholder" tattooed on their foreheads. Lawyers, and for that matter accountants and even consultants, often overlook the fact that stockholders are also people who may be prospective clients or at least possible sources who could spread the word about the fine law firm their company has representing it. In other words, they are individuals who should be recognized as such and who should also receive some marketing attention.

Here is a group of people who already should know the firm and have some idea of what it can do. So remove that categorical designation of "stockholder" and research and even cultivate some of them just as you would any other contact. That quiet man at the shareholders' meeting may own his own company, or that outspoken woman stockholder may be the new CEO of a business that is unhappy with its current legal counsel.

The same principle holds for boards of directors, whether they be of companies or of civic or nonprofit organizations. Too often the lawyer or lawyers who are involved in working with boards do not take the time to research and cultivate the individual directors as potential clients or potential sources of business.

SHOULD LAWYERS SIT ON CLIENTS' BOARDS?

Of course there is the other point, not at all unrelated to marketing, about lawyers serving on the boards of client companies or organizations. For many years, this was a common practice that was rarely if ever questioned. In recent years, however, serving as a director of a publicly held company has become a perilous, or at least more sensitive, responsibility for anyone—particularly attorneys. If a lawyer serves on the board of a publicly held company that is also a client, disclosure must be made of the fees paid the lawyer or the firm by the company. When even modest fees are involved, some people relish the opportunity to question the propriety of this perceived conflict or at least dual responsibility. Because this has become a significant if not pertinent issue at times with publicly held clients, some law firms have established the policy that their lawyers may not serve on the boards of client companies. Of course some publicly held companies have adopted the same policy in reverse: attorneys or consultants who serve the company may not be directors.

Speaking from a marketing point of view only, I can understand both sides of this issue. I have been, or currently am, on the boards of several companies, both public and closely held. In some cases the company's general counsel has also sat on the board. This type of exposure has usually been quite helpful to the other board members and, I believe, also to the attorney. Of course the obvious point could be raised that the attorney could attend board meetings but not be a director. That's true—but it just doesn't have the same impact.

The answer? I believe that each law firm or each sole practitioner and each company must make its own policy. In the case of privately held companies, I believe it is generally a good thing for the firm's counsel to be a member of the board if he, and/or his firm, are comfortable with that relationship. In the case of a publicly held company, I feel the issue must be more closely examined in the light of stockholder relations and even the broader concept of social accountability. If there could be the slightest question as to the attorney's perceived allegiance, i.e., to the stockholders or to company management, then I do not believe the attorney can serve effectively on a client's board.

Sources: How to Identify and Develop Them

Any law firm, large or small, specialized or general practice, has a number of different markets that it must recognize and market to if it is going to be successful. (For any of you familiar with another very specialized field of marketing, health care, you will recognize the similarity. In the case of hospitals, the various markets are called "publics.") In addition to current clients and prospective clients, sources are an extremely important market. Although law firms have historically depended on referrals from either clients or third parties as perhaps their single most important source of new business, it is surprising that so few firms have an organized marketing approach to outside sources.

A firm's principal sources of leads and referrals can generally be categorized as follows:

- Other lawyers or law firms
- Accounting firms
- Other professional firms
- Certain types of businesses
- Personal contacts, friends and relatives

Each of these categories should be analyzed for its current and potential value to the firm. Then marketing effort should be directed toward those sources that either have already referred business to the firm or are in a position to do so.

OTHER LAWYERS OR LAW FIRMS

This is such an obvious area that many readers may feel it is unnecessary to discuss it. However, while sourcing (and particularly sourcing with other lawyers) is not new as a business development technique, just as in the case of several other "traditional" marketing techniques, good marketing means developing a process for doing the job effectively. Sole practitioners and small law firms often have clients who either outgrow them or need specialized skills that are only available in other firms. Larger firms also must frequently refer out cases, either because they have a conflict or just cannot handle the matter for one reason or another (such as the size of the fee). Therefore, the larger or specialized firm can benefit from cultivating the sole practitioners and smaller firms, and they, in turn, can benefit from association with reputable larger firms to whom they can refer their clients. It's a situation, like all referrals, where both sides should benefit—as well as the client, who is the first person that must benefit.

It is always important to research the quality of your sources, particularly when you will be referring work back to them as well. In the case of other law firms or lawyers, however, it is vitally important. If you are going to refer out one of your own clients, contacts, or friends, you had better be sure that the source you are sending them to is, first of all, qualified and secondly will work well with them. Remember our earlier discussion on the chemistry that must exist between a client and his or her lawyer? The worst thing you can do when you refer business *to* a source is to have that source mishandle it in some way. The same principle works in reverse. You want to feel confident that the clients and matters that another lawyer or firm is sending you are the quality and type that you and your firm want to handle.

So, in addition to determining other lawyers who might be good sources, also research into what their reputation and quality of practice is.

The managing partner of one of our first law firm clients had what I consider the best—and also the briefest—description of the type of law firm that would be a good source: "Can do, won't steal, will refer." Keep that in mind as you develop your list of other law firms as sources; you won't go wrong.

ACCOUNTING FIRMS

Some lawyers, particularly those in the tax area, say that accountants are not only poor sources of business but competitors as well. Our firm has been consulting with accounting firms for over ten years, so we have a pretty good understanding of what accountants think. There *are* one or two areas these days where accountants and lawyers do compete against each other, but for the most part the two professions each have their own turf and complement each other. In other words, they can be very helpful sources for each other.

The departments that can generally receive the most business from accountants are General Corporate and Bankruptcy. Of course, Litigation can receive referrals from practically any source. Real Estate is another department that can obtain some benefit from accounting firm referrals.

Don't overlook the obvious. Determine who the accounting firm is for each of your business and institutional clients as well as your large-fee individual clients. You may find you have a number of clients in common with certain firms. If you don't already have a good source relationship with these firms, start with them as the best ones to initially cultivate. You already have something—meaning clients—in common.

OTHER PROFESSIONAL FIRMS

Other types of professional firms may also be good sources of new business, depending on the nature of the practice. Architects and engineers can sometimes be helpful if the law firm has a strong practice in real estate, development, or construction. Doctors can be excellent sources to a wide variety of prospective clients, particularly for tax-related work, estate planning, and of course for firms that have a strong base in health care.

Even management consulting firms, depending on their areas of practice, can be excellent sources of business for a law firm. Firms that specialize in pension plans, benefits, and compensation consulting can often refer tax-related work. Those that concentrate in the general area of human resources and personnel (the old name for human resources) can often refer not only tax work but labor work as well. Probably the best sources among consultants are those that specialize in the areas of general management, business strategy, financial management, and even crisis management—areas in which they either come in close contact with top management or assume management responsibility themselves.

If you feel that management consultants should not be regarded as professionals in the same sense as lawyers, doctors, and accountants, I won't argue with you. However, they can still be excellent sources of business—so just consider this paragraph as part of the next section below.

BUSINESS AS SOURCES

Many types of businesses can be good potential sources of new business for a law firm. Brokerage houses and investment bankers are two, particularly for firms that have a strong SEC and general corporate practice. Banks, particularly lending and trust officers, are generally considered good sources. In some cases workout officers are also important. We have had several client firms who have built almost their entire practice by cultivating a number of bank officers in the appropriate areas. Insurance agents and even some real estate brokers are frequently good sources of leads and referrals.

Beyond the basic business categories mentioned above, there are many others that might be good sources for a particular firm. Each firm should analyze its own practice and targeted areas for development to determine which types of businesses can be most helpful as sources.

PERSONAL CONTACTS, FRIENDS AND RELATIVES

It is amazing how many lawyers who might otherwise be excellent marketers overlook their own personal contacts, friends, and even relatives as potential sources of business. I am not talking about targeting them as prospective clients; that is discussed in another section. I am talking about cultivating them as "outside people" who can be alert to opportunities to spread the word about your firm and even make referrals and introductions. We should never overlook those people who are closest to us as potential sources of business.

Quite often a firm is not really aware of what outside sources have provided it with leads and referrals. One of the questions on the Strategic Analysis Check List in Part I is "Who are the principal outside sources of business?" This frequently draws the answer "We dont' really know" or "We don't have any." However, when the firm checks with the partners and sometimes also the associates, it generally finds it does have some sources that should be cultivated further. If no names materialize, it means that the firm is missing an important part of its marketing program.

HOW TO DEVELOP SOURCES

Once a firm has identified the various outside sources that are or can be important to it, how does it cultivate and develop these relationships?

Prior or existing personal contact is best. If you know someone in a source operation, start with that person. If not, start at the top—i.e., the president, the managing partner, the head of the commercial loan department, etc. Please remember: presidents of banks, God bless them, are generally not good sources (although they may be important as "Influentials"). You must get closer to the "firing line."

Research all potential sources before contacting them. If you already know the source, research again anyway. Learn as much as you can about their business or practice and also, if possible, about any clients or contacts you have in common. This helps identify what you don't know about the source and therefore want to inquire about. It also impresses the heck out of a lot of people and "sells" them on your interest in them, thoroughness, alertness, etc.

Be prepared with some ideas on what your firm could do for the source and what you believe the source could do for you. If possible, have examples of other similar source relationships, what has been done and what has been accomplished by both parties working together.

Also have in mind some kind of plan and program that you might discuss as a way of developing the relationship further. This could include meetings, lunches or dinners involving the source's people and yours, social functions, jointly sponsored seminars, etc. Think of things your firm and the source could do together. This results in far more people being involved than just you and your own personal contact and both strengthens and "institutionalizes" the relationship.

Do not treat the source as a prospective client, even if it could be. The approach and technique for cultivating a source is different in many respects from that used in cultivating a prospective client. Don't confuse the source—and don't confuse yourself—about which relationship you are trying to establish. If you approach someone as a potential source of business and develop the relationship along those lines, you will also have done a good job in developing that source as a potential client. The reverse is not necessarily true.

STEP RIGHT UP TO BAT

On your initial contact with the source, state your objective, which is to explore how the two of you—or your respective firms—can help each other. It is that simple and straightforward. Don't be timid about it. For some reason, lawyers often are. You are not promising the source any business, and you are certainly not going to guarantee that you will send the source every potential piece of business you could. But the basis for developing the relationship is that they might be able to help you and your firm, and, in turn, you want to know how you might be able to help them.

Then ask about them, everything they do, who their clients or customers are, what kinds of business they are looking for, and, very important, who are the key people in the source's operation. You can mention, almost casually, that you would also like to have the source as a client as well. But don't push that issue any further. Concentrate exclusively, except for that one casual reference, on the source relationship. As the source is talking, spot opportunities. Discuss your mutual contacts and experiences.

Then educate the source on what you and your firm can do. Do not limit your discussion to just what you think might be of interest to the source. Tell him or her everything your firm does. Use every golf club in your bag. You will probably emphasize certain apparent areas of interest, but don't hold anything back. Remember, you want to source to function as an "outside salesperson" for you and your firm, so the more the source knows, the better the source can help you.

If you discover areas of mutual interest and potential benefit, work out a follow-up program to maintain the contact and, if appropriate, involve others in your firm and the source's. Are there introductions either of you could make right now to prospective clients? Don't wait. Start the ball rolling right now.

KEEPING SCORE

Start a file on the source. Rather than keep it to yourself, make it available to the entire firm. The best place to do this is with the Marketing Coordinator (see later sections on implementation of the marketing plan) or in some other central place in the firm; some firms use the librarian or even the office manager. The file should contain information on the source's operations and qualifications, what they are looking for, and what help the source can give your firm. Also start a record of each source on the work referred to you. This record closely resembles a balance sheet. All of this information can go on a computer.

Finally, if you give the source's name to someone, let the source know. First of all, this is a courtesy to your source and equips him or her to react even more favorably if contacted. Secondly, the "someone" may never contact your source, but at least you will receive some credit from the source for giving the name out.

After a period of time, review and evaluate the business referred to and received from the source. If you have been on the giving end but not on the receiving, sit down with the source and attempt to find out why. If there is no good explanation, or if nothing changes, consider dropping that source and concentrating on another.

You can sum up a marketing strategy toward sources as: designate, educate, and cultivate.

Social Functions

Some law firms feel it is important to entertain their clients and other people, not just individually but also at group functions such as cocktail parties, open houses, golf outings, and the like. In other words, they adopt a marketing strategy of giving social functions.

The idea is fine. I am certainly not against enjoying a couple of drinks at a pleasant party or playing in a golf outing. The only problem is that much of the money spent on these social functions is wasted and some of it actually does more harm than good. This is because the well-intentioned firms that throw these functions forget the main purpose of the function and then plan and execute them poorly.

First of all, the purpose: If it is a social function, make it just that, social first and foremost. Don't seize the golf outing or open house for the new offices as an opportunity to buttonhole clients or friends of the firm and lay a heavy sales pitch on them. This is neither the time nor the place for that. The reason you invited people to your party was, ostensibly, for them to have a good time, a couple of drinks, see your beautiful offices, meet and chat with members of the firm or other interesting people, play golf, swim, or whatever the case may be. Your guests didn't accept an invitation to a business meeting; they accepted an invitation to a social event. So plan it that way, play it that way, and keep it that way.

Now I am not so naive as to think that some excellent chances to talk business will never arise during this type of event. They might, and if they do, go right ahead. That's the "hidden potential agenda" in any such event. But that must arise out of an enjoyable social function, not replace it. Quite frankly, if your clients and others find that your so-called social outings are really just excuses to give them a hard sell on the firm, you won't have to worry about their attending others in the future, because they won't be back. Your firm will have wasted a lot of money and time and done itself more harm than good.

So be sure that everyone planning the event keeps in mind that the only purpose is to make sure that your guests enjoy themselves. Pay attention to every detail. Have name cards if it's appropriate. Think of little touches that might distinguish your event from all the others your guests attend. Plan it as carefully as a party in your own home.

NOT AN OFFICE PARTY

Keep in mind that your event is not a private firm gathering. This means that every person in the firm must regard himself or herself as a host or hostess, not as a guest. They must go up to people and introduce themselves or take care of people who are standing alone, looking lost. Above all, the firm's people should never stand around in their own private little groups, talking among themselves and ignoring the guests. That will do more to alienate clients and prospects than cold hors d'oeuvres, weak drinks, or no place to put their coats—none of which should happen either.

If your guests leave your function feeling and saying that they had a good time, you have accomplished what you should have accomplished. It will do your ultimate marketing efforts more good to have your guests remember a pleasant time than to remember how two partners tied them up for half an hour on why your firm is the best one in town.

One final word on planning the event. Consider whether you want a large, mass function or a series of smaller, more intimate ones. If there are only ten of you, don't invite 300 with 200 expected to show. Then it won't really be your party, because you won't have enough lawyers to go around. Also keep in mind your own style as a firm. Do you want to be associated with the biggest bash in town, or are other kinds of events more appropriate for your firm?

Giving a successful social function isn't easy, and it can be expensive. That's why there aren't more of them given. Like anything else, however, if done right it can be a significant step in the marketing process.

Business Functions

Seminars, conferences, meetings, receptions to introduce the new head of the firm or a visiting dignitary, and similar events are really business functions which may have a social aspect included. The important point is to recognize that the business purpose must be accomplished even if the social purpose is never reached.

When your firm invites people to attend a seminar, presentation, or the like, they expect to receive some business benefit from it, even if that benefit is only to realize they should subsequently use your firm to work on their own particular case. They are giving up their time, perhaps a day or more of it, with the thought in mind that what they will learn at your business function will be worth more than what they could accomplish by staying in their office or at home.

So don't cheat them, don't disappoint them; give them their money's worth, even if it didn't cost them a cent. In other words, fulfill the billing and deliver the goods. If, for example, you invite people to a two-hour seminar to discuss how to fight an unfriendly tender offer, make sure the speakers (your people and any others) know their subject and cover it. If you are going to serve refreshments as part of the seminar, do it *after* the program has ended, not before or during the program. This will indicate that you have your priorities in order and that when you say you're going to talk business, you do talk business. It will also make the social part of the seminar, if there is one, more enjoyable as a change of pace for those who wish to remain.

LINE UP AT THE DOOR

If you are introducing the new head of your office or firm at a big reception, form a receiving line at the door and make sure that everyone who attends meets the "guest of honor" before they do anything else (other than hang up their hats and put down their briefcases). Sure, some of the people will come just to be there or to see who else is there. But carry the event off the way you announced it, and make sure you fulfilled the announced purpose.

If you are holding an open house to present your beautifully designed new offices, be sure everyone is offered a tour. That's why you supposedly invited them, so don't look foolish by not following through.

Guests at either social or business functions can see through a phony event in a minute. Don't let that happen to your firm.

The question sometimes arises about whether a firm should charge for a seminar, meeting, or symposium. As a general rule, I say no. You may think you establish a value to the function by charging for it, but you must remember that there are plenty of similar functions given for which no charge is made. Therefore, unless yours is either unique, several days long, or involves some highly recognized (and recognizably expensive) authorities, I would say you are only kidding yourself to try to charge for it.

To sum up: If it's a business function, make it business. If it's a social function, make it fun. Don't confuse the two.

Contributions

Contributions to various causes can be part of a firm's marketing program. Every law firm, like practically every other business entity, is besieged with more requests for contributions than it could possibly respond to. All or nearly all of them are legitimate, and every one is for a needy cause. So if we are going to give to some of them, either as a firm or as individuals, why not do it in a way that will further the firm's marketing efforts?

First of all, establish a budget. Some clients of ours, when they first hear this idea, recoil from it. Yet all major corporations include in their budgets an amount designated for contributions to various causes. Many individuals do the same in their personal budgets, at least for major causes that they know will solicit contributions from them and which they want to support. So why should the concept be ignored by law firms? For some strange reason it frequently is. It shouldn't be. Contributions are just as legitimate an item to budget as rent, utilities, or salaries.

The size of the budget to be devoted to contributions must vary with each firm. It depends, for one thing, on the profitability of the firm and the funds that would be available. It also depends on the priorities of the partners. There is no perfect amount or percentage of fee income to budget for contributions., It may even vary from year to year.

The next step is to agree on a list of organizations and causes that the firm will support and the amount budgeted for each. This is where the marketing considerations come in. Suppose that the firm has been making annual gifts of several hundred dollars to each of five law schools in the area. However, it decides that two of the schools have outstanding graduates and it wants to concentrate on obtaining a higher percentage of its new associates from these schools. It would seem wise to change the contribution basis to give greater amounts to these two schools and to reduce the amount given to the other three.

As another example, consider making substantial contributions to groups or causes that clients or prospective clients support (and perhaps even solicit your contribution for) in preference to others.

The firm should probably wind up with approximately 60 to 70 percent of its contributions budget earmarked for certain specific recipients and for some well-thought-out reasons. It is amazing how often firms have no idea of how much they contribute in a year or where or for what reason many of the contributions are made. The unspecified amount in the contributions budget should be kept for various other purposes that may come up in the course of a year, either from clients, prospects, influential people, or anybody at all.

If a firm has decided to position itself as a leader in its community, this careful budgeting and allocation of contributions becomes more important than ever. Call it public relations if you wish, but it still adds up to putting your money where it will do the most good, both for the recipients and for the firm.

Not all contributions need be made in the form of cash. In some cases it can be in the form of *pro bono* work. This can often be more helpful to the recipient than cold, hard cash, and may even cost the firm less. For example, a local orphanage might prefer to have a law firm handle its routine legal affairs than make a cash contribution. Or a nonprofit organization might appreciate a lawyer serving on its board even more than receiving another check. This type of activity should be considered where appropriate. The only drawback, from the law firm's viewpoint, is that such no-charge services are often overlooked or are almost taken for granted by some organizations, and almost never are publicized as much as a regular cash donation.

The question of political contributions will be taken up in the next section. As a parting word, let me make it clear that I am not a Scrooge who is against making gifts to any cause unless the firm obtains something in return. What I have been trying to say is that all causes that solicit your support are worthwhile and need the money. Therefore, since it's just about impossible to support them all, think and plan where your few dollars can both help some worthy organizations *and* aid the firm's image and marketing effort at the same time.

Political Activities

Lawyers are no strangers to politics, and many law firms have developed considerable new business over the years by becoming involved in political activities. In other words, they have used political activities as a marketing strategy.

Before adopting this strategy, however, a law firm should consider all the aspects and possible effects. To begin with, the firm should analyze its current practice as well as the potential business that could possibly be obtained as the result of political activity. If the practice as it exists today, or as defined in terms of the long-range objectives of the firm, would not benefit from political involvement, the firm would be wise to forget the whole subject and concentrate on other strategies. Politics is a win or lose situation. Whether you are working for a party, an organization, an issue, or a candidate, you can't win all the time or perhaps even much of the time. The partners in a firm that gets involved in politics must understand the risks and the rewards as well as the problems that can arise. They also must understand a very complex area and how to play the game.

The best place for a firm to start is to examine the two main approaches to political involvement and to develop a policy with regard to them. One approach is to support permanent political committees that do not involve campaigns of individual candidates. Local, county, and state party committees are among the best examples of these. The other approach is to support particular candidates and the temporary organizations and committees that are formed to support them. Similar to these are the committees, formed to support a particular issue or cause. The many groups formed in support of, or in opposition to, the Equal Rights Amendment, and the campaigns in various states to raise the legal drinking age, are examples. Quite often these special groups cut across party lines.

COVER BOTH SIDES

The first approach, supporting permanent committees, is the least controversial and least risky political activity a law firm can undertake. However, it still takes careful planning and execution. It also requires that one cardinal principle be remembered: "Cover both sides of the aisle." This means, of course, that the firm should support representative groups or committees from both or all of the political parties involved. There could be exceptions to this principle, but for the most part it is far more prudent to support all the major political groups in an area than to commit everything to one party or side. From a business standpoint, and that is what we are talking about, even the strongest supporters of one party will advocate that the firm cover the other side of the aisle as well.

When it comes to the second approach, supporting particular candidates, causes, and issues, the firm must exercise extreme caution and judgment. Clients and prospective clients often have very strong political or candidate preferences. The odds are that the firm will run the risk of being on the opposite side of the fence from some of its important clients. Many times this will not cause any problem in the relationships with those clients—but problems can arise. The firm should recognize this. Here again, even though it may sound ridiculous, a policy of providing at least some support to both sides may prove less dangerous to the firm.

A firm can be involved in the first approach, supporting permanent committees and organizations, without being involved in the second. On the other hand, it would rarely become involved in a particular campaign without first being active on a continuing basis for some permanent organization.

There are basically four ways a firm and its lawyers can be involved in either approach: cash contributions, volunteer work, running for office, and hiring former public figures.

CASH CONTRIBUTIONS

Contributions in the political area should be budgeted and planned just like those in other areas. But there is one additional factor to remember in the case of political contributions: In addition to, or separate from, the election laws regarding such contributions, the firm must develop a policy on the dollar limit and the places that the firm will contribute out of its own funds as well as the dollar limit and the places where the firm will "pass the hat" among the partners. In the latter cases, the partners have agreed to assess themselves a certain amount to be contributed either in the firm's name or in their individual names. Even if the firm has voted on this matter, collection of contributions from some partners may become a tedious and sometimes difficult task. Some people just naturally delay in coming up with their share of anything until pressure is put on them. Others may not agree with the policy even though the partners as a whole voted in favor of it. In these cases, be prepared for some collection problems.

VOLUNTEER WORK

In the case of volunteer or gratis work, there are several differences from the charitable or community area. First of all, this almost always has to be done on an individual, not a firm, basis. Second, volunteer work generally receives more recognition in the political area than in any other. To effectively execute this phase of the strategy, a firm must discuss with its lawyers—associates as well as partners—their interests and available time. In some cases this may require a reduction in the amount of billable time expected from certain people and can even involve having someone take a leave of absence from the firm if the volunteer work will require all that person's time. The latter case seems to arise most often during a campaign for a particular candidate.

Certain activities are really a combination of the cash contribution and volunteer efforts, such as giving a fund-raiser party for a party or a candidate. Such efforts are naturally conducted by one or more individuals rather than the firm itself.

RUNNING FOR OFFICE

The third and most involved area of political activity is running for office. Occasionally a firm will urge one of its people to run for a particular office or job, but this usually occurs as a result of an individual's initiative. This most frequently happens in local communities for offices which are nominally part-time, such as committee person, governing body member (such as township committee), or board member (such as a zoning or school board). These permit the elected person to continue his or her practice because they are, as noted above, "nominally part-time." However, the person considering running for such offices should recognize that many of them can consume a large amount of time, and not just in the evenings or on weekends. People who run for such offices are usually not interested in a political career as such. Nevertheless, they give up a great deal of personal, and sometimes business, time to serve their communities. Such political activity really can amount to a second full-time job.

Some lawyers, of course, have much loftier political ambitions than running for local office. Congressman, senator, governor (and beyond) are full-time occupations that require the lawyer to give up his or her practice—even to run for these offices. While probably none of the lawyers would ever admit it, we know of a few who ran for public office as a marketing strategy solely and entirely. They didn't expect to be elected or, if they were, they returned to their practices after their terms were over. Their main purpose was to raise their visibility, regardless of the outcome of the election, in order to have a larger law practice eventually.

HIRING FORMER PUBLIC FIGURES

A number of law firms have made a practice over the years of hiring former senators, former mayors, former district attorneys, and even former cabinet members. Whether these people are truly effective lawyers is not the main point. This is another way of marketing the firm, raising its image, and, hopefully, bringing it new business as a result. Sometimes it works, sometimes it doesn't. But we have known firms who have employed this strategy for years with good results.

It is another marketing strategy for some firms to consider. And they should consider it very carefully before doing it. Like all other politically related activity, it is not a strategy for every firm.

Membership in Trade Groups

The main reason for a law firm to become involved in trade associations is primarily the same as for becoming involved in community activities or for joining certain clubs: to be active outside the office in places where clients and prospective clients gather. There are other reasons that are almost as important. One is to learn more about a particular industry; another is to make contacts; a third is to have an opportunity, through participation in seminars and programs, to expose certain lawyers or the firm's expertise in that industry.

Lawyers are frequently surprised to learn that their clients are delighted when the lawyer shows an interest in the trade groups the client belongs to. It adds another dimension to the relationship and indicates to the client a further interest on the part of the attorney in understanding the client's business or field of work.

While some trade groups limit membership of any kind to individuals or companies that are part of that industry, many groups provide for associate memberships for individuals or companies that serve the industry. If a law firm has one or several clients that are members of a particular trade group, the best overture is to express to the client an interest in the group, and to ask if one or several people from the firm can either join the group or at least attend some of its meetings and functions. Some groups have only company memberships, which may include a few or many people from the member company; others have individual memberships. The differences and the costs in each case could be significant. As stated above, the clients will usually be delighted at the law firm's interest and, almost literally, will take its people by the hand, introduce them around, and try to get them involved if the group's policy permits.

To justify the time and cost of this marketing strategy, it is not necessary that a firm develop extensive expertise or a high profile in a particular industry. The firm could have only one client in an industry; if that client is important enough, it could justify employing the trade group strategy.

This is one of the easier strategies a firm could use and it is worth considering.

Trade Conventions and Meetings

One of the most expensive, time-consuming, and potentially least productive activities that lawyers can become involved in is attendance at trade conventions and meetings. What is the lawyer doing there in the first place? It may be that he or she is on the program, or attending at the invitation (or, more accurately, the suggestion) of a client, or in order to do some investigation and spadework. Whatever the reason, the money and time spent attending such events can very easily be wasted.

There are, however, some techniques that can be employed to increase the benefits that could be obtained, totally separate from the "good PR" of attending with a client.

If one or more lawyers from the firm appear on the program at a convention or meeting, it might be worthwhile for them to spend some additional time there. They have already obtained a certain amount of visibility by being on the program. To stay around, even a little while, and mingle with the attendees could develop new contacts and business opportunities. It also gives the speakers the opportunity to pick up additional knowledge or information about the group sponsoring the event.

Occasionally, one or several people in the firm will attend a convention in the company of a client. The prime reason for going is to further develop the client-firm relationship. Even in these cases, it is wise for the attorneys to take maximum advantage of the situation by learning as much as they can and by meeting as many people as they can during the convention. All too often the attorneys limit themselves entirely to the client and completely miss everything else around them.

Then there are occasions when a firm may send one or several people to attend a convention, either to basically research the group involved or to make some initial contacts, or both. I call this "The Lone Ranger" approach. Because a number of our clients have asked what their people should do to obtain maximum benefit from these trips, we have prepared some guidelines. While these guidelines were prepared for people who were attending by themselves, they also contain some excellent pointers on how to make the opportunity productive when speaking on the program or attending with a client.

In any of the above cases the firm may give a reception or provide a hospitality suite during the convention. (See the section on Social Function for some guidelines in this regard.)

Attending conventions is not a strategy to be used by every firm or on every occasion. If planned and controlled, however, it can be worthwhile.

Attending a Convention by Yourself

Sometimes you will attend a convention as a "Lone Ranger." The following is meant to be a guide for you in order to make this of maximum benefit to you and the firm.

By the term "Lone Ranger" it is meant you are attending the convention strictly as an individual observer and not—

—to make a presentation
—with a client
—to hold a hospitality suite

The main reasons for your attendance at a convention or meeting under this circumstance are probably:

1. To learn more about the industry or field.
2. To appraise the quality and type of convention for possible firm participation in the future.
3. To determine the level and type of executive attendance.
4. To favorably impress and familiarize attendees with the firm.

Since #4 holds under any circumstances at any convention, we discuss the other three reasons:

1. Prior to attending, check to see what clients the firm has in this industry. Are any of them expected to attend?
2. Meet as many people as you can. In conversation, determine why they are attending, their opinions of the convention, their thoughts on significant happenings in that industry or field.
3. Obtain copies of all programs, literature, and handouts. Pay

particular attention to what law firms, CPA firms, and consulting firms are present and what presentations, if any, they are giving.

4. Attend as many sessions or workshops as you can, particularly those with high attendance by the delegates. Take notes of the key points made.

5. Whenever you introduce yourself, also clearly identify the name of your firm. Be ready to explain, briefly yet clearly, the firm's principal areas of practice; also remember the various points in the firm's Positioning Statement and weave as many as appropriate into your conversations. Be ready to explain that you are attending the convention mainly to learn more about the industry in order to better serve the firm's clients in this area. Have plenty of *clean* business cards.

After the convention, follow up to insure that the expenditure of time and money will pay big benefits for the firm.

1. Communicate with prospective clients.
2. Communicate with appropriate lawyers in your firm.
3. Do a report on the convention, your contacts, observations, and recommendations.

Industry Specialization

The development of industry specialties has been regarded by most lawyers as a marketing strategy only for accounting firms. Nothing could be further from the truth. Any law firm can employ it. Even the sole practitioner can use industry specialization as a marketing strategy.

The first step is to find out what particular industry expertise the firm already has. This should have been determined during the Strategic Analysis phase covered in Part I. Most firms are surprised to learn the number of industries in which they have served clients. In other words, most firms, regardless of their size, have a degree of expertise or at least experience in more industries than they realize. This provides the base for further specialization in these industries.

In considering a strategy of industry specialization, a law firm should take advantage of opportunities that may be indicated in the Strategic Analysis. For example, most high-technology industries in the United States have been growing over the past few years and their continued growth is forecast for at least a generation to come. The various high-technology industries seem to cluster in certain regions of the country. Broadly speaking, health care opportunities exist in all parts of the country, although certain areas and communities may have a higher percentage than others. Both the high-tech and health care fields offer law firms abundant opportunities for industry specialization.

STARTING FROM SCRATCH

If a firm determines that specific industries have great potential for the firm, these could become targeted for development even if the firm has little or no client base in those industries at present. How can a firm without such a client base develop expertise and a reputation in a particular industry? There are several ways. One is to research the industry thoroughly and begin to make contacts in it. This is best accomplished by assigning one or more lawyers to take on this project. Memberships in trade groups and "Lone Ranger" attendance at conventions and meetings are two ways of accomplishing this. This is a slower way to develop an industry specialty, but it could pay off sooner or later. Remember, you only need obtain one client in a particular field to give you the opportunity to become a self-proclaimed expert in that field!

A second and quicker way to develop expertise in a new industry is to bring into the firm, at the partner or senior associate level, a lawyer who has extensive experience in that industry. In other words, a lateral entry. This may not necessarily bring the firm any clients in that industry, but it does at least make the expertise available in-house.

A third way is to acquire a firm that has a client base and also some reputation in the industry. This has the advantage of quickly giving the firm both specialists and clients in the industry and, in a short period of time, a reputation in that industry as well. Depending on how long it takes to locate and negotiate with the firm, this could be the quickest way to develop an industry specialty. In the short run, it might also appear to be the most expensive; in the longer run, however, it is sometimes far less expensive than either of the other two alternatives.

TWO SKILLS NEEDED

In order to obtain maximum benefit from a program of industry specialization, a law firm must attain two types of expertise in each and every industry it represents: technical and marketing. Technical knowledge is an understanding of the unique problems of an industry—financial, operational, and legal—which will enable a firm to work effectively with clients in that industry. Marketing knowledge is an understanding of the industry as a whole, what its trends are, who its leaders are, and how best to obtain visibility and recognition for the firm in that industry.

Both of these two distinct areas of industry expertise are required if a firm is to succeed in a program of industry specialization. In most firms both areas, technical and marketing, must be combined in one person or a small group of lawyers who may even be in different departments. The industry expert must keep up to speed with all the technical knowledge required and also have at least some ability to market this expertise. Since few lawyers possess equal ability in both areas, some compromises or trade-offs will be necessary. In these cases, obviously the technical knowledge must be given priority, because if a firm doesn't know how to do the work once it gets it, then it shouldn't be marketing its alleged expertise in the first place.

IDENTIFY THE SPECIALISTS

How does a firm determine who has particular industry expertise among its partners and perhaps associates? First, examine each attorney's current client responsibilities. The chances are that certain people have been assigned clients from particular industries for one reason or another. Second, determine each attorney's prior client responsibilities, either with the firm or in their prior professional experience. These two analyses will indicate which people have experience, although not necessarily expertise, in which industries.

The firm should make a definite decision as to which industries it is going to emphasize in its industry specialization program. There is a limit to what a firm and its people can handle. It is better to take fewer industries and devote more time to each than to take a larger number of industries and merely skim across the top of them.

INDUSTRY COMMITTEES OR TEAMS

Once it has been determined which industries a firm wants to develop (in marketing terms, "penetrate further" or "increase its market share"), how does the firm go about marketing to those industries? If the size of the firm permits, it is a good idea to form a committee or team of lawyers to concentrate on each industry, both to develop further technical knowledge and also to market to current and prospective clients in that industry. In many cases, the "committee" will consist of a single person, who will generally be a partner but who could be a fairly senior associate. A description of the functions and activities that an industry specialty committee (or team) should address is included at the end of this section.

When it comes to marketing, many of the strategies discussed in this book for the firm as a whole can also be applied to particular industry programs. Developing a reputation in the industry and personal contacts, as stated earlier, are the most effective marketing strategies. Ultimately all other strategies, if effective, result in some form of personal contact. But it is not enough to build a marketing program on personal contacts alone, or even on reputation alone. Participating in seminars, writing articles, giving talks, membership in trade groups, attending conventions and meetings, newsletters and special publications, direct mail pieces, even advertising are some of the marketing tactics that can be employed to implement an industry specialization strategy.

One final very important point. The development of industry committees or teams will cut across departmental lines; they will include lawyers from each area of the law that is involved in an industry. For example, health care: This team could involve lawyers from the business, tax, labor, litigation, environmental, and pension areas—to name some but not all.

I believe that this trend of industry specialization, which is just starting, will increase, particularly in large firms. Get accustomed to it. It really amounts to establishing specialty firms within the law firm itself—and is the best way to market against these specialty firms.

Industry Committees or Teams

A. Objectives
   1. Develop list of target clients (along with key executives and directors).
   2. Select specific areas of the law for marketing emphasis.
      a. Develop, or recommend, new areas.
   3. Develop strategy on how to develop target clients.
   4. Establish and implement formal programs—professional and trade associations, talks, seminars, mailing lists for publications.
   5. Maintain communications on prospects.
   6. Evaluate results in January and July.
B. Suggested Methods for Accomplishing
   1. Have every member of committee working on at least one assignment at all times. Don't overload anyone. If two or more are assigned to same project, designate one as responsible for coordinating, assembling, and reporting.
   2. Have each department advise committee on its expertise in the industry and how to talk about this to clients and prospects.
      a. Involve heads of these departments to address committee.
   3. Keep advised of new developments in the industry.
   4. Invite guest speakers from the industry to address committee.
      a. Combine with visits to clients and prospects.
   5. Limit meetings to one hour except evaluation meetings, which might continue for two hours.
   6. Route industry bulletins and newsletters, important industry publications to all members.
   7. Follow a set agenda format.
   8. Keep same secretary for six months, then rotate.
   9. Minutes—as brief as possible (ABAP) and as soon as possible (ASAP).
   10. Meet monthly.
C. Suggested Agenda Format
   1. Target clients or prospects

      a. Selection
      b. Report on contacts
      c. Strategy
  2. Other prospects and clients
  3. Developments and matters in the industry.
  4. Formal activities—reports and assignments.

Area of Law Specialization

Specialization by area of the law is both one of the easiest and, at the same time, one of the most difficult parts of the marketing plan to work with.

It is one of the easiest primarily because most law firms are organized more or less along departmental lines and because lawyers tend to think in terms of legal specialties or at least areas of concentration. Many smaller firms specialize in only one or two areas of the law. (This is often referred to as finding a "niche" in the market. It is a good marketing as well as a good legal strategy.) But it is difficult because, while some specialty areas actually define the target markets (school law, health care, maritime), many are so broad that the markets are hard to define and, in some cases, even harder to reach. Take labor law for example, The market is obviously any business, institution, or organization that employs people. Beyond this, however, the market is so broad that it is difficult to target. Or how about divorce law, now being euphemistically referred to as domestic relations or family law. The market is obvious: those couples contemplating divorce (or, in the growing area of prenuptial agreements, those contemplating marriage); but how do you target or market to this market segment? You can't very well run an ad stating "Special this month! Two divorces for the price of one!"

Another factor that makes the marketing of specialty areas difficult is that not all areas of the law can be marketed in the same way. The tactics and techniques of marketing a workers compensation practice are quite different from those of marketing an environmental practice; the method of marketing the Estates and Trust department has little or no similarity to the way insurance defense work would be marketed; a criminal lawyer markets his practice much differently from a bankruptcy lawyer.

So, having defined the problems and their difficulty, how do we go about solving them?

BEGIN WITH THE DEPARTMENT

Marketing specialized areas of the law begins with the department. Each department in the firm should have some kind of marketing program. Most specialty areas either have their own department or come under a department with other related, it not similar, areas. Divorce, while it can involve litigation, is generally a department by itself. The same is true of workers comp. On the other hand, labor, environmental, and products liability are more often than not grouped in the litigation department. (I know that some firms have such a large practice in these areas or others that they constitute a separate department. I am, however, talking about the structure that exists in the majority of general practice firms). If the department has a marketing program, then the subspecialties within that department have either a program they can adapt to their own needs or at least an environment that can assist them in their own particular marketing needs.

The starting point is, of course, experience and a track record. The more specialized the area of practice, the more important this is. One matter is sometimes all that is needed to establish some kind of expertise, reputation, and basis on which to build a further practice. Without experience and a track record, no matter how large the potential market may appear to be, it is almost impossible to market a specialized area of practice. If a firm doesn't possess the necessary expertise, it must first acquire it by lateral entry or merger before it can market the area. As the old-time door-to-door merchants used to say, "You can't do business from an empty wagon."

If a firm doesn't have the expertise in a specialty area and can't acquire it, forget the whole thing. Put the time, money, and marketing effort in areas where you have something to market.

Some of the marketing activities discussed eslewhere in this part of the book apply to many specialty areas. Seminars are excellent marketing tools for certain areas—corporate, taxation, estates, and environmental, to name a few. Published writings are always excellent marketing tools—if only to establish or further develop a lawyer's reputation in a particular area. A book, even if it isn't a "best seller," is usually a great marketing device.

Newsletters are excellent for some areas and absolutely useless for others. Corporate, labor, estates, and workers comp, for example, all seem to generate enough material to justify newsletters. On the other hand, how do you publish a newsletter on divorce (and whom would you send it to?), fire subrugation, or aircraft defect?

THE ONE ESSENTIAL

One marketing "tool" that is an absolute must for every area or field of practice is a Practice Area Resume—a description, often fairly detailed, of the firm's expertise in a specific specialty area. These can be slipped in as part of a general firm brochure (see later section on Brochures), provided to all lawyers in the firm, and given to outside third parties (including lawyers) and prospective clients who make inquiries. Merely the fact that you can prepare several pages of qualifications and experience in a specific practice area is an impressive marketing weapon. Be certain to include the pertinent credentials of the lawyers involved; this is one place where a discreet amount of self-promotion is not only permissible but necessary.

Another marketing activity, which can work in certain areas far better than others, is publicity. Litigation is one of the prime ones. In fact, other than published writings and membership in appropriate legal groups, publicity within and outside the legal profession is one of the few marketing tools available to a litigator. Anti-trust and Mergers and Acquisitions are two other areas that can often provide material for appropriate and effective publicity.

ESTATES AND TRUSTS

One area that most firms are having trouble with is Estates and Trusts. The main reason, besides changes in the tax laws, is that competition has arisen both from within and outside the profession and has captured a lot of the business. On the one hand, legal clinics have so systematized the writing of a will that they can grind out literally thousands of wills at a very low price. On the other hand, accounting firms have practically attacked the estate-planning area and are charging fees that estate and trust lawyers consider unbelievable. They (the accounting firms) have even raided the competition and hired lawyers into their estate-planning operations. Other sources of competition have also arisen outside the profession; insurance companies, financial planners, financial consultants, and whatever stockbrokers used to be called are all cutting into the business that the estate and trust department of a law firm used to think was theirs. The only way to combat this is to, in effect, "join the competition" by repositioning the estates department into an estate and financial planning department and provide many of the same services, at the same profitable fees, that the accounting firms and others do.

INDIRECT MARKETING

One final point about the marketing of specialized areas of practice. Frequently the marketing effort is not directed to the potential client but to other lawyers. The more specialized the area, the more this is true. People with a specialized legal problem will either ask their lawyer for a reference or will be advised by their lawyer to take the matter to a specialist in that area. It's the same as in medicine when someone needs a specialist; they generally ask their family doctor or close friend who to go to. Unless, of course, they know someone else who has had the same problem; then they will ask that person.

Which leads me to add one more final point: Clients. Never forget the marketing impact of a delighted (not just "satisfied") client. Even if you will probably never serve that client again, as in the case of a serious personal injury matter for example, make every effort, throughout the matter and when it is completed, to be sure that your client feels you served him or her well. You may need that client for a future reference—or you never know when someone, faced with the same kind of problem, may ask that client, "What lawyer or law firm did you use?" A ringing endorsement from one client can be worth more than a whole raft of seminars or published articles.

Personal Letters and Notes

This is a personal marketing tactic rather than a firm one. In my seminars on marketing for law firms, I begin this section by announcing, "It may startle some lawyers to learn that their clients, prospects, and contacts are human beings just like they are. Therefore, these clients, prospects, and contacts respond to some of the same things that other human beings do."

The sarcasm, or as I like to call it, "dramatic emphasis," in that opening statement is meant to grab the attorneys' attention and focus it on a point that so many of them miss. Their clients do have the same human feelings, concerns, and desires as their friends and relatives. Therefore they frequently respond to or appreciate human and personal gestures—even from a lawyer! A congratulatory note after a promotion or award, a thoughtful phone call inquiring as to the welfare of an ill spouse or child, a greeting card on a birthday or anniversary—these little personal gestures are generally appreciated if done with the right touch. They also distinguish the person who does them from most other people, lawyers included.

There is, of course, a danger in this. It can be overdone or it can bring an unfavorable reaction. In my own experience this seems to occur most often with insurance agents. There is one who sends me a birthday card every year, personally signed, even though I only met him once about fifteen years ago and never hear from him (other than receiving the annual premium notice) at any other time. My reaction is quite the opposite of what I'm certain he wants; I feel that his annual card is really saying, "I'm glad you're still alive this year so you can pay another premium."

NOT FOR EVERYONE

This is certainly not a marketing strategy to be used by everyone. Many people are just not comfortable sending cards, writing letters, or making calls to business acquaintances on personal matters. These people should never use this strategy, because their discomfort will show through and the recipient will feel it, no matter how thoughtful or appropriate the gesture. On the other hand, there are quite a few people who would feel very natural making some form of personal gesture toward a business acquaintance, client, or prospect, yet hesitate because they feel it may be resented. In these cases, I invariably recommend that, if they feel comfortable doing it, go ahead. More than likely, it will be received in just the way they intended and hoped for.

I have known several lawyers who have developed their own very comfortable and effective style in this regard. One of them must own stock in several greeting card companies, while the others have just the right knack for writing a short note on the occasion of some special event, either happy or sad.

To summarize: If you are at all uncomfortable with this idea, don't do it. If you are comfortable, go ahead.

Publicity
and Public Relations

Now to enter the interesting, complex, and often comtroversial area of publicity and its relative, public relations.

These terms, along with "advertising" and "promotion," are often misused and misunderstood by lawyers (as well as by other professionals). The following definitions could certainly be refined and improved upon, particularly by practicing professionals in each of the fields. Nevertheless, I prefer these particular definitions (or explanations) because they distinguish each activity from the others.

Advertising: Makes use of existing media (print, radio, television, Yellow Pages, etc.). You create the message, you pay for the space (or time), therefore you control what the message is, within obvious ethical or policy restrictions.

Promotion: I am referring to all physical pieces that carry a message from or about the firm. These are generally printed pieces and include brochures, pamphlets, newsletters, even business cards and stationery. Promotion creates its own medium, i.e., the physical piece itself. You create the message and you produce the piece or object. Therefore you control the message (again, within ethical restrictions), but, because you are not employing a medium that already exists, you must compete for the audience's attention with the medium you create.

Publicity: Makes use of the existing media (print, radio, etc.). You do not create the message. You do not pay for the space (or time). Therefore you do not control the message.

Public Relations: A much broader term that embraces all forms of nonadvertising communications used to convey messages about the firm to the general public or to specific audiences. This includes publicity.

To understand what publicity and public relations can do and cannot do for a firm, it is important to examine the implications of the above definitions further.

USUALLY IT ISN'T FREE

To begin with, under the definition for publicity, it says that you do not pay for the space and time. This does not mean that publicity does not cost anything. It may or may not. You may have obtained some publicity about the firm without doing a thing or spending a dime. On the other hand, you may have employed an outside public relations agency to arrange for the publicity. While you will not have purchased any space or time, I can assure you that this will cost the firm something. P.R. agencies, just like law firms, charge for their services.

Perhaps even more important than the economic implications are the editorial ones. Because you do not create or deliver the message, and because you do not pay for the space or time in which it is delivered, you do not control how the message comes out. Naturally you are going to try to exert as much control or influence as you can. The best example of this is when you send out a news release. If it is picked up and run, in whole or in part, the release will generally be used pretty much the way you (or the agency) wrote it. In fact, that is one of the secrets of getting releases run: Write them in a professional style that enables the particular medium involved to use them with little or no work. As long as the subjects of your releases are appropriate and the writing is good, the medium will be likely to use them. If a release needs work, it won't get used.

In many cases, however, publicity involves someone from the media writing an article about the firm, interviewing someone from the firm, or quoting a member of the firm about some issue or subject. These are the cases where you have little or no control over what is written. You can ask to see the final piece before it appears, but I urge that you do not. This is unprofessional and implies that you want to control the media (which of course you would like to!). The only responsibility that the media has—and it is a significant one—is to be accurate in reporting facts or in quoting someone. You have every right to require accuracy, even to the point of having the writer verify any quotes or facts being used.

IT'S A TWO-EDGED SWORD

Publicity is a double-edged sword, and one side can hurt. If an unfavorable piece of publicity appears, or if an otherwise favorable piece is given a tilt that the firm feels does not reflect favorably, there is not much that can be done. Remember, the function of most media, except certain trade and professional publications, is to report what they consider to be news, not to promote or publicize a particular source such as you or your firm. The general public places a lot more credibility in ''news'' than it does in advertising. That is its big advantage. But be aware that publicity can also hurt you. And much of this is out of your control.

This is a good place to address a few words to those attorneys who are strongly opposed to any kind of public relations program.

To a certain degree, publicity is not a marketing tactic that a firm employs. Quite often, publicity *happens* to a firm whether it wants it or not. Sometimes this is in connection with unfavorable developments in a case or matter the firm is handling for a client. For this reason, an increasing number of law firms are developing a public relations policy and program in recognition that there will be publicity whether or not the firm seeks it and that it is in the interest of the profession and the firm to ensure, as much as possible, that information carried in the media is accurate.

Of course, a publicity program also involves a deliberate attempt to increase the visibility of the firm. But to many lawyers, who might otherwise oppose such a program, it is the *defensive* and *corrective* benefits that publicity can provide that make them support and even participate in such a program.

WHAT YOU CAN DO YOURSELF

There is a lot in the way of a publicity and public relations program that a firm can do for itself without engaging an outside public relations consultant or agency. Routine releases on partner announcements, people joining the firm, seminars, awards, etc., can be written by someone in the firm and mailed on the firm stationery to the appropriate media list. Most firms have at least one partner, associate, or even staff person who has the ability to do this.

In terms of media contact and press relations, much good work can be done over an occasional cup of coffee or lunch, particularly with the local media. Editors and writers have great need for editorial material, although not always on the day when you might like something to appear. Contact them, invite them out for coffee or lunch, tell them you are interested in obtaining publicity for your firm. Ask them what types of news items they are looking for. This is the key question and the only way to express it. Remember that the media is interested in publishing news. If you are going to obtain publicity for the firm, it must be newsworthy in the eyes of the media. Ask them what form they want news releases in—written prose or just factual outlines. Ask if they use photographs. Even ask what days of the week (if it is a daily paper, radio, or TV station) they generally have more editorial space or time available. There are definite patterns. You can increase the chances of your material being used if you target it toward those days.

In addition to the above, tell the editors or reporters as much as you can about the firm. Educate them, give them an idea of the kinds of stories or comments they could obtain. If you have some recognized authorities, or at least knowledgeable experts in certain fields, let the media know. If the editor needs some background or wants some quotes regarding a new development in toxic waste disposal, for example, why shouldn't he or she call an environmental lawyer in your firm rather than one of your competitors? Most important of all, let the editor know there is someone specific to contact in the firm, even if it is the managing partner, who can provide information and comments or can find someone in the firm who can.

If you do the above, you will have established a good working relationship with the media and will receive, sooner or later, regularly or occasionally, a higher percentage of desirable exposure than firms that are not doing this. A beautiful thing about this strategy is that it does not necessarily require a partner to take the time to handle it. This is often an excellent assignment to give to an associate who has the judgment and skills to handle it or to the marketing coordinator (see later section). We have even seen office managers and secretaries who do an excellent job in handling routine publicity and in maintaining good press relations.

WHAT NOT TO DO

Now, after all the "do's," it is time or a couple of "don't's." If you have contacts on the advertising side of the media, or even if you advertise in the media, don't ask the advertising people to put in a word for your firm with the editorial people. These are totally separate functions in just about every newspaper, magazine, radio or TV station. Each resents the other's interference in their own department. The only thing this can do is kill your relationship with the editorial side.

Furthermore, never thank an editor for running something about your firm. This may strike you as just the opposite of what should be done, but editorial people consider themselves professionals. They believe, or try to believe, that the material they use is news and of interest to their readers, listeners, or viewers. In point of fact, if they are going to continue to hold their jobs, they must fulfill this requirement. When you thank them for using some material of yours, you are telling them, in effect, that they did it as a favor to you, or, in other words, that they were not being professional. This can boomerang against you.

What should you do instead? Compliment the editors on how they reported something, or let them know the impact and importance their story had: More often than you will ever realize, editorial people do not receive favorable comments on what they run. They only hear from people who find fault for one reason or another.

In addition to press relations, someone within the firm (generally the marketing coordinator) can be given the broader public relations assignment of contacting various community organizations to see if they would like speakers for some of their meetings. This requires some research to determine which organizations would be desirable, which people in the firm are qualified on which subjects, and also who has the ability to speak in public. Pretty soon the firm has developed its own in-house speakers bureau. Warning: Once this gets going, the requests will far outrun the firm's ability to provide speakers. Judgment and tact are then called for in turning people down.

WHAT CAN A P.R. FIRM DO?

It is reported that approximately 15 percent of all the law firms in the United States currently use outside public relations counsel and that the number is growing. This can be an individual consultant or a public relations agency employed on either a retainer or project basis.

The logical question is: "What can a public relations firm do for our firm?" The answer is "a lot."

In terms of internal publications, they can design and write firm brochures, design and edit practice area resumes, design and write newsletters. They can write or edit monographs on legal issues and can also even write or edit books and articles under the by-lines of lawyers in the firm.

In terms of external publications, they can work with the general consumer press, the business and legal sections of newspapers, industry publications, the general business press, and even legal publications and directories. They can write and distribute news releases; develop relationships with reporters and editors on behalf of the firm; place by-lined articles by lawyers in the firm; and develop and place third-party articles about the firm. They can also arrange for guest-authored columns by the firm's lawyers and arrange for interviews or background briefings with members of the press.

Some but not all P.R. firms can do even more. They can write or edit speeches for the lawyers. They can act as a "speaker's bureau" for the firm. Some can develop, promote, and coordinate seminars. Many can design and produce special announcements and mailings and also arrange for radio and TV interviews.

In terms of press relations, broadly speaking, I believe the most effective public relations person is almost invisible. He or she should act as a "facilitator" who brings together the editor or reporter and the appropriate lawyers and then steps back to let this relationship develop of itself.

SELECTING A P.R. FIRM

The next question is: How do you select a public relations agency or consultant?

P.R. firms are a lot like law firms; they come in all sizes and types. There are the giant national or international firms. There are smaller, specialized firms that concentrate in a particular field such as financial or health care. Then there are the generalists, either agencies or individuals. You may need a very large firm—or a free-lance individual.

Begin by asking around your own firm. Find out which people, particularly the partners, have contacts in public relations agencies. Also, ask some of your clients who are using P.R. agencies. Evaluate their comments and recommendations. The firm may even have one or more agencies as clients. Examine them, although we all know that it can become ticklish to have a client who is also a subcontractor. What happens if you eventually have to fire them? If this process has not produced any satisfactory leads, obtain a copy of O'Dwyer's Directory of public relations firms. Also, contact the nearest chapter of the Public Relations Society of America. They won't specifically recommend anyone, but they will give you the names of their members in the area, some information about them, and the name of someone to contact.

Then contact the prospective candidates, preferably on the phone. Ask them to send you some material about themselves. Avoid meeting with them until you have received the material and compared it with that of other candidates. Then call those you are interested in meeting and set up the first interview. In this interview you should give them information on your firm, including appropriate sections of your marketing plan. You should also have developed a list of questions to ask. Here are some suggestions.

1. How would the P.R. firm propose to work with your firm?
2. What are the P.R. firm's objectives, services, and methods of operation?
3. Who are its clients?
4. Ask for some samples of its work—and what the objectives and results were.
5. Ask for a list of references to contact.

6. What will the P.R. firm do for its proposed fee?
7. What is its fee structure and billing procedure?

Any agency or individual that declines to reveal at least some of its clients—or will not give you references—should be dropped from consideration immediately.

What should you look for? In terms of their clients, look for professional firms and service businesses or organizations rather than product-related companies. An agency that has served accounting firms, law firms, banks, designers, architects, consultants, and nonprofit organizations will probably be more appropriate than one that has served retail stores, automobile dealers, or hardware manufacturers. Also be on the lookout for conflicts; a public relations or advertising agency should not serve competitors.

ONE OR THE OTHER

In addition, pay particular attention to any agency that presents itself as both a public relations and an advertising agency. These are very different specialties. Most firms that handle both generally have greater skill in one area than the other. Find out which area is the larger one in the particular agency; that is generally the area the agency is stronger in. Always avoid agencies who use the same people for both advertising and public relations work; the odds are very high that they are not very good at either.

How will P.R. agencies or people charge? Their fees are determined in pretty much the same ways as a law firm's, because they basically offer the same thing—the time and skill of people. Therefore they will bill for the work done or proposed, based on the actual (or estimated) time to complete it. They will also charge for out-of-pocket expenses, which may include telephone calls and travel as well as photography, special consulting, and other things. Many firms will propose a retainer, and they should define what the client would receive for this on a regular basis. P.R. firms prefer to work on retainer, just as accounting firms like to obtain audit engagements. But most of them will accept project work if the project is large enough to be profitable. The cost to the client for a project will probably be higher than if the project were included in a retainer, but the total cost for several projects may still be less than the total cost of a retainer arrangement. P.R.

agencies are accustomed to preparing estimates of the cost for a project. They aren't crazy about the idea, of course, but they know that many of their clients want or require estimates. *So don't hesitate to ask for estimates* before you approve their starting on a project.

How do you select the right P.R. agency? The same way that many of your clients selected your firm. That means after you have checked client lists, type of work, references, etc., you will select the agency with which you feel most confident and comfortable. There is no scientific way to do it. It all comes down to what amounts to the "right chemistry."

How do you work with an agency? The same way, to a great degree, that you would like your clients to work with you. Define for them your objectives and your budget. Tell them any particular policies they must adhere to. Educate them on the ethical rules they must observe. Then step back and let them do their job. It is the only way you can evaluate their work. You don't want your P.R. firm practicing law, so you shouldn't try to practice public relations; that's what you hired them for.

Brochures and Newsletters

This chapter was written by one of my associates, Donna Greenfield, along with Burkey Belser. They are specialists in marketing communications for professionals.

Consumers of legal services need information. Imagine buying a car without knowing which models were available or, having discovered a model you like, not being allowed to look inside to inspect its features. That is the uncertain condition of most prospective clients. Corporate clients may be more sophisticated than an individual, but all prospective clients need information about your services to reduce their uncertainty. Furthermore, individuals and corporations today are shopping around for legal counsel. Some form of communication informing prospects about your firm becomes an absolute necessity if you are going to compete effectively.

Once the firm considers how to provide needed information to its public, some choices have to be made. You must decide where and how you wish to distribute your message and how clearly you want to distinguish yourself from your competition. These questions of distribution and style go right to the heart of a firm's identity. They require you to determine who you are and where you're going, perhaps for the first time as a single firm. These issues usually cause heated controversy within the firm—a sort of an identity crisis—before the questions are finally settled.

Promotional materials should be created as soon as you have a promotional strategy but not before. Your strategy will position your firm within its competitive environment, target the types of clients you wish to develop, and suggest how best to reach them. Your marketing consultant or a knowledgeable communications consultant (design firm, P.R. firm, advertising agency) should develop a promotional plan with you before you create any materials for the firm.

Every communications piece your firm creates, from the letterhead and business card to a firm brochure or newsletter, communicates an image of the firm. You can control public perception according to your marketing goals.

The Golden Rule of Style, whether you choose a traditional idiom or an innovative approach, is: Don't be afraid to be creative. You want your firm to develop a single, coherent, and *distinctive* image over time, one that will be recognized as your own. Gaining an institutional identity increases the public's perception of your importance. And if your image is creative, as well as tasteful, you will be perceived as a creative firm as well.

THE COMMUNICATIONS TOOLS

Announcements, newsletters, reports, brochures, and reprints all contribute to identifying your firm and explaining your firm to your client or prospective client. They are the tactical tools of your marketing strategy. They increase client awareness, demonstrate professionalism, and demonstrate understanding—critical elements in the marketing of legal services.

LETTERHEADS

All firms use letterheads and business cards. The overwhelming majority of law firms adopt the traditional style of letterhead, imperceptibly different from one another in paper stock, typography, or engraving. As a result, almost all law firms look alike and miss a marketing opportunity to use basic tools to reinforce a unique position. Firms today are choosing to focus on brochures and newsletters to establish their separate identity. But if it will be a while before you publish a brochure or newsletter, consider starting with your letterhead.

ANNOUNCEMENTS

Commonly, announcements are sent out as new partners are accepted into the firm. A change of address may stimulate another engraved card alerting clients to the move. Announcements act secondarily as gentle reminders of your firm's existence. Even the most conservative partner would not flinch from these venerable "news releases." You know what these messages mean to *you* when you receive them. But ask, what do they mean to your client? Will your client read them and understand their implications for your firm or your service? Does your client know something important to him or her as a result of getting your announcement? How could they be improved to enhance client awareness? At a minimum, be sure to identify what experience the new partner or associate brings to the firm and what his or her area of practice will be. You may want to consider a new format for an announcement that gives a full biography of the newcomer.

THE FIRM BROCHURE

A well-designed and well-written brochure can say much more about a firm, its capabilities, and its "style" and say it more widely than its people could say in person. It is also the cornerstone of a cross-selling strategy aimed at selling additional services to current clients.

The brochure is literally a "silent salesperson" for the firm. When a firm has committed itself to caring about its clients' needs, it is hard to imagine being without a brochure, since nothing demonstrates so clearly the desire to inform and educate the client about your work. It is the marketing communications tool most commonly used by law firms today.

What should your brochure say? The brochure should state or convey every point in the firm's positioning statement. The positioning statement, which has been developed as the capstone of your marketing strategy, is the kernel of your identity.

To expand and develop its essential theme is the responsibility of the copywriter. Do not expect that the copy will flow easily or be easily accepted by members of your firm. Copy development is, without question in our experience, the most difficult promotional activity you will encounter. If every partner is involved, the process will inevitably be painful, alienating, and protracted.

We suggest forming a small committee to oversee the creation of the entire brochure. If you have a small firm, assign the task to an individual. The committee or individual can then report to the firm for feedback and approval according to a predetermined schedule. In no case should members of the firm write anything other than abstracts concerning their specialties which can be used by the copywriter. Writing letters, briefs, or articles is *not* writing copy. One skill does not imply the other. Trust your copywriter. For the duration, he or she is another of your partners. If the message is somehow not coming through in the copy, examine why not. Have you given the writer all the necessary information? Have you avoided answering the hard question of telling who you are in favor of simply telling what you do? Is your positioning statement an honest definition of your goals and skills? have you so many fears about promotion that you're not letting the copy say anything at all?

Other details concerning copy: A brief history is useful and interesting if it's very brief. A firm biography, however, is less interesting than how you meet clients' needs. Keep the material short. Restrict yourself to the benefits your firm offers the prospective client and the tangible aspects of your experience and approach that make you qualified to do your prospect's work. If possible, list your services in benefit categories rather than placing your benefits under service categories; for example, let a headline read "Our Computerized Litigation System Operates Nationwide" instead of the uninspiring "Mass Litigation."

Write biographies of partners, especially if the partners want them or if you are a small firm whose identity is very much allied to the personalities who make up the firm. Biographies will mean a lot to referring attorneys, if they will make up a large part of the distribution list for your brochure.

We generally recommend that practice area resumes as well as partner biographies appear in a pocket in the back of a brochure. This offers several advantages: (1) the text of the brochure may be completely and effectively used to develop the positioning statement and create a style or image of the firm; (2) practice area resumes may be selectively included in the brochure to target presentations or mailings to specific audiences; (3) loss of partners or the addition of important new partners will not embarrass the firm or date the brochure; (4) as new services are developed, new inserts can be created for the back pocket. You should hope for an active shelf life for your brochure of at least two to three years. If your brochure is to work for you as an active marketing tool, you will want it to be flexible and enduring.

DESIGNING IS FUN

If writing copy seems to be the most painful aspect of your brochure's creation, having it designed may be the most enjoyable. It is, after all, a chance to play with paper, color, images, tone, and so on. Don't be afraid to be creative. This attitude is especially important in your brochure's design. Many law firms we've worked with will spread out a pile of brochures they've collected from other firms and then point to the one they want duplicated. Although the exercise may be valid to help you understand the options available to you, it defeats the goal of creating a unique position in your market. Attorneys rely so heavily on the verbal and the written that they tend to downplay the visual in favor of the written content. *But the image your firm communicates through your brochure will have been established before the first word of copy is read.* Successful brochures have a strong, immediate visual impact. Copy informs the intellect. Design stimulates the emotions. Do not discount its importance in the selling process.

Who should design your brochure? Advertising agencies frequently maintain design staffs who create collateral material to support their clients' advertising campaigns. Design studios differ from advertising agencies in that their principal source of income are fees resulting from designing such print collateral and not commissions received from placing ads. Free-lance designers are individual artists performing similar, if more limited, functions as design studies. Agency, studio, or free-lance designers may suit your needs. The graphic artists who work for printers generally are not the best available design talents in your area.

How do you find a designer? Ask your corporate clients who they use for their work. Call the local Art Directors Club for references, or select a designer whose work you like from the *Club Annual* (a special selection representing the best work in that market for that year). Even check the Yellow Pages.

Then meet with the candidates. Ask to see portfolios. Find out if they are familiar with the unique problems and concerns of law firms. Review their work. Be sure to get estimates for the design work and ballpark fees for printing (final printing prices will always depend on the exact specifications of the approved design). Select a few whom you believe can do the job, *then hire the person you like the most.* Creating a brochure can be a long and difficult partnership. If the chemistry is wrong, the brochure will never be right. You'll need a friend, someone who can listen to you and your partners' needs and problems.

How elaborate must *your* brochure be? How do production values affect cost? There's no easy formula, but you may expect to pay 1/4 of your total budget for copywriting, 1/4 for design and illustration or photography, and 1/2 for printing. Four-color printing, glossy paper stocks, die-cutting and embossing, elaborate illustrations or complex photography will be expensive. If you are not a regular buyer of graphic design, sit down. You may be in for a shock. The graphic designer you choose, however, will work with your budget or create a proposal to answer your needs. We feel the best results are achieved when our clients tell us honestly how much they would like to spend and what they want, rather than leaving us guessing. You enjoy a partnership with your clients to improve their business, service, or product. Trust your designer to feel the same way. As for budget, creativity does not depend on a fat check but on an inventive mind. You can work wonders on a shoestring.

NEWSLETTERS

A newsletter is an effective way of becoming known and staying known if (1) it appears periodically, not just occasionally and (2) it contains information your clients and prospects will find interesting and/or useful. A newsletter about the office softball team, new receptionist, or copying machine is an in-house memo, not a newsletter. A newsletter about new developments in areas of interest to your clients, whether legal or business or political, is a useful tool your client will appreciate.

You may wish to have partners write articles on matters of interest, or you may reprint articles by members of your firm that have appeared in other journals. Whatever you do, make it readable. Write in language that nonlawyers will understand and enjoy. If no one in your firm has that facility, give rough drafts to a copywriter who can then give you an editorial style. We feel the most important reason for having a newsletter is to "show off" in a tasteful way the credentials and expertise of the people in the firm. That means that the articles should have by-lines and even photographs. The people in the firm generally welcome the recognition and publicity that an article in the firm's newsletter gives them, even though they may complain about the additional work or the tight deadline.

Don't neglect the design of your newsletter. A graphic designer can create a preliminary design for you, including a masthead (or title design) and interior layout. Many of our clients preprint the title in two colors, then have a quick-printer print the copy in black as each issue is ready, saving money and time in the long run. The correct choice of color, paper, and design will certainly spell the difference as to whether your newsletter is read or just received. Try hard to include pictures, even old engravings of your city or town if photographs are not available. We often illustrate individual issues with original drawings or get permission to reprint cartoons with appropriate themes and humor (e.g., from *The New Yorker*.)

CRITERIA FOR DISTRIBUTING

The introduction of new communications materials into your firm represents a change. So that your firm reaps maximum benefit from its new communications materials, new systems and practices will be needed to manage their use and distribution.

A distribution system for your communications materials is a key resource for your firm. It is important because it involves your clients and your staff. A distribution system consists of practices that form the basis of long-term client relationships. To effect the widest dissemination possible, it requires commitment from *all* firm members. We recommend the following ideas for distributing new communications materials:

Involve all firm members including nonprofessional staff. Distribute copies of the materials to each firm member and selected nonprofessional staff. Make sure all staff members are aware of benefit statements, special features, and general client uses for the materials. You may want to set distribution goals for firm members. If an approval system is necessary for distribution to clients and prospects, establish one. Draft a prototype letter for mailing your communications materials to prospective clients.

Keep the reception area supplied with the new material clearly visible and available to all. Consider including communications materials with a few select invoices.

Make your materials available. Bring copies to seminars and other public meetings you attend and to those you give. If you give speeches, make your marketing materials available there and alert your audience from the podium that the materials are available. Use the materials on client calls as an outline for conversation and guide your client or prospect through the process of your services.

Send your materials to your referral sources. These may include individuals, other firms, professional associations to which you belong, and trade associations in industries of interest including headquarters and regional offices.

Systematize your distribution efforts. Develop a prospective client list and establish a time for reviewing it. Also establish a time for reviewing your current client list and target specific clients for marketing efforts. For example, at the end of the month when you review clients for billing, also review for distribution. If you are preparing a final bill, you may wish to include a copy of your communications materials with it informing your client of other services offered by your firm. When your client is waiting for long periods of time for a court date, a statutory waiting period, etc., reinforce your relationship by mailing your communications materials to them with a note emphasizing your continued concern for their interests and your firm's capabilities to service their needs. Whatever the situation, establish a system for selecting clients for distribution and accompany your materials with a letter.

Monitor your distribution system. Develop a method for recording the names of communications materials recipients and indicate how the materials were distributed—in person, by mail, by a referral, etc. Change can be managed, and if instituted within your form in a proper way, your firm will realize many returns from its new communications materials, including satisfied clients and a satisfied staff.

Advertising

This chapter was co-authored by myself, Donna Greenfield, and Burkey Belser. Sounds like a committee in a law firm, doesn't it? Ms. Greenfield and Mr. Belser are principals in the Washington, D.C., Marketing Communications Firm of Greenfield Belser Inc.

Stanley Ulanoff in his book *Advertising in America* defines advertising as "a tool of marketing for communicating ideas and information about goods or services to a group; it employs paid space or time in the media or uses another communication vehicle to carry its message; and it openly identifies the advertiser and his relationship to the sales effort." The major categories of media are print, radio, television, Yellow Pages, direct mail, and outdoor (generally meaning billboards). The print medium is further classified into magazines, newspapers, and trade. As with other communication devices, the marketer (or in this case, advertiser) controls what is said and the way it is said but within the policies of the particular medium (magazine, newspaper, network) and, in the case of law firms, within the ethics of the profession.

FEAR OF ADVERTISING

When is advertising suitable for a law practice? Advertising is suitable whenever your marketing plan targets an audience or group that can be reached through an established medium; for example, your real estate practice can be advertised to reach developers and realtors in *Builder* magazine. The real issue is not so much whether you can advertise but whether you *should* advertise; and, if you chose to advertise, the tone and style of your advertisement.

Most law firms still bear a mortal terror of advertising (and in fact mistakenly characterize all marketing promotion efforts as "advertising"). Law firms who fear advertising generally fear the disapprobation of their colleagues and clients, remembering the days when advertising was against the code, therefore *bad*. However, the Bates decision clearly stated that consumers would benefit by information made available about legal services. That is to say, advertising by law firms is in the public interest!

How do you assess the risks you perceive in terms of harm to your image? Advertising can be appropriate, tasteful, beneficial to the firm, and enthusiastically accepted by the target audience. Advertising can and should enhance your image. Opinion survey research has shown that other lawyers do not object to advertising as long as it is dignified and tasteful and consumers desire information with which to make informed decisions. We therefore conclude that tasteful, highly informative advertising will not harm your image.

You must recognize the limitations of advertising, however. It cannot be a firm's only marketing strategy. Some may claim that advertising is all that is needed in order to build a practice. It just isn't so. Advertising can create greater recognition of the firm and can bring inquiries by prospective clients about the firm and its services, but it cannot do the whole marketing job. Your professional presentation, quality work, good service, and good client relations are what will bring the potential client to the firm.

USE A PRO

Can a law firm prepare its own advertising? Yes. *Should* it prepare its own advertising? No, except for a possible "tombstone" ad announcing something like a new partner. If you are going to advertise, retain the services of an advertising professional to plan, create, and produce your ads, and that even includes radio. The Yellow Pages people do have reasonably qualified experts in layout, copy, and art. Since the Yellow Pages are a very special type of media, and also since the cost of Yellow Pages advertising includes these services anyway, a law firm is generally well-advised to have the Yellow Pages experts design, write, and produce those ads. But be sure to work with them to be sure the end product is tastefully done. If Yellow Pages ads suffer from anything, it's overkill or glare. In the cases of all other forms of advertising, however, use an advertising agency or a qualified creative person. If you are considering a very large budget, you should have the agency write a media plan which proposes how the money will be distributed among different media.

If you are running print advertising, obtain additional copies (called "proofs") of the ad to send to your mailing list, include in a proposal package, or just have available in your reception areas. Having paid the production cost of the ad, you should make that ad work for you in every way possible. Proofs costs very little compared to production, so spend the few pennies more and use the proofs to get extra mileage out of your print ads.

How do you select an advertising agency? Follow most of the steps discussed in the Public Relations section on selecting a P.R. agency, then dig further. Check the agency's history and growth; ask how many accounts they have and the size of their budgets. If your budget is small in comparison, you will not receive the best work and services, no matter what the agency tells you. You may be better off with a smaller agency where yours will be an important account. Ask to meet the person who would be your account manager, your prime interface with the agency. Be sure he or she understands the unique concerns of a law firm as well as the legal ethics of what you do. Also, remember that agencies that have both advertising and P.R. departments are generally better in one area than the other. In the end, just as in choosing a P.R. agency, the final decision will be to some degree a "gut" one.

How does an ad agency charge for it services? The old traditional way was that it received a commission on the advertising it placed. If you ran an ad that cost $1,000, you paid the agency the $1,000 and it paid the medium $850, retaining $150 as its commission—the 15-percent commission that ad agencies have received since they first came into being. Agencies still receive commissions for placing ads, but with the rising salaries and other expenses that agencies face, commissions rarely generate enough income unless the advertiser has a gigantic media budget. As a result, since the late fifties or early sixties, agencies have been charging a fee in addition to a commission; the fee is based on the time it takes to create the material and what the people involved are paid—the same system as that used by a law firm. Ask any prospective agency to spell out what their fees are and how they are paid.

SUCCESSFUL ADVERTISING

Are there basic rules for creating successful advertising? Yes—and we will list them—but you must realize that successful ads can also break these rules:

1. *Good ads are visually exciting.* They capture the reader's attention from the clutter of other appeals. Because the reader scans the page quickly, a single element or image should dominate the ad (headline, visual, or text) and demand to be read. Dull, uninteresting ads may satisfy the advertiser's requirement for taste or dignity but fail completely to satisfy their purpose: to stop and command the reader's focused attention.

Naturally it will help if your ad is easy to read. Keep the body copy type as large as possible—no smaller than 10 point if possible (the point size of most magazine type). Avoid reversing the type—that is, white type on a black background. Studies show that readers find this hard to read.

2. *Know what you are selling.* This means you must know who you are selling to—small businesses, farmers, specific industries, married individuals, and so on. If you identify the service you wish to promote, then you can identify your target audience. Let your ad speak to your prospect directly.

3. *Promote benefits, not features.* Address your audience's *needs.* Tell the readers what you can do for them. Listing your services does not lead the readers to align their needs with your service. You must identify how your service meets those needs; for example, "We handle estates and wills" will obviously not snag the reader like "Effective estate planning can reduce your estate taxes."

4. *Talk personally.* An effective ad addresses the individual, the "you," not the madding crowds. Use the first or second person, "we" or "you." Keep the headline and copy conversational—write short sentences and short paragraphs. Now is not the time to impress the reader with your erudition. Make it easy—avoid a fifty-cent word when a simple word will do. In other words, be as considerate of your reader as you would a friend. It is not necessary to talk down to the reader to achieve this, either.

5. *Know the current ethical guidelines in your jurisdiction.* Puffery and platitudes should not form the basis of any ad—legal or otherwise. Readers turn off and tune out. Many jurisdictions now follow

the Federal Trade Commission rule for advertising, simply prohibiting deceptive or misleading statements or conduct.

THE BUDGET

How much should you budget for advertising? There is no definitive answer to that question. (John Wanamaker often said that he know that half of his advertising was not worth the money it cost; he just wished he knew which half.) Advertising is too new to the legal profession for any budgetary guidelines to have been developed. Some firms use a figure of one-half percent of gross fee billings, while a few use a figure of one month's gross profit. Others project potential fees as a multiple of the advertising's cost and see if the figure looks reasonable, particularly for a "product" ad (such as a will). Whatever the system used, it isn't very scientific.

The amount to be budgeted for advertising should be evaluated as part of the total marketing budget. The most practical recommendation is to budget as much for advertising as you can afford to spend for some period of time without necessarily seeing any measurable results. After this period, stop and evaluate the results against your objectives. Over time, you will improve at calculating the return on investment you need for your dollars spent. This holds true for practically every marketing strategy you employ.

Ask the advertising agency or media planner you work with to justify whatever figures they suggest for an advertising budget. You should get a media plan recommending which media should be used to carry your advertising. You should be able to tell, theoretically, how much of your targeted audience is expected to be reached and how often, based on information available from the selected media in which the advertising is placed.

THE FUTURE OF ADVERTISING

The future for advertising for law firms is wide open. We encourage clients to think about using advertising, especially business-to-business advertising in trade and business publications where the medium's demographics show their target market can be reached. Radio is a highly targeted medium with good ratings during specific times of day among managerial and other professional-level people. It is much cheaper than television and an excellent conveyor of informational type advertisements. If you are prepared to invest the money and wait through the awareness-building period, and then to do critical follow-up work, advertising could pay off for you.

Much of the creativity in your advertising will come about in the rethinking of your services to make a creative appeal. What kind of inducement can you offer that will make it worthwhile for someone to try your firm? Can you offer an audit of a company's exposure to risk of employment discrimination claims for little or no cost (a variation on the theme of free initial consultation)? Deferred fee payment arrangements? A special package of services for the start-up of a new business? You are equipped to think creatively about the features of your services because you deal every day with the clients who use them and you know their needs. Discuss them with your marketing consultant and ad agency while doing the concept work for your advertising.

Some of the most successful advertising experiments to date are so-called co-op TV advertising systems. Generic TV spots are generated for, say, a personal injury law firm and licensed for use to a single law firm in each television market. The law firm pays a licensing fee, production costs that are much cheaper than if it were to produce its own spots from scratch, and the TV time to air the spots. One user of a co-op system reports a 50-percent increase in inquiries about the services of the firm and a 35-percent increase in the personal injury caseload. The system used TV and newspaper advertising in tandem in a series of thirty or so informational spots about understanding the law and the lawyer-client relationship. At this writing there are many TV markets to be sold the co-op ads.

DIRECT MAIL

Direct response is a major part of most *corporate* marketing activities. As a marketing technique, it has capabilities no other tool can offer. First, the results are precisely measurable, making this technique more of a science than public relations, advertising, sales, or other communications efforts can ever be. Second, direct response is concentrated. The sender can target and select the audience by neighborhood, job category, or even personal taste. Third, its effect is immediate, creating a response as soon as the mail is opened. Fourth, the letter can speak *directly* to the person the sender wishes to reach, and can even address the individual by name with today's word-processing capabilities. These are powerful advantages.

Why is it then that direct mail is not used by attorneys more frequently?

Two reasons. While many local bar associations have altered their ethical codes to allow many forms of marketing, there may still be prohibitions against solicitation that uses direct-response advertising. Check your local code. Most codes tend to be less restrictive about communications to existing clients. Since the expansion of your existing client base represents perhaps the greatest immediate possibility of new business, you should consider this tool as a strong option in your marketing efforts.

The second reason that direct response is underused is its equation with junk mail. Yours need not be. You can alert clients to the range of your expertise and services and to the specialties of other partners. For example, you can increase your practice in a given area with a special offer on a service all individual clients need: wills and estate-planning. We have seen this strategy create an enthusiastic response from the recipients of a direct-response package which included a personalized letter, an explanatory and educational brochure, and an estate-planning questionnaire. Not only did the attorneys generate new business, their clients appreciated the effort as thoughtful, interested counsel—the kind of counsel, in fact, one expects from one's lawyer.

A direct-mail package typically includes a letter, a descriptive brochure of some type (from very simple to very complex), and some reply mechanism calling the reader to immediate action—a reply card, a coupon, or anything that will aid in stimulating a response.

Can you do this yourself? For once we feel absolutely not. Work with a professional—a graphic design studio, advertising agency, or shop specializing in the creation of direct-mail packages. While principles remain the same for all direct-response packages, their application can be as varied in taste and creativity as you make them. If you are planning a broad-scale campaign, discuss pretesting techniques with the professional you work with. You can test how different direct-mail packages pull by using sample audiences if you have a sufficiently large target market.

Target Prospects

I am a great believer in developing a target prospect program. Some lawyers are in favor of many of the marketing strategies discussed in this book but are very much against this one. I understand how the idea might disturb them at first. Once they understand how a target prospect program really works and how effective it can be, however, most of them appreciate it and become enthusiastic about it.

I believe in it first of all because it brings results. In our own firm we obtain, in a period of a year, over one-third of the prospective clients we target. Some of our client firms obtain as many as 50 percent (which probably proves the old adage that the pupil should surpass the teacher). Another reason that I endorse such a program is because it gives priority to some of the marketing activities of the people in the firm and makes them more efficient. Since no firm, no matter how large, has all the time and money it could use for marketing, anything that maximizes the use of its resources should be considered.

The key to making a target prospect program work is the selection of the potential target prospects. Certain criteria must be applied:

1. Could your firm realistically perform the work if it obtained the prospect as a client? A general practice firm of even 100 lawyers might love to be the head counsel to General Motors but it would never be selected. A sole practitioner who has an excellent individual tax practice could never handle the tax needs of a ten-store department store chain.
2. Is it realistic to believe that the prospect would consider changing to your firm? If the managing partner of the current firm is the brother-in-law of the president, the chances are not too good. If the prospect is publicly held and your firm has no S.E.C. clients and does not even have anyone on staff with that kind of experience, better save your effort for a more likely prospect.
3. Do you really want the prospect as a client? Is there a potential conflict? If the prospect has serious financial problems, you might not get paid, or your firm might prefer not to have that type of client. Some firms, for example, will not take a client who has any direct involvement in the gambling industry.

The application of these criteria by everyone involved will generally save a lot of time and wishful thinking in developing a good target prospect list.

PROSPECT WORK-UP

The procedure we have found most effective is to ask each partner and senior associate to prepare a list of key prospects. Remember that line on the lawyer's profile? The list should be amplified, however, with some notes as to who that person knows in the prospect's organization, what they know about the prospect, and why they think they are a likely prospect. These lists should then be reviewed at the departmental level, if the firm has separate departments, to arrive at a departmental target list which will obviously be much shorter than the total of all the individual prospect lists. Finally, these lists should be reviewed by the practice development committee (or its equivalent). At this point a target prospect form should be filled out; see the sample at the end of this section. After reviewing all the potential target prospects, the P.D. committee should select a limited number for the firm's target prospect list.

Be careful at this point. Don't select too many. No matter how large your firm or particular office may be, it is pretty difficult to work with more than ten target prospects. In the case of a smaller firm or office, the list should probably be shorter. Remember, the various departments and each of the individuals can still have their own target prospects that they are working on without total firm (or office) support.

The list should then be distributed confidentially to all the lawyers in the firm above a certain level. It is a fairly sensitive list, so you do not want it floating around the mailroom or the reception area. It is often wise to include several of the support staff people who may be able to aid the program.

THE PROSPECT FILE

A file is then started, or assembled, on each of the firm's target prospects. The file should either be retained by the head of the P.D. committee, the marketing coordinator, or the "team captain." The latter is the person who agrees to accept the responsibility of coordinating the firm's efforts to obtain this particular prospect. He or she also has the prime responsibility for strategy development, researching the prospect, updating the file continuously, and keeping track of the activities of anyone in the firm in connection with this prospect. On the prospect form that we recommend, it is this person's name that goes on the line marked "PA," which stands for "Person Accountable." The reason for the one central file on each prospect should be obvious: Anyone who wants to know the status of the project, what has been done, what contacts are known, etc., can go to one spot and be brought up to date quickly.

Some of the most important material that should go in this file are annual reports, 10–Ks, etc., if the prospect is a publicly held company; any newspaper clippings or articles about the company or its people; and reports of any contact with or presentations to the prospect. Also important is a list of personal contacts that anyone in the firm might have that could be helpful. Some secretaries in a firm can do an excellent job as a "clipping service" by watching for anything that might appear in print about a prospect. (They are usually better at this than even the team captains.)

Of course, all this effort cannot stop with the preparation of a list and the starting of files. Everyone, the team captain in particular, must keep alert for opportunities to move the firm along toward the ultimate goal of having the prospect as a client. Executives in the target prospect organization, starting with house counsel if there is any, should be on the firm's mailing list. Opportunities should be sought to establish or develop relationships with target prospect people. The whole idea of a firm's target prospect program is to bring as much of the firm's resources to bear on the prospect as possible.

Why It Works

Probably the main reason that a target prospect program works is that it raises everyone's awareness of certain prospects. This alone is important. As a result, things begin to happen. Perhaps because your people are "sensitized" to anything relating to the prospect, they soon start noticing news stories or hearing important things about the prospect. They suddenly find themselves meeting people connected with the prospect.

My favorite story in this regard is about the litigation partner of a large firm who one day shared a cab with a stranger. He happened to ask the other man where he worked and discovered he was the house counsel of a target prospect company, a man no one in the firm had ever met. Our alert partner was able to convert that twenty-minute cab ride into a lunch date several weeks later. This was followed by several other social visits over the next few months. Finally the house counsel invited the partner and other lawyers in the firm to meet with him and his department. At this point our partner was well equipped with background on the company and some of its key legal problems. At the meeting, the house counsel discussed some of the company's other problems. Several weeks later a proposal was requested, and several weeks after that the law firm's target prospect became its newest client.

TARGET PROSPECT PROFILE   (PA_____)

Name _____ SIC or Industry Code _____

Address _____ Phone _____

_____ No. of Employees _____

Other Locations _____

Subsidiaries _____

Description of Business _____

_____

Sales Volume Last Year _____ Fiscal Year _____

Union(s) _____

No. of Shareholders _____ Public (Exchange) _____

Private _____

On File: Current Annual Report __ _____

Latest 10-K _____

Proxy Statements _____

Accounting Firm _____ Bank _____

Law Firms _____

Investment Advisers _____

Key Officers: On Mailing List?

_____ ___ _____ _____

_____   _____ _____

_____   _____ _____

_____   _____ _____

Directors:

_____ _____ _____

_____ _____ _____

_____ _____ _____

_____ _____ _____

Notes:

Alumni

Whether or not it is a personnel or human resources policy of the firm, maintaining contact with its alumni should be part of the marketing program. Some former firm members may wind up as prospects or clients; others could be excellent sources of business. If a firm burns its bridges with its alumni, it will someday also see some new business go up in smoke as a result.

Regardless of how an alumni relations program is implemented, the most important point is the attitude of the firm toward its former members. Except in those cases where the departure was truly unpleasant, the firm should make every effort to keep in touch with its alumni in order to maintain, or restore, their positive feelings toward the firm. Let the alumni ignore or reject the overtures; the firm should make a sincere and continuous effort to continue some kind of pleasant and constructive relationship with them.

Far too many firms take the opposite viewpoint. Once a person leaves the firm, he or she is immediately written off and forgotten. A cloud is neatly deposited over that person's head regardless of the circumstances. In addition to being poor human relations, this is also bad business.

An alumni relations program is not complicated to set up. Depending on what is involved, it might become difficult to maintain an up-to-date address file. Other than that, it is one of the easiest marketing strategies to employ.

All alumni should be on a mailing list to receive newsletters and general announcements. This is the bare minimum of contact; it is also quite impersonal. A further step, and a more personal one, is to include alumni on the invitation list of a big annual event such as a Christmas party or summer picnic. If the alumni list becomes too big, it may be necessary to drop some names off after several years. In the meantime, however, they will still feel wanted and that, of course, is the whole point.

The most effective technique is one-on-one personal contact by someone they were close to in the firm. Nothing will keep alumni more positive in their thinking about the firm than an occasional visit with a close friend or working buddy from the firm. When someone leaves, assign a "running mate" to keep in touch with that person several times a year at least. Not every one of the alumni will respond to this effort, but then it is they who have made the choice, not the firm. Those that do respond to the overtures will, sooner or later, help bring additional business to the firm.

This, by the way, is an excellent program to assign to a senior associate to organize, implement, and administer. It's way of giving a nonpartner some significant marketing responsibility—if the firm takes the program seriously. The enthusiasm and follow-through that an associate can bring to this program will open a lot of people's eyes and prepare him or her for further assignments in the future.

Prospect Presentations

The major accounting firms have been writing proposals and making presentations to prospective clients for years. In the case of very large prospects, these proposals resemble bound volumes of an encyclopedia and the presentations become elaborate productions including even audio-visual material. Lately, smaller accounting firms as well are having to prepare formal proposals and make comprehensive, if not elaborate, presentations to even their smaller prospects.

And so too are law firms!

Yes, it has finally happened. Whatever the reasons (there are several, but they aren't important anyway), lawyers and law firms today are now faced with the necessity of making presentations to prospective clients and even submitting written materials that look somewhat like a proposal.

For those Dedicated Lawyers and Anti-Marketing Attorneys described in Part I who find this just too much to take, I suggest you skip to the next section. Let others in your firms read this one, because, like it or not, it is becoming a necessity at times in the marketing of a law firm—and *somebody* has to know how to do it correctly.

WHAT IS A PRESENTATION?

Let me define what I mean by a "presentation." For a large firm courting a large prospective client, this could mean a stand-up or at least formal presentation to house counsel, the in-house legal department, and/or top management of the company. For a small firm or sole practitioner, it could involve a discussion, over lunch or in the office, of what the attorney or the firm can do for the prospective client. Whichever form it takes, or anything in between, it amounts to a presentation on the firm (or the lawyer), its qualifications, and the reasons why it should be retained.

To put it bluntly, it's a sales pitch.

I well realize that opportunities to make or solicit presentations to prospective clients must be circumscribed by both rules of ethics and the boundaries of good taste. They are also impacted, to a great degree, by the style of the law firm as well as its analysis of the prospective client. Nevertheless, each contact with a potential client should be viewed as an important opportunity to sell the firm and its entire range of legal skills, whether it is a formal presentation or not. This means that each planned contact should be prepared for just as if it were a formal presentation. And, let me repeat, particularly for those firms seeking the larger or "institutional" clients, a presentation will probably be required somewhere along the way.

Actually, if you think about it, making a presentation is kind of fun. It is an opportunity to say frankly and openly how good you and your firm are. Just about every lawyer feels this way anyway. The idea of having to organize it may not be appealing, but the chance to discuss just how good you are should appeal to most lawyers.

Based on a number of years of working with both accounting firms and law firms, I have a strong conviction about presentations and proposals. Accounting firms all too often do not begin their real marketing effort until they start work on a proposal. Everything is then poured into a frantic effort as if the proposal were the only basis on which the prospect will make the decision, when actually the marketing effort should have started long before. In a law firm, however, the presentation is often the result of a great deal of marketing effort that has been conducted beforehand. For this reason, and also because the idea of making presentations is new to most lawyers, law firms approach this task in a rather casual manner. My warning to you is—DON'T! This may be your only real "at bat" with your prospect. This is where you can—and must—go on stage and tell your story. It is at least as important, and possibly moreso, than the proposal presentation by an accounting firm. So don't take it lightly.

THERE SHOULD BE A PROCEDURE

Each presentation and its supporting material must be prepared and executed to the best of the firm's ability. While each must be custom-tailored to a particular prospect, some of the work involved is repetitious; therefore, a procedure can be developed which makes the presentation less hectic and much more effective.

The most important steps are the following.

In many cases, you will be making the presentation (formal or informal) to a target prospect or, at the very least, to a person or prospective client you have had some prior contact with. Therefore, some marketing activity should have already been done with regard to this prospect. So . . .

1. Check with the appropriate person in the firm to be certain that other lawyers are not working on a similar presentation to the same prospect. If this is a designated target prospect, check with the "Person Accountable." If not, then check with the Chairman of the Marketing Committee or the Marketing Coordinator.

2. Select an appropriate team, if called for, to develop and make the presentation. If there is no Person Accountable, select one of the partners who is participating in the presentation as the team leader to organize the effort.

3. Research all material in the firm's marketing files on the prospect. Also, check around to see who in the firm has any contacts with the target prospect and its personnel or has any other information that might be pertinent to the presentation.

4. The team leader, along with any other lawyers in the firm who have particular knowledge of or contact with the prospect, should develop a list of practice areas in which the prospect is already or may be interested in having assistance from the firm. If there has been effective prior contact with the prospect, these areas may have already been defined.

5. General information on your firm should be assembled, together with biographies of the lawyers who might be closely involved with the prospect if it retains your firm. Include relevant material such as reprints of articles, pertinent publicity, etc.

6. Practice area resumes that contain specific examples appropriate to the needs of the prospect should either be pulled from the marketing files or prepared.

7. The materials assembled in 5 and 6 above should be collected into a folder, firm brochure, or some other tasteful vehicle (not a file folder!) to leave with the prospect.

8. All members of the team who will be participating should get together to plan and rehearse the presentation. This may be the most important step of all. A slipshod or disjointed presentation will almost guarantee that the firm will *not* obtain the prospect as a client.

THAT'S NOT ALL

Here are some other important points to remember.

Don't try to sell what the prospect does not want to buy. For example, if you are a general practice firm meeting with a prospect who is interested in your capabilities to do tax work or bond work or to handle their labor matters, don't make a pitch to become general counsel as well. It's not ethical if they already have general counsel. If you need an additional reason, it's bad marketing as well. You can only sell a prospect what they are interested in buying. Of course, you can—and should—let the prospect know about the full range of the firm's practice, but then concentrate only on what you have determined the prospect is interested in hearing about.

Include only pertinent experience and references of both the firm and the individual lawyers who would be working on the prospect's matters. For example, if the prospect is a hospital, they don't particularly care about your experience with clothing companies, retail stores, or bowling alleys unless it reflects your general reputation for integrity and service. The prospect is interested in your experience relative to the health care field and related problems such as perhaps tax, bonds, or corporate reorganization for hospitals. The same principle holds for the individual biographies included in the leave-behind material. Keep them short and relevant. Save all the ego-flattering awards, technical articles, and such for the appendix.

Be a little humble. Don't say, "We will do this; we will take care of that." I know that this is directly opposite to what most so-called professional sales training programs teach. That may be correct for selling automobiles or insurance policies but not for selling legal services. Talk and even write in the conditional tense, i.e., "If you select our firm, this is what we would do . . . this is how we would approach that matter." Don't talk—or write—as if you already have the client. Show that you realize that you must earn the right to represent them first.

OTHER IMPORTANT POINTS

Who will determine the type of presentation? The prospect, of course, but the law firm generally will suggest an appropriate form. For example, if only one lawyer has been in contact with the prospect, it might be effective to suggest that several of the client's attorneys or executives meet for dinner with several of the firm's attorneys. This would set the stage for a rather relaxed presentation over, or at the end of, dinner after everyone has gotten to know each other a little. On the other hand, if there has been a great deal of prior contact between prospect and firm people, a formal meeting in the firm's offices with a more formal presentation would seem appropriate. Generally speaking, the firm should take the lead in suggesting the meeting and also the format. Let the prospect accept or suggest an alternative setting.

And a final point. Be patient, particularly after the presentation. The speed with which the prospect will make its decision will depend most of all on the urgency of its situation. If it is faced with impending litigation or has a critical matter that must be addressed immediately, it will probably make its decision promptly. On the other hand, if it is merely exploring several law firms for expected future needs, the prospect may not make a decision for some time. Don't press the issue after the presentation. Stay in touch—and read the later section in this book on Selling to Prospects. But above all, be patient.

Fees, Pricing, and Billing

The entire area of fees, pricing, and billing has a major impact on firm operations. For this reason law firms are increasingly bringing in management or financial consultants to assist them in straightening out this part of their operations.

Why then discuss the subject in a book on marketing?

The reason is that fees, pricing, and billing are not only important from an operations viewpoint, they are also extremely important from a marketing viewpoint. The receipt of a lawyer's bill is often greeted with the same kind of enthusiasm as a long-postponed appointment with the dentist. It is often a jolt, even if the final amount is less than the expected or projected fee. The receipt of a bill often results in numerous questions from the client that, in many cases, could have been avoided. Sometimes a carefully developed client relationship is seriously and unnecessarily damaged by the manner in which the statement for services is rendered.

LET'S START WITH FEES

A discussion on fees could probably fill an entire book, because, like advertising, everyone has a viewpoint on the subject. I will try to treat it briefly yet appropriately here.

In other forms of marketing, meaning consumer and some industrial marketing, price is one of the four P's of the marketing mix. The others are product, place (i.e., distribution), and promotion. Price is extremely important in the marketing and delivering of legal services today. (More on this in the next section on Cost Containment.) Because of this, a firm's hourly fees and overall pricing of its services must be considered both from a profitability aspect and a marketing aspect.

I believe that law firms should have an established hourly rate for each lawyer, based on the lawyers' experience and skill in addition to their salaries, even if the firms do not bill on an hourly basis. Hopefully the lawyer's salary will reflect the lawyer's experience and ability, but in many cases this is not so. Without getting into that can of worms (compensation is for management consultants, not marketing consultants), let me only state that the hourly rate for each lawyer should reflect his or her *value* to the client. Some firms have two rates—"required" and "desired." The required rate is the minimum rate (allowing for write-offs) that the firm should bill in order to make that lawyer's work profitable. The desired rate is the rate that the particular lawyer's experience and skill should commend. When quoting the hourly rate to a client or prospective client, it is important to know which rate to use. Since this can often lead to confusion, I personally prefer that there be only one hourly rate established for each lawyer, but I understand that there are compelling financial reasons for having the two-tier system.

One of the best ways to avoid subsequent problems over fees is to discuss them at the beginning of the client relationship. This is often a difficult experience for many lawyers who feel that is it unprofessional or makes it appear that the lawyer is more interested in the money than in helping the client. Actually it is the mark of a truly marketing-oriented professional who thinks from the client's viewpoint. I believe that the lawyer should always make an effort to discuss the expected fee—or at least the hourly rates—with the client before starting the work, particularly if it is a new client. If the client doesn't want to discuss the subject because he or she is preoccupied with the problems they have, at least the lawyer has shown the courtesy and sensitivity to raise the subject. In today's competitive and expensive legal market, most clients will welcome and appreciate the lawyer's discussion of the fees at the start.

Remember also that there can be an important difference between hourly rates and the total fee. Some clients tend to place almost total emphasis on the hourly rate they are charged, while others, generally the more knowledgeable and sophisticated clients, look more at the total cost. Sometimes it will cost the client less to have a partner who has a high hourly rate spend four hours on a matter than a much less costly associate who might have to spend twenty hours on the matter. And, of course, there is the issue of quality of the work as well.

TYPES OF PRICING

There are basically five ways in which a firm can price its services.

1. *Hourly rates.* This is the customary way and applies to most types of work. The hourly rate must also be the basis for developing any other pricing approaches, hence my earlier statement that each lawyer should have an established hourly rate.
2. *Fixed-fee retainer.* This commits the firm or lawyer either to provide specified services on a continuing basis or to be available to serve the client when called upon. Frequently the time actually spent is recorded against the retainer and billed to the client if it exceeds the retainer on a monthly, quarterly, or annual basis.
3. *Flat fee.* Legal clinics generally price most of their "products" on a flat-fee basis such as wills, uncontested divorces, personal bankruptcy, etc. Some of the traditional types of law firms are also using this approach at times. It requires that you know how many hours it will take to perform the service and what your actual costs are. Legal clinics must know this. Many traditional firms do not appreciate that fact and establish fixed fees without either knowing their costs or having systems in place to minimize the time required.
4. *Contingency.* Compensation is based on the result achieved. This method is most often used in litigation on the plaintiff's side such as in personal injury.

5. *Value.* Compensation is based on "the responsibility assumed and the result achieved" (to quote one lawyer who frequently prices his services in this manner). Naturally, in this case, it is difficult or unwise to project the fee at the start.

I realize that there are some types of legal work in which the method of pricing or even the hourly rates are pretty well established by the marketplace. Worker's compensation and insurance defense, particularly on behalf of insurance companies, are two examples where the firm has little maneuvering room in establishing its rate or pricing its services. But there are a number of other areas in which law firms that have traditionally charged on an hourly basis can explore other types of pricing. Quite frankly, the client doesn't really care how much time the lawyer spent; it's the result the client is interested in.

One of the most knowledgeable authorities on the pricing of legal services is Thomas J. Harrington, President of Legal Financial Management Services, Wellesley, Mass. The following is quoted from a newsletter on the subject that Tom himself wrote.

THE ART OF PRICING LEGAL SERVICES

The pricing of legal services is a fine blend of cost recovery, net profit and the quality of service the client desires. There is no mathematical formula to combine these ingredients. The right mix is born of experience, insight and a certain willingness to break new ground.

Some guidelines to consider in the practice of this art:

1. Do not let hourly time and rates alone be the determinant of your services. Such a basis demeans both the attorney and the service.
2. If a particular service is continually underpriced, either the service should be dropped or the quality increased to allow for a profitable higher fee. Estate Planning is a primary example.
3. Research and development costs for developing new services or systems in all fairness are to be borne by all clients who benefit.
4. There is sufficient data in your timekeeping system to establish profitable prices for almost all your repetitive services.

5. The price of a service is best expressed in round figures—the nearest $10, or for larger amounts the nearest $100 or $1,000.
6. Client disbursements should be absorbed into the fee when they are very small or less than 1% of the fee.

BILLING

Bill regularly and promptly or, as one brilliant managing partner puts it, "While the glow of appreciation still shines in their eyes."

When possible, use descriptive billing, rather than the traditional and terse "for professional services." It reminds the client of what you have done and it also has an important psychological effect: the fee becomes smaller in relation to the work described.

I know there are many cases, particularly with large corporations or clients with house counsel, where the law firm must submit detailed and itemized statements. But don't use this type of bill when it is not required by the client. It can become quite tedious as well as expensive, not just to prepare the bill but also in postage costs to mail out a large envelope bulging with detailed printout sheets. When not required, itemized billing is also a marketing mistake. Many clients do not want all the details on how your bill was arrived at. Quite frankly, you don't want to provide them either, because it could lead to a lot of hassle over rates, time spent, etc. What many clients do want to know is what did you do. A descriptive bill provides adequate explanation for these clients. Once a descriptive billing procedure is in place, it should take the responsible or billing attorney only a few minutes to prepare the bill or, better yet, to check the bill that the secretary has prepared from the records.

For those cases where descriptive billing is possible—and there are plenty of them—here is an example.

Harris, Jones and Trialawyer

International Consolidated Manufacturers, Inc.
10056 Longwinded Boulevard
Holtz, PA 19999

For professional services in connection with obtaining zoning variance for building of new plant in Pittsburgh. Includes six meetings at the company, three meetings with the zoning hearing board, preparation of variance request forms, and attendance at two public hearings.

$13,500

Cost Containment

Although one of the shortest sections in this book, this is also one of the most important.

It's no secret that the cost of legal services is mounting. Clients of all sizes and types—from major international companies to elderly widows—are looking for ways to control the cost of using a law firm.

Beat your clients, particularly your corporate clients, to the punch on cost containment. Many in-house counsels are under pressure from their management to reduce legal costs. As a result, law firms across the country are receiving comments and even letters from their clients insisting on lower legal bills and, in some cases, even dictating how savings will be achieved.

You can very possibly lose some of these clients if you don't take some firm and noticeable steps in controlling your fees to them. Review your internal systems and procedures. Use lower-cost personnel—lawyers, paralegals, legal assistants, nonprofessional staff—whenever possible. Budget time and money. Suggest litigation budgeting, project cost billing, or the use of alternative resolution techniques. Think of new ways to lower the cost of your services without affecting your profitability—or the quality of your work.

Show your client that you realize how expensive legal services are and that you are effectively addressing the matter wherever you can. In other words, cost containment should not only be an ongoing operations procedure in your firm, it should also be a marketing activity of your firm.

Routine Firm Operations

Many law firms spend a lot of time and money developing excellent marketing programs only to ruin them by their failure to attend to some nitty-gritty details of the firm's operations.

Since the telephone is probably the most frequent form of contact the client has with the firm, let's start there. Call your office sometime and listen, really listen, to how the phone is answered. Does the operator or receptionist have a professional yet pleasant manner, or does she sound hesitant, bored, or annoyed? Does she get the caller's name correct? Does she acknowledge frequent callers or clients with a greeting? Does she leave the caller on hold without checking back? I could go on and on, but the point is this: The way phone calls are handled in your office creates a much stronger impression than you could imagine. Top quality, professional phone manners can create a favorable impression that will go a long way, while poor phone manners can irritate callers and cost your firm money—and even clients!

While we're on the subject of phone calls, let's not forget the professional staff, particularly the partners. Nothing irritates people more than to leave a message for someone to call back and for the call not to be returned. This seems to be a special prerogative, or failing, of some partners. Yes, we all have a few people who seem to constantly bug us on the phone. For the most part, however, when people want us to call them back they have a reason. Think how bad your practice would be if no one ever called! When a lawyer doesn't return phone calls, it is generally because he or she isn't client-oriented and considers clients an interruption to work rather than the reason for it. If any of your lawyers have this failing, start a campaign to have phone calls returned and follow up on it.

One way to reduce the number of phone message slips on an attorney's desk is to introduce other members of the firm, including his or her secretary, to the client. The lawyer should inform the client that if he or she is not available, the client should mention the reason for the call, because often the secretary could either answer the client's question herself or find someone who can. At worst, she can brief the lawyer on the reason for the call before he or she returns it. It comes as a terrible shock to many lawyers to learn that their clients don't always want to speak to them—they just want an answer. If the secretary is properly trained, if she is introduced to the clients (and even prospects), and if they are encouraged to tell her their reason for calling, she can often handle the matter. Results: delighted clients and fewer message slips on the lawyer's desk.

Also about phone calls: When clients are meeting with the firm's professionals, particularly partners, in the office, do the lawyers accept phone calls during the meeting? It is distracting to many people to have their meeting interrupted when a lawyer takes a phone call, particularly when the client knows that he or she is being billed for the time. It is a sign of courtesy and respect for the client if the lawyer refuses all phone calls during a meeting with that client. Furthermore, when the client calls in and is informed that the lawyer can't take the call because he or she is meeting with a client, the caller will believe it and respect both the lawyer and the firm.

How do your offices look to an arriving visitor? I am not referring to the design and decoration. I am referring to the cleanliness, neatness, and general condition. Once a week or so, walk into your office as if you had never been there before. Look at everything through the eyes of a client or prospect who is visiting your office for the first time. Is the lettering on the front door dirty, scratched, or even missing a few letters? As you enter the reception area, is the rug clean, the receptionist neatly groomed and pleasant, the furniture (regardless of its style) in good repair? Are the magazines and publications recent and in good condition or old and tattered? Are they all technical or legal publications, or are there some general interest magazines as well. Is the visitor greeted promptly and pleasantly or made to wait while the receptionist finishes a personal phone call?

The way that routine firm procedures are carried out can help or hurt the firm's marketing program. The support staff can help greatly in this regard. If they are marketing oriented, routine matters will be handled with the client or prospect in mind. One excellent idea is to have the office manager or firm administrator hold a meeting with the support staff to explain the firm's commitment to marketing and the importance of the role they play. You may be surprised at their positive response and also at the good suggestions they will have.

The Name of the Firm

Like many subjects discussed in this book, this is a sensitive one. It is also something that certain lawyers may feel has no connection with marketing. The fact is, however, that the name of the firm—or, to be specific, the length and difficulty of the name—can often have an ef- fect on its marketing efforts.

Some firms have extremely long and/or difficult names. Where the name is long, it has probably gotten that way because each new part- ner's name was added to the firm's name. The result is often a firm name of five, six, or seven individual's names. If some of the names are long or of foreign extraction—like Demopolous, Ildefonso, Gert- stenmettler, Chung Lee How, and Valdez-Portera—it becomes a mouthful to say, let alone a chore for clients to remember.

The name of the firm is, of course, a matter affecting the egos of the "name" partners. Many firms that have a long name often shorten it conversationally, or other people, when referring to the firm, will shorten it themselves to one or two names.

There is a trend today for law firms to officially shorten their firm names. I think it is a good one. The name of a law firm is very impor- tant in terms of marketing. If it is hard for people to remember, or long and complicated to say, this has an effect on clients and other outsiders. Business can even be lost. Sometimes a person who has received glowing references about a firm that he or she never heard of will fail to contact that firm because they couldn't remember the name.

Another point: It is the desire of many firms today to "institu- tionalize" their clients, to have these clients think in terms of the *firm* rather than a particular attorney. A long or complicated firm name just adds one more obstacle to achieving this.

I know it is a delicate issue. But if the name of your firm is long, complicated, or both, see if you can obtain the partners' approval to simplify or shorten it. Then keep it. Every time you add to or alter the name of the firm it complicates your marketing program and, more importantly, can diminish its results.

Mergers

While it might seem surprising to see mergers discussed as part of a marketing program, our firm frequently includes a merger strategy as part of the marketing program we develop for our clients. The reason is quite simple. A marketing program is a program for growth. Generally it is assumed that the program will focus on *internal* growth. Nevertheless, the Strategic Analysis will frequently indicate areas of opportunity that a firm can only capitalize on through a strategy of *external* growth—i.e., mergers. For this reason, mergers are a proper subject for consideration here.

There could be a number of reasons for a law firm to consider a merger strategy as part of its growth plans.

1. The firm wishes to expand into a different geographic area from its principal office. This could be a suburban area (if the main office is downtown) or it could be in another city or another state. The firm may or may not already have a sufficient client base in that area to support the office for a while, but the internal growth prospects are slow and costly. In these cases the firm should consider acquiring a firm in that area, one that has a client base to start with.

2. To acquire expertise in a particular area of the law. Many times the Strategic Analysis will indicate substantial growth opportunities for a firm in a particular area of the law in which it possesses little or no expertise—for example, bankruptcy, labor, taxation, or SEC. To develop this expertise internally might be a long and costly process; even if it could be eventually developed in this way, the opportunity might be lost by that time. In these cases, it is often much better, as well as less expensive, to acquire a firm that already has the needed expertise and, hopefully, a strong reputation and client base as well.

3. Many firms today have a considerable "age gap" between the senior partners who are nearing retirement and the younger partners. This age gap often translates into a lack of sufficient experience, expertise, and reputation to carry the firm through the next five or ten years. In these cases the firm should consider acquiring another firm that has partners who fill the age gap and

can provide the needed factors and leadership until the younger partners develop more.

4. Another reason for acquiring a firm is to broaden the client base. Some firms make the determination that they need to expand the client base sooner than an internal program might accomplish. In these cases, acquisition of a firm with a compatible client base could be a sound decision—and also a more profitable one.

5. A firm may have identified a particular industry that could provide great growth potential but in which it has little or no client base and reputation, whether or not it has the needed expertise. In these cases a merger that brings into the firm a solid client base in that industry as well as additional expertise in the industry could be a wise move. Some examples are the high technology field, transportation, financial institutions, and agribusiness.

6. Mergers are sometimes consummated because it is the only way for a firm to acquire one or more particular lawyers who it feels would add a great deal to the practice for any of a variety of reasons.

There are many factors that must be considered in a potential merger, not the least of which are the compatibility of the lawyers in both firms and the current income levels. This is not a book on mergers, however, and I am not qualified to discuss the subject in the depth it requires. Nevertheless, from a marketing viewpoint, let me list some points to keep in mind. By addressing them early—or even adopting them as basic policies for consideration of a merger—a firm can save a lot of time and money.

1. The merger should provide expertise in areas of the law that the firm has either targeted for development or in which it feels its skills need upgrading.

2. The merger should be with a firm either located in the firm's principal geographic area or in areas targeted for entry.

3. The merger should equal or improve the firm's profitability in no more than two years.

4. If located outside the immediate geographic area, the incoming firm should have lawyers who already have established practices and can successfully market in the particular area.

5. If located outside the immediate geographic area, a member of

the acquiring firm should probably transfer to the new firm's office to provide leadership and indoctrination in the policies and procedures of practice of the acquiring firm.
6. The quality of practice of the acquired firm should be up to the standards of that of the acquiring firm.

In summary, mergers are both a management and a marketing decision. Examine them in both lights.

Product Development

In many marketing-oriented companies, product development is a function of the marketing department. If the company is in a medium- or high-technology industry, marketing will still have a shared responsibility with the research and development function. Similarly, product development becomes an important marketing function in a law firm as well.

Product development can refer to several things: the development of needed expertise in a new field of law, the development of experience and reputation in a particular industry, or the development of new services. Whatever the area, a firm cannot go to sleep in considering and developing new legal "products." It is, to some degree, an opportunistic situation in which a firm either detects opportunities to grow or is confronted with the need to expand its capabilities to keep from losing some of its clients. Whether the reasons are offensive (to take advantage of an opportunity) or defensive (to keep from losing business), a continuing program of product development prepares a firm for a smooth and profitable expansion of its capabilites. In other words, keep looking ahead. In this way you can be ready when the opportunity or need arises. Sometimes a firm doesn't get a second chance.

To have an effective product development operation requires relatively little. Most product development work occurs within the major departments—litigation, corporate, estates and trusts, etc. Therefore the lawyers in these departments must be constantly on the alert, within their major fields of law, for trends and developments that require them or the firm to possess additional capabilities. For example, health care has become an important specialty area of the law in recent years. Only a few firms, however, have developed expertise in the new subspecialty of corporate reorganization. Because of their alertness in developing this legal product early in the game, these firms have gained a big leg on other firms that may have health care expertise but have not been as farseeing or as aggressive in their product development.

Whether it originates with the marketing group or the individual departments doesn't matter. What does matter is that a firm keep alert in examining and developing new products.

Integrated Marketing

During the seminars that I conduct on marketing for lawyers and accountants, I ask the attendees if they have ever heard of "integrated marketing." Practically none of them ever have. I then ask them what they think it means. Most of them come up with the obvious answer, in one form or another, that integrated marketing refers to a marketing program that integrates some or all of the strategies and activities discussed in this book.

This is the wrong answer. The right answer is important for every lawyer to know and understand.

Integrated marketing—a term that comes from the health care industry—means that the people who deliver the service are also the people who must market it. There is no separate marketing staff in a clinic, hospital, or nursing home (although there may be a public relations department). The professional staff—the doctors, nurses, etc.—are the ones who care for the patients and provide the necessary services. They are also the only people who can market the services. In other words, the marketing of the service must be integrated with the delivery of the service.

This principle is just as applicable to the legal profession.

Another way of saying it is that *it takes a lawyer to market legal services.* No one else can do your marketing for you. Outside marketing specialists such as advertising agencies, public relations agencies, or consulting firms like ours can provide marketing support services, but we cannot market for the firm. The members of the firm must do *most* of the marketing and all of the selling themselves.

Many lawyers, of course, resist this principle. They are in favor of marketing as long as someone else does it for them and delivers the new business to them; all they want to do is open new files. Unfortunately, it just doesn't work that way. Fortunately, more and more lawyers realize this and know that they, themselves, must devote time and effort to marketing.

There is a Catch-22 to the whole situation. The more successful you are at marketing, the more work you have to do—and the less time you then have for marketing. Yet, in the successful and growing firms, it all works out somehow. You can't have one without the other.

Integrated marketing has become a basic fact of a lawyer's life.

PART III
THE MARKETING PLAN
FOR THE SMALLER FIRM
OR SOLE PRACTITIONER

Overview

A "plan" of any kind for a law firm can be defined as "the organized use of the firm's resources." The marketing plan identifies growth opportunities and presents an organized use of the firm's resources in order to obtain maximum benefit from these opportunities.

Basically the marketing plan for a sole practitioner or smaller firm is the same as that for a large firm.

(For simplicity's sake, let's define a smaller firm quantitatively—25 or so lawyers. In specific cases, however, the style and organization of a firm is more important than its size. I have worked with firms of less than 20 lawyers that were organized like, and praticed like, firms many times their size.)

As stated in the early sections of this book, the steps in developing the plan (the process) are exactly the same for large and small firms, beginning with the Strategic Analysis and concluding with the Tactical Plan. The form of the plan is also the same: a statement of objectives, the action steps to accomplish them, who is responsible, the time frame, and the budget, both in terms of hours and expenditures.

The differences, which are naturally the result of size, are in the structure and the complexity of the plan.

1. The large firm may—and I do mean "may"—spend more money on its marketing program.
2. The large firm will probably have mini-marketing plans for each of the departments.
3. Since many large firms have more than one office, each office should have a marketing plan of its own that integrates into the total firm plan.
4. The large firm may—and again I mean "may"—be more formal and structured in the implementation of the plan.
5. The large firm may—once again I use that term deliberately—designate certain lawyers whose prime responsibility is marketing, not billable hours.
6. The large firm may undertake more marketing activities.

These differences call for different techniques in structure, implementation, and administration of the plan. This part of the book deals with the requirements of the sole practitioner and small firm. The next part deals with those of the large firm. Readers who are members of large firms—by whatever definition you wish to employ—may skip the next few sections. Those who practice alone or in smaller firms may skip Part IV. Any readers who are currently with a smaller firm which they expect will become a large firm should read both parts.

Sample Plan

The idea of drafting a formal, written marketing plan overwhelms many lawyers, most of whom are, of course, no strangers to preparing lengthy documents. In the case of a large firm, the marketing plan is indeed a sizable document. Although there is no such thing as an "average"-size plan, the plans that we develop for a firm of a hundred or so lawyers generally run 80 to 90 pages including the appendix. For larger firms, particularly those with several offices, the plans have been over 150 pages long. The size and complexity of these firms require that the plans be that extensive.

On the other hand, the plan for a sole practitioner or very small firm can consist only of several legal-size pages of handwritten notes. "The form of the marketing plan is not nearly as important as the substance and the thought that go into its preparation" (Part I, section called The Steps in Developing a Marketing Plan). Regardless of its length and the form in which it is finalized, the plan should include each of the elements discussed in that section:

1. Strategic Analysis Marketing Report
2. Firm Strategic Objectives—three to five years ahead
3. Firm Strategic Marketing Objectives
4. Basic Policies—"Rules of the Road"
5. Basic Marketing Strategies
6. Positioning Statement
7. Tactical Marketing Objectives for the year ahead
8. Action steps to accomplish

These should be presented in separate sections in the above order, which is the sequence in which the plan should be developed. The sections fall under the three main parts of the plan—Part I is also section 1; Part II, the Strategic Marketing Plan, includes sections 2 through 6; Part III, the Tactical Marketing Plan, includes sections 7 and 8.

The Strategic Analysis Marketing Report may be the largest single part of the plan. It can take a variety of forms. The important thing is to follow the major categories as shown in the Strategic Analysis Check List and to address each one of them:

I. Internal Factors
   A. Personnel and Organization
   B. Fees and Hours
   C. Client Data
   D. Marketing
   E. General
II. External Factors
   A. Opinions and perceptions of the firm
   B. Firms considered as competition
   C. Economic and social evironment in the market area(s)
   D. Leading industries, businesses, and organizations in the market area(s)
III. Opportunities for Growth

Because the Strategic Analysis Marketing Report is usually quite long, I do not include an example here. If you follow the check list in doing the analysis and follow the above outline in drafting the report, you will do a thorough and competent job.

The earlier section on The Strategic Marketing Plan included examples, or at least adequate discussion, of each section of this part of the plan.

The Tactical Marketing Plan, also discussed in an earlier section, is really quite simple—although many marketing professionals would prefer lawyers didn't realize that! It merely takes each of the tactical objectives and discusses the action steps that will be taken to achieve that objective, together with expected dates of completion for each step, the person or persons responsible, and the hours and money budgeted. It must also include a means to control the program and monitor the results.

The exact format that is used is, once again, not nearly as important as just getting everything down on paper in some form. Every firm's plan is different. As a guide, here is a sample tactical marketing plan in the format our firm normally uses.

1. *To adopt and implement an organized firm Marketing Plan.*
   A. Appoint a Marketing Committee
      1. Define its charter as follows:
         —To develop a commitment through the firm to a sound and reasonable growth program.
         —To identify opportunities for growth.
         —To develop an organized Marketing Program that includes appropriate strategies that will capitalize on these opportunities.
         —To provide the necessary assistance to all lawyers in the firm in implementing this program.
         —To monitor and direct the program and to evaluate the results.
      2. Membership to consist of three partners.
      3. Appoint a Chairman who is also a member of the Executive Committee. The other two members should be from other departments.
      4. Appoint a Marketing Coordinator. Suggested duties and responsibilities as shown in (Appendix X).
      5. Complete all of the above by _____.
   B. Each lawyer develop a Personal Marketing Plan. See (Appendix XI). Members of the Marketing Committee can assist the lawyers in preparing their plan.
   C. The following are expected to be the minimum hours each year spent on marketing activities:
      —Partners: 250 hours
      —Senior Associates: 100 hours
      Certain lawyers may be requested to devote more time. Their goals will be adjusted accordingly.
2. *To develop an external awareness of the firm by our involvement in both professional and community activities.*
   A. Each partner and senior associate is expected to be active in at least one professional organization or activity.
   B. Seek and fulfill appropriate speaking and writing opportunities with professional and business forums.

      1. Obtain reprints of speeches and articles for further distribution.
  C. Each partner and senior associate is expected to become actively involved in at least one civic, charitable or community activity.
      1. Members of the Marketing Committee available to counsel lawyers in their selection of activities.
      2. Marketing Coordinator to be advised by lawyers of new activities they have become involved in.
      3. Lawyers are reminded that the maximum benefit to the firm is when they are active and visible in an activity they enjoy.
  D. Contribute to activities and organizations whose goals are in harmony with the firm's and which also offer appropriate visibility and recognition for the firm.

3. *To implement external Marketing Communications about the firm and its capabilities.*
  A. Develop a firm brochure. Complete by _____.
      1. Distribute to all clients and friends. Complete by _____.
  B. Develop lawyers' biographies to be included with the brochure. Complete by _____.
  C. Develop practice area resumes to be included with the brochure. Print on firm letterhead.
      1. Complete selection by _____.
      2. Complete writing by _____.
  D. Conduct informative seminars for clients and other contacts on pertinent subjects.
  E. Develop a public relations program—managed in-house.
  F. Each lawyer have at least one breakfast or lunch a week with a client, prospect, source or contact.

4. *To develop and implement a Target Prospect Program.*
  A. The responsibility for initiating prospects rests with every lawyer in the firm. In developing his/her list of target prospects, each lawyer should be guided by the objectives of the firm in this regard, i.e., to place particular emphasis on certain industries as well as new high growth companies early in their history.
  B. Each lawyer will discuss his/her list of target prospects with appropriate department lawyer and Marketing Committee member.

C. The lawyer should then develop preliminary analysis of these prospects. Evaluate needs and develop strategies.

D. The Marketing Committee will review and select about eight target prospects for the firm together with a lawyer or team of lawyers (with a captain) responsible for the effort. Develop a file on each prospect to be retained by the Marketing Coordinator. Marketing Committee to review status and progress monthly.

E. Each lawyer is encouraged to continue working on his/her own prospects on an individual basis.

F. Structure meetings with target prospects.

5. *To establish and implement an organized program for client development that will result in one-third of our clients using at least two of our services.*

A. Establish and implement a formal client review program for all major clients and key clients.

1. Designate clients to be classified as "major" and "key." Major clients are defined as those with significant fees and/or significant matters; key clients are defined as those with significant potential for additional fees either through growth of their own operations or their ability to refer new business. Complete by _____.

2. Select partners to conduct Client Review in accordance with the procedure outlined in (Appendix XII). Copies to department head chairmen and Marketing Committee. See Appendix for format. Select partners by _____. Complete reviews by _____.

B. Identify opportunities for cross-selling of other services in order to further "wed" the client to firm.

1. Discuss these needs with client to obtain further background and stimulate interest.

2. Review with appropriate lawyers what would be involved.

3. Arrange for introduction of appropriate client executives to appropriate lawyers.

C. Initiate other activities relative to client retention and development.

1. Arrange early contact with new executives when changes in management occur.

2. Watch for clients that may be tender offer targets or potential sellers.

3. Identify clients that may be potential buyers or changing their business objectives and offer assistance.
4. Keep abreast of client employment of other law firms.
5. Visit with major and key clients frequently by phone, in their offices or socially.
6. Expand contact throughout client organization, particularly with present and future decision makers; involve younger lawyers as soon and as intensively as possible.
7. Invite clients to speak to our lawyers about their organizations.
8. Maintain frequent contact with client's bankers and accountants.
9. Develop a Client Profile for each major and key client. Sample in (Appendix XIII). Develop effective system whereby client lists could be kept current and used for announcements and other information retrieval use.
10. Review each major or key client at least annually with client responsible lawyer to determine if attention is being paid to above points.

6. *To develop a Management and Marketing Information System that enables us to manage and evaluate both firm and individual performance.*
  A. Necessary marketing reports include the following:
     1. Client profiles—responsible attorney complete
     2. Fees by client, by major area of the law—annually
     3. Fees and number of clients by industry—annually
     4. Fees and number of clients by geographic area—annually
     5. Number and names of new clients and fees—semiannually
     6. List of new clients and nature of legal work—monthly
     7. List of new matters for current clients—monthly
     8. Origination—annually
     9. Skills index of each attorney's qualified areas of practice—update annually.
     10. Attorneys' biographies—update annually
     11. Professional and nonprofessional activities and clubs with names of attorneys involved—annually
     12. Profitability of each major practice area—annually

      13. Referral summary, in-and-out, for law firms, accounting firms, banks, insurance agents, commercial real estate brokers, and investment advisors. Marketing Coordinator to maintain—semiannually and annually.

  7. *To improve marketing communications within the firm.*
    A. Marketing Committee to meet monthly
      1. to monitor and evaluate program
      2. to develop new ideas
      3. to consider suggestions from members of the firm
      4. Marketing Coordinator draft minutes. After Chairman approves, distribute to all members of Committee.
    B. Executive Committee to include a report on marketing as part of its regular agenda once a month.
    C. Marketing Coordinator to be the hub of the marketing communications wheel by maintaining necessary files as well as up-to-date status of all firm and individuals' marketing activities.
    D. Marketing Coordinator to prepare and distribute internal marketing memo at least monthly or more often to include:
      1. new matters for existing clients
      2. new matters for new clients
      3. current firm and individual marketing activities
      4. other marketing information and follow-up

ADDITIONAL RECOMMENDATIONS

In addition to the Marketing Plan presented here, the Marketing Committee invites suggestions for additional marketing activites from all lawyers. Those currently before the Committee are:

1. Publish a general newsletter for clients and friends of the firm. To carry brief articles by the lawyers on topics within their practice areas.
2. Periodic in-house training seminars on marketing.
3. Additional social functions with selected clients or client groups.

In the example above, all forms, check lists, etc. referred to would be included in the Appendix to the Plan. Some firms prefer to include them in the body of the Plan. It makes no difference.

Organization, Administration, and Communications

Even for the smaller firm there are a number of things to consider in organizing, directing, and administering the marketing program. The most important point to keep in mind throughout the process is to avoid letting the administration and paperwork get in the way of the marketing. It won't if you organize it properly at the start and keep on top of the process.

The next is the matter of responsibility. Everyone in the firm is responsible for the marketing program. It is the same as their responsibility for the legal work. No lawyer can say, "I'm not responsible for the quality of my work; it's someone else's responsibility to check my work out." The same holds for marketing. Certain people, however, must take the lead, commit to the program, and create the atmosphere that will get everyone else involved. This means the partners and, in particular, those partners who are regarded as the leaders in the firm. This is an easier job in a smaller firm because everyone is under one roof. Several committed partners who believe in the program and who have the respect within the firm can get the ball rolling.

Everyone in the firm must participate if the marketing program is to achieve maximum effectiveness and results. This includes support staff as well. Spouses should also be informed about the program and made aware of how they can help if they are interested.

GETTING SPOUSES INVOLVED

In this regard we have found the following to be very effective. Once a year hold a firm meeting of the lawyers and support staff; invite the spouses too. The best time is generally late in the afternoon. Take everyone over to a meeting room at a local hotel. Present the results of the past year—omitting, of course, specific figures about fees and income. Tell everyone what the major functions of the firm are, the major areas of law, who the important clients are, and the major industries in which the firm does work. Discuss what the objectives for the next year are, such as 20-percent increase in fee income; three new corporate clients; launch a new area of the law; open a new office, etc. Tell them about the marketing effort, what the objectives and strategies are. Show them any materials that have been developed—brochures, practice area resumes, newsletters. Tell them about any new clients the firm has obtained. Answer questions from anyone, including the mailroom personnel and the spouse of the newest associate. After the meeting, which should take only an hour or so, serve refreshments and perhaps dinner, then end it all by early evening. This is primarily a business meeting with a social ending, not a firm party.

Many good things happen as a result of this kind of meeting. Total firm morale is raised, both in the office and at home. Everyone in the firm appreciates being informed of the total picture and of what they can do to help the firm. Spouses feel involved. They have a greater appreciation of what their husbands or wives are doing in their careers. They also become more understanding of the long hours and time away from home that the practice of law, and the marketing of the firm, often require. Finally, it also helps the marketing program greatly, particularly with the spouses. Because they now have some understanding of the firm and what it is doing to make the firm grow, they can often become helpful in being alert to opportunities, developing contacts, and in general furthering the impact of the marketing program.

New members of the firm should be involved from their first day with the firm. Of course they cannot become actively involved in the marketing program for their first year or so if they are recent graduates. However, from Day One, they should be aware that their professional development and career advancement will depend on both their legal *and* their marketing skills. They should also realize that, as entry-level associates, they can start contributing to the marketing program right away by being alert to opportunities for additional business as well as by "talking up" the firm.

THE PERSON IN CHARGE

In order to get the program developed and rolling, someone must be named to organize it and direct it. Whatever the title, Director of Marketing, Chairman of the Business Development Committee, or what have you, this person must have enough "clout" in the firm to get people involved and doing things. The tendency in many firms is to pick the best "rainmaker" for this responsibility. This is often a mistake. It's the old story: the best salesperson is often not the best sales manager. It is better to select someone who may not have all the personal selling skills but has management ability and understands everything involved in marketing, not just the personal selling aspects. Naturally, this will be a partner. It is best not to select a department head if possible; the person will have enough to do between client and marketing responsibilities without having to direct a department as well.

If the firm has a governing body, such as a management committee or executive committee, it is important that the partner heading the marketing effort also be a member of that committee. There are several reasons for this. There are times when that committee's approval is needed for some activity. It also makes the marketing program important to the firm. Finally, it ensures that firm management will be kept continually informed of the firm's progress in marketing.

What does the Chairman of the Marketing Group do? To help answer that question we have developed a job description for that position (see below). It is quite comprehensive and, particularly at the start, may include more than would be involved at the time. Eventually, however, most or all of what is shown there will become a reality if the program is successful.

JOB DESCRIPTION

POSITION:	Director of Marketing/Chairman of Marketing Committee
GENERAL DESCRIPTION:	Overall responsibility for developing firm (or office) marketing program. After Partner approval, responsible for implementation and evaluation.

SPECIFIC RESPONSIBILITIES AND DUTIES

1. Initiate necessary research, evaluate and maintain necessary files.
2. Prepare and submit to the Partners—
   Positioning Statement
   Marketing Objectives, both Strategic and Tactical
   Annual Marketing Program
3. Implement Marketing Program, after approval by the Partners, using all members of the firm as appropriate.

4. Identify important outside activities—civic, charitable, political, clubs, etc.—where firm should have representation in accordance with its Marketing Program. Work with Managing Partner in selecting appropriate persons for involvement and persuade them to become involved.

5. Discuss with each member of the firm his particular marketing activities within the overall firm program. Encourage involvement.

6. Monitor completion of the Client Review Program. Evaluate reports and submit this report to the Partners or management group.

7. Recommend firm target prospects. Maintain complete files on all target prospects and actively monitor the progress on each.

8. Responsible for all intra-firm communications on marketing.

9. Responsible for all exterior firm communications of a marketing nature such as—
   Newsletters
   Announcements
   Brochures
   News releases
   Public relations
   Advertising

10. Maintain files and keep updated.

11. Develop, with the appropriate department heads, marketing programs for each department if desired; with each office head, marketing programs for the particular office.

12. Plan and conduct Marketing Meetings.

13. Keep informed of—and handle if appropriate—all firm/office marketing activities such as speeches, articles, seminars, receptions, etc.

14. Provide or arrange for sales training of lawyers.

15. Identify firm members who are best suited for extensive marketing activities.

16. Strategy development on key prospect situations.

17. Contact and relations with the press.

18. Counsel and strategize with individual firm members on marketing opportunities and problems.

19. Participate in sales calls as appropriate.

20. Recommend sales teams for various target prospects and presentations.

Taking charge of the marketing program is an important responsibility and it is going to take time to do the job right, particularly in the early stages when you are getting the program underway. The partner selected should probably have a lower billable hours goal than the other partners. How much time will this take? The factors are different in every firm, but probably several hundred hours. The larger the objectives, the more complex the program and the more time will be required. It is a necessary investment. There is no way around it.

Of course there will probably be a committee. The committee should include at least one person from each department if the firm is organized along departmental lines. This ensures that every part of the firm will be involved. The firm administrator should also be an ad hoc member of the committee.

MARKETING COORDINATOR

One of the greatest aids to any marketing program is a good marketing coordinator. This is a person who is responsible for marketing support services and serves as the administrative assistant to the marketing group and the partner responsible for marketing. Generally this person comes from the support staff or is a paralegal who has the interest and ability to take on this responsibility. It is a real plus if the person has some experience or at least education in marketing. Since knowledge of the firm is very important in this position, it is better to select someone from within the firm without a marketing background than to hire someone brand new with it. Sometimes the firm administrator makes an ideal marketing coordinator.

At the start this job will take up to 50 percent of a person's time. After the program is underway, it can either become a full-time position or continue to be included along with other duties. The important point about having a marketing coordinator is that this person can save a lot of lawyer time—and probably handle many matters at least as effectively as a lawyer.

Here is a sample job description.

Duties of Marketing Coordinator

1. Conduct necessary research and evaluate for the Marketing Committee.

2. Monitor completion of the Client Review Program. Summarize reports for the Marketing Committee.
3. Administer all exterior firm communications such as newsletters, announcements, brochures, news releases.
4. Maintain necessary files:
   a. all Marketing research material and reports
   b. profiles of members of firm, their activities and their interests
   c. copy of Client Review reports
   d. copy of client profiles (eventually should go on computer)
   e. files on target prospects
   f. file of individual lawyer's target prospects
   g. lawyers' biographies
   h. file of designated nonprofessional activities and who in firm is involved.
5. Development of data and reports to be put on computer.
6. Handle arrangements for major activities such as firm seminars, receptions, etc.
7. Prepare and distribute marketing memos.

INVOLVE ALL LEVELS

As discussed earlier, all levels of the firm should be involved in the marketing program. This includes paralegals and support staff; they often have as much contact with clients and outside parties as some of the lawyers do. With the younger lawyers and support staff, it is a case of emphasizing effort and awareness as much as results. Each professional level in the firm also has an appropriate peer level on the client side that they should concentrate on. This builds a solid communications network both with the client and within the firm. It also helps institutionalize the practice. This relationship is shown on the chart at the end of this section.

Of course files are needed. This tends to become quite extensive, but let me suggest the minimum files that should be maintained and urge you to keep as close to that minimum amount as possible:

Profiles of the lawyers—update annually
Biographies of the lawyers—update annually
Client profiles (in firm's central files)

Client review reports
Target prospect files for firm-wide prospects
All activities, organizations, clubs—with names of lawyers involved
Personal marketing plans (see next section)
Minutes of marketing committee meetings
Copies of reports generated (see Reports: The Marketing Information System)
Support material—brochures, practice area resumes, newsletters
Sources and references—qualifications and record of referrals in/out
Skills index of the lawyers—update annually
Copies of any publicity
Background and research on target industries

COMMUNICATIONS

Good marketing communications within the firm are important. This can become a mess if there is no system. Fortunately there is a very simple system that works in *every* case. We call it the Wheel Principle.

If you picture a wheel with the Chairman or head of marketing at the hub and the people in the firm at the end of the spokes around the rim of the wheel, you understand the principle. All communication should either go into the head of marketing or out from that person to the rest of the firm. The head of marketing (or, for many matters, the marketing coordinator) is the only person that anyone else in the firm should worry about communicating with in regard to marketing. This person should either have the answers or know where they are on file or who in the firm would know. This person must also take the responsibility for advising other people, or even the entire firm, about marketing matters. Keep the wheel principle in mind—communicate into the hub, communicate out from the hub—and you won't have any problems with your internal marketing communications.

Reports should be kept to a minimum. The purpose of the marketing program is to build business, not an administrative nightmare. There are two important communications vehicles that can help achieve this: marketing meetings and internal marketing bulletins.

Marketing meetings, or if the firm is large enough, meetings of the marketing committee, should be held on a regular basis and minutes should be kept. There should be a basic agenda. Here is a sample:

Reports from each person (verbal, as much as possible)
Reports on departmental activities
Reports on firm target prospects
New activities to consider

The marketing coordinator should keep the minutes, draft them as soon as possible afterwards, and, after they are approved by the head of marketing, distribute them to all partners.

In the early stages of developing the program it will probably be necessary to hold these meetings every two weeks. They should not be held more frequently, unless certain conditions require, to avoid taking too much time and also to allow time for things to be accomplished between meetings. Later on they may be moved to a monthly schedule if possible. No meeting should run longer than two hours except when the plan is being developed or reviewed. Most meetings should run less. If they are running longer, determine the reason. Perhaps the attendees are just talking too much, or unimportant items are wasting time. If it appears that more than two hours is required, then schedule the meetings more frequently until the agenda can be shortened. More frequent, shorter meetings accomplish much more than less frequent but longer meetings.

There should be some form of internal marketing bulletin. It should contain news of anything relating to marketing: new clients obtained or significant new matters from current clients, external newsletters or bulletins being published, significant marketing activities of individual lawyers, etc. The purpose of this bulletin is not just communication; it is also to raise everyone's awareness level of the marketing program and what is being done. The bulletin should be distributed at least monthly, and more often when there is important news. A major new client is worthy of an immediate special bulletin. The marketing coordinator can draft the bulletins—saving lawyer time—for approval by the head of marketing. Here's another tip. Since intra-firm memos are usually done on white paper, put the marketing bulletins on colored stock. They will stand out from all the other paper that flows around the firm.

Finally—follow up. The program won't run itself.

BUILDING A COMMUNICATIONS NETWORK
WITH A CLIENT ORGANIZATION

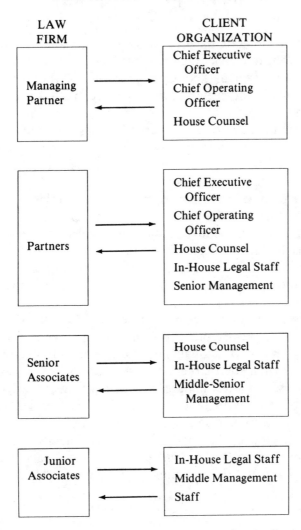

Implementation—Getting the Program Underway

A plan is something on paper. A program is a plan that has been implemented. The difference between the two is one word: *action*. Many firms claim to have a marketing *program* when all they really have is a marketing *plan*—and even that may be more in a few people's minds than down on paper.

Therefore, in order to turn a marketing plan into a marketing program it is necessary to implement the plan, which means getting it off the ground and getting people involved. This is a critical step. Here is how we recommend the smaller firm go about it.

After the plan has been developed by the marketing group or even all of the partners, hold a firm meeting that includes all the partners, associates, and even the more senior paralegals. One purpose of the program is to have the partners formally accept and approve it. Another is to sell the program to the entire firm, explain it in detail so everyone understands it, obtain everyone's commitment, and then start the ball rolling.

It may be necessary to begin this meeting with a discussion of why the firm needs a growth plan. It is important, at some point early in the meeting, to stress that quality of growth, rather than growth for its own sake, is what the marketing plan is all about. It may even be necessary to spend a few minutes discussing the many ways in which the firm could grow in order to point out the considerations and choices that had to be made in developing the plan.

As the managing partner of one of our client firms said at this point in a similar meeting, "The point of all this is to teach everyone to forget the Eleventh Commandment for lawyers: 'Thou shalt not market.'"

WALK THROUGH IT

After these introductory parts of the meeting, the plan should be presented. In most cases, it will have been distributed beforehand, in total to all the partners and parts of it without fee figures to associates and paralegals. Everyone should be walked through the entire plan, starting with the Strategic Marketing Analysis and winding up with the Tactical Plan. It is most effective if as many people as possible are involved in the presentation. If there is a marketing committee, each member should take a section of the plan, present it, explain it, and field questions. If the partnership has functioned as a committee of the whole, each partner should have a role in the presentation.

The meeting must conclude on the note that the plan is now a program. If necessary, have the partners vote to adopt it. It becomes an integral part of the firm's operations as of that moment. Everyone is expected to do whatever he or she can do to make it work.

Depending on the size of the firm and the personalities of the people, this meeting could take as little as two hours or as much as five. It is time well spent. Hold it beginning in mid-afternoooon or on a Saturday. But be sure you hold it.

FOLLOW-UP MEETING

After the program has been in effect for a while, many of the lawyers will realize that they need help. They will be confronted with more opportunities to talk to prospective clients and they will also be making more cross-selling presentations to current clients. They will also realize that they need some help in how to handle all of this and what to say.

In other words, they will realize they need some sales training.

Part V of this book is devoted to this subject. Whether you have an outside consultant conduct this training or have the lawyers in the firm attempt to handle it, respond to the need and address it.

One effective way to provide some in-house training is to have several of the most successful marketers give brief presentations on their own personal marketing activities and techniques. Pick these people carefully so that you get a good cross section of new-business getters (rainmakers), client lawyers, one-on-one salespeople, target prospect developers, seminar givers, writers, etc. After each lawyer's presentation, open the floor for questions. The objective of this meeting is to point out to the entire firm that there is no one way to develop business and that each person can be effective using his or her own personal style. This is always the result of this meeting, too. It is one of the most popular meetings a firm can hold in relation to the marketing program. However, it cannot be held until the program has been underway for a while and the attorneys realize the need for it.

PERSONAL MARKETING PLAN

After the original meeting to present the plan, it is important to immediately follow up and have every partner and associate over one year prepare a personal marketing plan. This is where each person commits in writing to what he or she is going to do as part of the marketing program. It is where the principle of accountability comes in. Some lawyers may feel this is pushing the people too hard. Until this is done, however, many people will avoid doing anything and the program won't be nearly as successful as it should be. There is no way to avoid it.

The members of the marketing group should be available to counsel the lawyers on their plans. This step greatly accelerates getting people involved and, therefore, getting the program underway. It also provides a basis for reviewing each person periodically, at least once a year, to see if they are actually doing what they said they were going to do.

A suggested format is included here.

GET STARTED

From this point on it is a case of diving in and starting. Priorities must be established, of course, but here is a suggested list of some of the things to do early on.

1. Identify growth clients, those who are prospects for additional services. Begin cross-selling to them.
2. Prepare client profiles on all new clients and start developing them on all "major" and "key" clients (see section on Client Development Program).
3. Develop target prospect lists for individual lawyers, departments, and finally the firm. Start files.
4. Start the Client Review Program.
5. Identify the civic, social, and business activities where clients and prospects participate. Identify who from the firm is active in them. Identify others in the firm to become active and encourage them to get started.
6. Identify lawyers for writing and speaking assignments. Encourage them and lend assistance.

7. If you are not using a public relations firm, select someone to establish and maintain press relations, write releases, and originate ideas. This liaison person can even be a senior associate or an experienced paralegal.
8. Update the mailing list; review once a year.
9. Arrange for training in personal marketing skills (sales training). This must be continuing, not just one-shot.
10. Identify those with greater marketing skills. Encourage them to do more. Provide time and incentive.
11. Begin contacting sources and developing a network for referrals.

This is not by any means a comprehensive list of how to start, but it is representative. As you launch your program, keep the following in mind.

1. Aim for a few quick successes to develop early confidence in the program. Actually bringing in a few small clients is more important than just hoping for a big one. Getting a client newsletter actually published is better than talking about it for a year.
2. Some results will take time. Many parts of the marketing program are really planting seeds that will lead to a bountiful harvest later on.
3. Publicize all activities and successes within the firm.
4. It is better to tackle a few things and do them well than to attempt a lot and execute everything poorly. A well-done client review program and a successful cross-selling program might be enough for some firms to accomplish in the first year.
5. Keep at it, don't let up. Enthusiasm for the program should be high at the start. But it won't stay that way unless the marketing group keeps pushing—and some results are seen.

One other important consideration in getting the program implemented is the structure of the marketing group.

It often takes one kind of person to develop a program but another kind to make it work. The group that initially develops a marketing plan must be comprised of lawyers who are highly marketing-oriented and determined to get a plan developed and approved. They may not actually represent all departments in the firm. Once the plan is approved, however, the marketing group may require some restructuring. Different personalities may be needed. All departments in the firm should be represented. It is a good idea to include a senior associate or two; this emphasizes that associates are expected to market too. Besides, associates are often more enthused about the program and more committed than some of the partners.

Get as many people involved as possible. Quite often you will have more volunteers than there are places on the marketing group. Use these people for special projects such as developing a brochure, researching an industry, planning a seminar program, etc.

And keep pushing. It's more difficult to get a program started than it is to keep it moving along once it has momentum.

PERSONAL MARKETING PLAN
FOR THE YEAR ENDING JUNE 30, 198–

NAME: _____

The categories listed are to stimulate your thinking. Feel free to list your plans on this form or in a different format if you prefer.

Describe in detail your personal marketing plans and goals for the coming year. Be specific. Name organizations that you will join or are considering joining and in which you will be *active*. What companies and contacts do you intend to cultivate? What is your luncheon program, etc.?

CIVIC AND CHARITABLE ORGANIZATIONS _____

_____

PROFESSIONAL ORGANIZATIONS _____

_____

*TRADE ORGANIZATIONS*_____

_____

*CLIENT CONTACT PLAN*_____

_____

SPEECHES AND/OR PROGRAM PARTICIPATION _____

_____

POSSIBLE CONTACTS IN TARGET COMPANIES _____

_____

DO YOU HAVE A PLANNED LUNCHEON PROGRAM OR PLAN?
EXPLAIN. _____

_____

CONTACTS WITH OTHER LAWYERS, BANKERS, ACCOUNTANTS,
ETC. _____

_____

ARTICLES YOU INTEND TO WRITE _____

_____

OTHER COMMENTS AND GOALS _____

_____

_____

Reports: The Marketing Information System

The Marketing Information System is a fancy name for the reports
that should be generated periodically to measure the results of the
marketing program. They provide the scoreboard by which the program is, in part, evaluated. *They are absolutely necessary.* A law firm
is also a business. It commits certain resources, i.e., time and money,
to a marketing program. Like any business it must know the return it
is getting on its resources. The only way it can know this is by developing and generating certain reports that measure the quantitative
results. Of course there are qualitative results to be measured as well.

A firm actually begins developing the base-line data for these
reports long before it even completes its initial marketing plan. You
may recall some of the data that is called for in order to conduct the

Strategic Analysis. This is not one-shot data that is requested by a diligent marketing group or even a demanding marketing consultant! In addition to providing a quantitative basis for analyzing the practice at that time, it also provides the starting point on which to build the Marketing Information System that is needed to track the progress and results of the marketing program.

In addition to this base-line data, the firm has also developed the yardsticks by which the results will be measured when it established the Strategic and Tactical Objectives. You may recall that, several times in the early sections of this book, I stressed that the objectives should be made as definite and quantitative as possible so that the results could eventually be measured. "You cannot measure the results of a program that has vague or mushy objectives."

TWO TYPES OF REPORTS

In every business—and remember, practicing law is a business as well as a profession (if you didn't believe that, you probably wouldn't be reading this book)—there are certain reports that measure the results of the marketing program. Generally these are some form of sales and cost reports. In a law firm, however, the picture is both more complex and more subtle. Therefore, different kinds of reports are needed. Many are quantitative and these are the types of reports usually referred to in the term "Marketing Information System." Some, however, are qualitative. They must be included in the M.I.S. as well.

Here are what I consider the essential reports—and their frequency—that a smaller firm needs to monitor and evaluate its marketing program.

Report	*Frequency*
Fees by client, in descending order of magnitude	Annually
Fees by client, by area of law	Annually
Fees by client, by industry	Annually
Fees by client, by geographic area	Annually
New clients and their fees	Semiannually
New clients and nature of work	Monthly
New matters for current clients	Monthly

Report	*Frequency*
Origination—new clients and their fees, by originating attorney	Annually
Profitability by department	Semiannually
Firm target prospects and status	Monthly
Summary of referrals in/out, by source	Semiannually
Progress toward Strategic Marketing Objectives	Annually
Accomplishment of Tactical Objectives —total firm —by department	Annually
Accomplishment of each lawyer's Personal Marketing Plan	Annually

The first 11 reports listed above are quantitative. Most or all of them can be generated as part of the firm's regular operating reports if the system—manual or computer—is set up properly. They are actually operating reports themselves, reports on the marketing operation. For this reason they should be regarded as basic and essential as any other reports that are generated.

The last four reports on progress and accomplishment are qualitative, which means that they are written, at least partially. The quantitative reports—the numbers—will provide a substantial amount of the input needed to prepare the qualitative reports. But since there are many parts of a law practice that cannot be reduced to quantitative measurement, there are also many parts of a law firm's marketing program that must be evaluated qualitatively as well as quantitatively.

The quantitative reports will generally be prepared by the firm's administrative or financial operation. The qualitative reports will generally be developed by the marketing group or, in a very small firm, by the attorney responsible for marketing. These reports should be submitted to the firm's management body and then subsequently, *in totum,* to the entire firm.

We have been asked if a separate or specially designed computer system is necessary or desirable in order to develop the Marketing Information System. Our answer is always "no." It is a totally unnecessary expense in both money and time to develop. The best

Marketing Information Systems originate out of the firm's basic system, not a separate system.

Finally, there is one more step (there always seems to be, doesn't there?). Monitoring and evaluation. So go on to the next section.

Monitoring and Evaluation

No program should be set in motion without a process to monitor it and to evaluate how it is doing.

The monitoring process is relatively easy if it is followed. The one that our firm favors is a monthly review of what is being done and also what the results are. Have the client reviews been started? Is the brochure being developed? Has each lawyer submitted a personal marketing plan? What new clients have been obtained? A series of prepared, brief reports at the marketing meetings is an ideal way to stay on top of things.

If the marketing objectives have been clearly stated with action steps, timetables, and responsible parties indicated, the monitoring process becomes just that, a monitoring process, not an initiation process.

A marketing program cannot be evaluated in a short period of time. In truth, it really takes a couple of years before the entire program bears fruit. However, no firm can wait that long before evaluating the program, nor should it. Six months after the program has been launched, the marketing committee should do a report for the partnership on participation, activities, and early results. At the end of the first year a comprehensive review must be held.

(To repeat the point one more time, the marketing objectives must be as specific or quantitative as possible. A firm cannot evaluate the results of a program that has vague objectives.)

The annual review of the marketing program should cover the following:

1. Review of each objective for the year and whether or not it was accomplished.
2. A review of the participation in the program by each person in the firm.

3. A review of the results, both quantitative and qualitative.
4. A review of the actual expenditures in time and money versus the budget.
5. An assessment of the program.
6. Recommended objectives for the next year.
7. Recommended plan for the next year.
8. The strategic (longer-range) objectives should not be changed unless the office is running way ahead, or way behind, the rate at which it should be going to achieve them.

If there is a marketing committee, the evaluation should be done by the committee and submitted to the management committee or entire partnership. If there is no marketing committee, the attorney responsible for marketing must do it. The report should be realistic. It cannot overlook where the program has fallen down; it cannot sidestep people who are not contributing. But it must also accurately assess where the program is working and where it must be "fine-tuned," some degree of which is always necessary.

PART IV
THE MARKETING PLAN
FOR THE LARGE FIRM

Overview

The marketing plan for the large firm is somewhat different from that of a smaller firm or sole practitioner *although the basic format is the same.*

To begin with, the plan will certainly be developed by a committee (perhaps with the aid of an outside marketing consultant!) which must address all departments and offices of the firm. The strategic analysis, designated opportunities, objectives, and activities must cut across the entire firm, no matter how large. They must also draw on the resources of the entire firm, wherever they exist. For this reason it is desirable that all departments be represented on the marketing committee; if there are other offices besides the main one, they should be represented as well.

Furthermore, it is a complex plan—although I want to stress once again that the format is the same for any plan, regardless of the size of the firm. It is complex because it must be developed from four different aspects:

the total firm
each department
each individual lawyer
each office

There *may* be individual department plans included. There *should* be a marketing plan for each office included.

It is a large task, particularly for the multi-office, national, or international firm. Because of this, many large firms have not addressed the task from a total-firm point of view. They have let the marketing program evolve in some informal manner except possibly for the employment of a public relations firm. It is no coincidence that these firms have generally experienced little or no real growth (other than by merger) in recent years.

Sample Plan

The written marketing plan for the large law firm will be very similar in format to that of the smaller firm. The approach and some of the substance, however, will be somewhat different.

The plan will require every lawyer to devote thought and time to developing and executing a personal marketing plan. It will be based almost entirely on planning and implementation at the departmental level and in each office. The task of the firm's Marketing Committee is to establish marketing objectives, policies, and strategies; provide assistance in the planning process; and coordinate the overall firm effort.

The Strategic Analysis Marketing Report should follow the same sequence as that for a smaller firm (see the Sample Plan section in Part III). It may actually be a shorter report because it will probably summarize only, leaving the details for an appendix.

The Strategic Objectives will probably affect each department or office and may even provide very specific objectives. Here are some examples from a Strategic Marketing Plan developed for a three-year strategic planning period:

1. Establish national recognition of the firm as one of the leading multi-office, full-service firms.
2. Develop expertise in all pertinent new areas of the law as they emerge and make this expertise available to all offices and, through them, to all clients.
3. Achieve 750,000 billable hours as follows:
    360,000—main office
    106,000—city A office
     84,000—city B office
     63,000—city C office
     58,000—city D office
     55,000—city E office
     24,000—new office to be opened
4. Achieve a balanced, full-service practice in which no one department accounts for more than 46% of firm billable hours.
5. Develop a broader base of larger-fee clients, i.e., over $500,000/year, as follows:

    eight such clients—main office
    three such clients—city A and B offices
    two such clients—city C, D, and E offices

6. To develop a broader base of clients in each city, with particular emphasis on medium-sized companies ($25–100 million sales) both publicly and privately held.

7. Open one additional office by the beginning of the third year of the strategic planning period.

Let me point out a few things about these objectives and how they were developed.

They address the entire firm. Some of them are quantitative. They do not go into the detail that the strategic objectives for a smaller firm might, but they are quite specific for the points they address, such as billable hours for each office. Since they refer to, or set specific objectives for, each department and each office, they were developed with the participation and ultimate approval of the head of each department and office. The objectives for a large firm cannot be hammered out by a small group of partners and then given to the rest of the firm. It is a basic management principle that the strategic planning in a business must be done by those who will be responsible for implementing the plans and achieving the objectives. The same should hold for a law firm. If objectives are going to be established for departments and offices—and they should be—the heads of these departments and offices must participate in the process.

The Tactical Marketing Plan for a large firm will probably not go into the detail that it would for a smaller firm, because many of the details must be worked out in the department and office plans. However, just as with the strategic objectives, certain tactical objectives must be quantified wherever possible, otherwise they will never be accomplished. Here is an example of the Tactical Marketing Plan for a very large firm:

1. *Implement an Organized Firm-Wide Marketing Plan*
    A. This Plan has been adopted by the executive committee for concerted firm action and the senior leadership has indicated its commitment to the Plan. The Marketing Committee has appointed a Marketing Coordinator with a 50-percent time commitment to

start. Her duties and responsibilities are set forth at the end of this attachment.

B. Each lawyer who has been with the firm more than three years will be encouraged to develop an individual, personal marketing plan, and each specialty group (profit-center) within each department to prepare its own plan. These are to be reviewed individually with the department and office chairmen and their respective Marketing Committee representative. A draft of the suggested format of such a personal plan is attached. These should be completed and reviewed before _____.

C. The Marketing Committee, in conjunction with office or departmental chairman, should review and approve expenditures purporting to be for client development for that office or department. Appropriate management reporting information will be developed to facilitate this review. The Marketing Committee will report annually in this effort to the Executive Committe.

D. Each department and office will create a marketing committee to develop, from its individual lawyer and specialty group reports, its own overall written business development program for review and coordination with other office and departmental plans by the firm Marketing Committee.

2. *Establish and Implement a Structured Program*
   for Client Retention and Development

A. Establish and implement a formal client review program for all major clients and key clients based on department and office reports.

1. Designate clients to be classified as "major" and "key." Major clients are those with significant fees and/or significant matters, and key clients are those with significant potential for additional fees either through growth of their own operations or their ability to refer new business.

2. Select partners to conduct Client Reviews in accordance with a standard procedure. See the attached draft of report form. Copies to department and office chairmen and firm Marketing Committee.

B. Form specialty teams within firm to develop separate industry game plans. See memo on the health care industry which follows.

C. Identify opportunities for cross-selling of other services and offices in order to further "wed" the client to the firm.

1. Discuss these needs with client to obtain further background and stimulate interest.

2. Review with appropriate lawyers in the departments and offices that would be involved.

3. Arrange for introduction of appropriate client executives to appropriate lawyers.

D. Initiate other activities relative to client retention and development.

1. Arrange early contact with new executives when changes in management occur.

2. Watch for clients that may be tender offer targets or potential sellers.

3. Identify clients that may be potential buyers or changing their business objectives and offer assistance.

4. Keep abreast of client employment of other law firms.

5. Visit with major and key clients frequently by phone, in their offices, or socially.

6. Expand contacts throughout client organization, particularly with present and future decision makers; involve young lawyers as soon and as intensively as possible.

7. Invite clients to speak to our attorneys about their organizations.

8. Maintain frequent contact with client's bankers and accountants.

9. Develop a Client Profile for each of top 100 clients for entry into computer. Develop effective system whereby client list could be kept current and used for announcements and other information retrieval use.

10. Review each major or key client at least annually with client responsible lawyer to determine if attention is being paid to above points.

E. Client Review Program

1. All clients designated as key clients and major clients should be included.

2. The review is accomplished by holding a meeting with the client to obtain the client's reaction to and opinion of the firm and its services.

3. If possible, the client review should be conducted by the client responsible attorney accompanied by another partner.

4. Each person should do it in his own way. The important questions to ask are:

(a) Client's opinion of our firm and services.

(b) Client's opinion of members of the firm with whom they have had contact.

(c) Does the client feel we have been prompt? Kept him informed? Have followed up and properly staffed his work?

(d) Have we helped the client in other areas besides these matters?

(e) Does the client feel we have let them down in any way?

(f) Would the client recommend us to other people if asked?

(g) Review the client's attitudes toward our bills, billing frequency, format.

(h) Review firm specialties as they fit with the client's plans for future programs; search for changes in client's business which might indicate emerging specialization of legal work; review in detail possible cross-sale opportunities.

(i) Review interrelationship between house counsel and firm.

5. Do written report afterwards, distribute as described in A-2.

3. *Develop and Begin Implementing a Target Prospect Program*

A. The responsibility for initiating prospects rests with every lawyer in the firm. In developing his/her list of target prospects, each lawyer should be guided by the objectives of the firm in this regard, i.e., to place particular emphasis on medium-sized ($25–100 million sales) companies, both private and publicly held, as well as new high-growth companies early in their history.

B. Each lawyer will discuss his/her list of target prospects with an appropriate department and office marketing committee person.

C. Each committee should then develop preliminary analysis of those prospects with high potential for significant future business, using Annual Reports, 10-Ks, and personal contacts. Evaluate needs and develop strategies.

D. Each committee will review and select about ten target prospects together with priorities and justification for the effort recommended and a lawyer or team of lawyers responsible for the effort. Develop a file on each prospect to be retained by the chairman of each department or office marketing committee. Submit department and office list to the firm Marketing Committee for review and overall coordination.

E. Marketing Committee review and select about ten as firm target prospects. Provide support as requested or appropriate to department or office committee and responsible partners.

F. Each lawyer and department or office is encouraged to consider his/her/its prospects on a continuing basis.

G. Structure meetings with target prospects. See attached report as example.

4. *Develop a Firm Brochure for Use in Marketing and Recruiting and Complete Initial Distribution*

A. The Marketing Committee has designated a Brochure Committee.

B. The rough draft of the Brochure and underlying Positioning Statement is attached hereto. The final draft should be distributed for approval at the June Partners' meeting together with a plan for its use.

C. Brochure Committee select outside agency to develop and produce.

D. Select printer and complete printing by _____.

E. Complete distribution to clients and other parties by _____.

5. *Develop a System of Internal Marketing Communications*

A. Department, office, and firm Marketing Committees to meet monthly to:

1. Review ongoing activities.

2. Select clients for review and cross-sales and analysis.

3. Initiate new client contacts, new means of practice, new methods to assist each other in the firm.

B. Executive Committee to include a brief status report from the Chairman of the Marketing Committee on the agenda for each meeting and at least one full session of review each year.

C. Firm Marketing Coordinator to be the hub of the marketing communications wheel by maintaining necessary agendas, meeting dates, files, and status reports.

6. *Complete a Computerized System of Information on Lawyers and Skills*

A. Complete filing of all skills questionnaires.

B. Program computer to retrieve and search for professional biographical and skills information.

C. Provide all attorneys with procedures for obtaining output for use in client services and cross-selling.

D. Obtain information from all new attorneys and purge information on withdrawing lawyers.

E. Aid in preparation of printed biographies for recruiting and business development.

F. Develop periodic, computer-generated reporting forms for updating and reviewing a skills index with provision for reporting new skills through the internal firm newsletter.

7. *Begin Developing Greater Awareness of The Firm and the Individual Lawyers Both Nationally and in the Individual Office Areas*

1. Select with approval of Executive Committee outside public relations counsel to develop and execute an appropriate program for the firm nationally and for the individual offices. Review specific selection and budget as separate agenda items.

2. Develop a sound public relations policy and program in recognition that there will be publicity whether or not the firm seeks it and that it is in the interest of the profession and the firm to ensure, as much as possible, that information carried in the media is accurate. A communications plan should be developed with the advice of such counsel, including a "catastrophe plan" to be implemented when serious adverse news reports or articles are published about us.

3. Chairman of the Marketing Committee to maintain liaison with the firm's Executive Committee, the public relations firm, and when appropriate, the press.

4. Give consideration in the future to certain offices using a local public relations firm for programs in their particular areas.

In the above example, all forms, check lists, and samples referred to would be included in the appendix to the plan. Some firms prefer to include such items in the body of the plan. It makes no difference.

Department and Office Programs

A higher percentage of marketing activity must be generated at the departmental or functional level in a law firm than in any other type of professional firm, including accounting. This is particularly true in the large law firm. There are a number of marketing objectives, strategies, and tactics that must be adopted for the entire firm. There is also the growing need to cut across departmental lines for certain strategies such as the development of industry teams (discussed in Part I, Industry Specialization section). Nevertheless, the individual departments must also do a large share of the marketing or the total plan will not achieve the success it should.

This isn't based on any marketing principle. It is simple common sense. Other than successful cross-selling throughout the firm, each department must be marketed somewhat differently. The litigation department cannot market itself in the same way as the corporate or business department. The estates and trust department must market differently from the bankruptcy department.

On other words, each department should develop its own marketing program to supplement—not replace—the firm program.

How can this be accomplished? Initially, during the development of the firm plan, by addressing the particular markets, needs, and potential marketing activities of each department. Subsequently, by including a representative from each department on the firm's Marketing Committee. The latter approach gives each department a voice in the firm's marketing program and also a closer awareness of what the firm and the other departments are doing. Some departments will respond more quickly than others; the corporate or business department is generally one of the leaders in developing its own marketing program. The answer to this generally lies in the hands—and the attitude—of the department head or administrator. If he or she believes the department has to market itself in addition to the firm, it will get moving. If not, little will happen—until that department starts to fall behind the others that are actively marketing themselves.

Usually the firm marketing program must get underway before the departments can develop their own programs. But as soon as the firm plan is approved and implementation begins, the departments should get to work on their programs.

Individual office programs should be developed in the same manner. They too can be best developed after the firm program is underway.

New Offices

The opening of a new office, whether through merger or by start-up, has become a more costly investment than ever. In addition, many of the offices that are opened are never as successful as was hoped. For these reasons, firms are now doing considerably more analysis and pre-planning before making such a major commitment.

It is interesting and also fortunate that the marketing group in the larger firms is now being involved in this process. This is a sound approach because the selection of an area for a new office is, to a great extent, a marketing decision. Many of the studies and analyses that should be performed are of a marketing nature. While no amount of strategic planning can assure the success of a new office, the addition of the marketing approach to the process raises the odds that the final decision, whether to go or no-go, will be the correct one.

THINGS TO CONSIDER

Although innumerable factors must be considered before and even after the decision is made, there are a few that should be addressed early in the process.

1. What is the current composition of the firm's practice? Much of this information should already be available from the strategic analysis which was the first step in preparing the marketing plan. Specific areas to address in this case are:
   - Fee income and profitability of each department.
   - Fee income and number of clients by industry.
   - Current clients who are headquartered in the area being considered.
   - Fee income and firm profitability from these clients.
   - Work currently being performed for these clients and potential for additional work for them.

- The outlook for these clients' operations.
- Current clients headquartered elsewhere who have facilities in the area being considered.
- Projections of what additional fee income and profitability the firm could anticipate from these clients if a new office were opened in that area.
- Projections of what fee income and profitability would be lost if an office were not opened.
- Manpower currently required to service these clients.
- Manpower that would have to be based in the new office to serve these clients.
- Projections of clients' savings in fees and expenses as a result of the new office.

2. What is the economic condition of the area, both current and projected?
3. What are the principal industries and types of business in that area?
   - How do they compare with the firm's current practice?
4. Who are the largest employers in the area?
5. List of all the operations in the area that might be considered as possible future clients: businesses, nonprofit organizations, health care facilities, government bodies, etc.
6. Further information about the possible clients: size of operations, profitability (if appropriate), trend of operation, current law firm, etc.
7. How do the industries and possible clients match the firm's current practice?
8. What new services or expertise would be needed for the firm to acquire some of these possible clients?
9. What contacts does the firm already have in the area?
   - Which have been sources of new business?
10. Other law firms in the area—national, regional, local.
   - How long have they been there?
   - What is their size, trend of operations, nature of practice?
   - Who are their clients?
   - How are they currently regarded?
   - Are any others opening offices in the area?
11. Are any of these law firms potential merger candidates?
12. Does our firm have any recognition or even reputation in the area?

13. Are any current clients relocating to the area?
14. Are other operations relocating to the area?

SOURCES OF DATA

Much of the data and information about the area is already available from a variety of sources such as business directories. Much additional information can be obtained from local organizations in the area such as the chambers of commerce, local industry groups, banks, and local development authorities. They are generally more than willing to provide information, both "hard" and "soft," to any business that is considering entering the area. Should the firm eventually open an office there, these contacts should be helpful in making further contacts in the area.

At this point the firm should stop and analyze the results and indications so far. The basic questions the firm must address at this point are:

1. Is an office needed to retain the clients the firm now has in the area?
2. What are the prospects for further development of these clients if the firm opens an office in the area?
3. Does the firm have enough current business in the area to support an office of the size that would be required to serve those clients?
4. What is the market potential of the area over and above the current clients?
5. Could the firm expect to achieve some part of this market potential, i.e., gain a significant share of the market? To put it another way, are the law firms established in the area vulnerable to competition?

This is no time for wishful or even fuzzy thinking. This is no time for hopes or maybes, nor is this the time to consider the marketing strategies that would be employed in the area if the office were opened. This is the time to attempt to determine, based on as much hard data and information as can be assembled, if a new office could be successful given an adequate marketing effort.

NEW OFFICE CRITERIA

The criteria that our firm likes to use are the following:

1. Can the office be profitable the first year with just the current business the firm has in the area?
2. If not, can the firm carry the office for at least two years while it seeks additional business?
3. What level and expense of marketing will be required to make the office profitable by the third year?

If the answers are strongly on the favorable side, then the next steps should be taken. Probably the first one to explore is whether to enter the market by merger or by start-up. If the decision is by merger, then prospective merger candidates should be explored. If these efforts do not provide any likely candidates, then the firm should reevaluate if it wants to enter the market by start-up.

After serious merger possibilities have been identified, or the decision made to explore a start-up, a preliminary marketing plan should be drawn up. This must start with the firm's establishing some strategic objectives for the potential office and then must proceed through the rest of the steps in developing a marketing plan.

STAFFING

Although it is primarily an operations decision, the staffing of the office, whether in a merger or a start-up, also has significant marketing implications. If the office is to grow, there must be at least one person in the office, if not several, who has strong local contacts and the marketing ability to develop these into business. In evaluating merger possibilities, this must be looked at. In a start-up, consideration should seriously be given to bringing in one or more lawyers who are already practicing in the area and who have the required contacts and marketing ability as well as their own client base. In addition, at least one person (preferably a partner) should be assigned to the office under either circumstance to instill the firm's procedures, style, and philosophies. That person should also be a good marketer.

These are only some of the criteria that should be used in making and implementing the decision to open a new office. They are basically marketing criteria. If they are not met, the chances of the office's succeeding are greatly diminished.

START-UPS ARE VERY DIFFICULT

In their urge or need to expand, a number of firms in recent years have opened new offices in other geographic areas via the start-up route.

Few have succeeded. Many have even been closed. In a number of cases, the firms even followed the sound procedure of both transferring a partner from the main office and bringing in one or several lawyers from the local area. Still, in many of these cases, the office was not successful, drained the firm (and the partners) of money, and, to some degree, damaged the firm's reputation.

The sad point about these situations is that the *strategy* might have been right but the *tactics,* i.e., the execution, was wrong.

In other words, to start up an office in a new geographic area is a tough, tough way to go. The chances of success are low. And the total cost, over several years, is quite high.

Mergers present their own set of problems. Nevertheless, when a firm is considering "branching out" and opening other offices, it should consider the merger strategy first and foremost. It may not be right, but, if it appears that it is, the chances of success are far higher—and the total cost lower—than a start-up.

Organization, Administration, and Communications

The same principles, techniques, and guidelines that apply to a smaller firm also apply to a large firm—so, since you probably skipped it, go back and read the Organization, Administration, and Communications section in Part III.

To the points made there a few others should be added.

Recruiting will—or should—take a slightly different perspective in the marketing-oriented large firm. In addition to seeking the top students from the top law schools (what large firm would admit to anything else?), the firm should also look for potential marketing skills in its candidates. Large firms have historically omitted this qualification in screening candidates, while smaller firms, because they need more versatile and well-rounded lawyers, have unconsciously included them. The point is that all firms, but particularly the large ones, must include potential marketing skills in evaluating candidates. The most brilliant young lawyer who cannot communicate his or her ideas to clients, let alone prospective clients or the public in general, is going to have a more limited role in the large law firm of the future. There are too many fine firms that can provide excellent legal services today. The advantage—and the growth—will go to those firms whose lawyers can communicate their legal brilliance and also market themselves and their firms.

The Marketing Committee may, very possibly, be restructured in order to effect implementation of the plan. The valiant group of marketing-oriented "vigilantes" who can move a large firm forward into approving a marketing plan are often not the same group who can administer and monitor a marketing program. In addition to the style and skills of the committee members, the makeup of the committee is also extremely important. Every department and every office must have a representative on the firm's Marketing Committee. This need not be the department or office head—in fact, except for very small departments or offices, it is far better if it is not the head.

The same basic files are needed, but of course there will be more of them. In addition to the firm's Marketing Coordinator there should be a marketing coordinator for each office. In the case of a very large firm, the firm Marketing Coordinator's position (whatever it is called) could be a full-time job. Each department and office should have its own marketing committee and chairman of that committee.

Implementation—Getting the Program Underway

Just as in the previous section on Organization, etc., the same principles, techniques, and guidelines that apply to a smaller firm also apply to a large firm. So, once again, go back to Part III and read the section on Implementation.

Naturally, since large firms have different problems than small firms, some additional points need to be made.

Let's start with the group responsible for marketing. In a large firm there will be, no doubt, a Marketing Committee or the equivalent (business development committee, etc.). It doesn't matter what it is called as long as the principle is understood that the role of this committee is *not*—I repeat *not*—to do the firm's marketing. It is a characteristic of large firms, much more than of small firms, that the lawyers expect the marketing committee to do *all* the marketing and deliver new files and new business to their desks. 'Tain't so. Everyone in the firm must participate in the marketing program.

The Marketing Committee should have a charter which defines its responsibilities. Here is a representative sample:

1. To develop a commitment throughout the firm to a sound and reasonable marketing program.
2. To identify opportunities for growth.
3. To develop an organized marketing program that includes appropriate strategies that will capitalize on these opportunities.
4. To provide the necessary assistance to all lawyers in the firm in implementing this program.
5. To monitor and direct the program and to evaluate the results.

I realize that the above is a repetition of one of the steps under Objective One in the sample marketing plan given earlier in this Part of the book. It is so important, however, that it deserves being restated here. The members of the Marketing Committee will be active in marketing, just as every other lawyer in the firm is expected to be. In addition, they accept the responsibility for getting the whole firm involved in the plan. This means they already have a double portion of marketing on their plate. It is unrealistic—and unfair—to expect them to do everyone else's marketing as well. And it won't work either.

THE CHAIRMAN

Next comes the chairman of the Marketing Committee. Since all large firms have some form of management or executive committee, it is extremely important that the chairman of the Marketing Committee also be a member of the firm's management group. For the first year, it is better if a person who is already on the executive committee be given this responsibility. It shows real commitment to the program and generally means that the Marketing Committee chairman is an important partner with some degree of "clout" in the firm. After the first year, the Marketing Committee chairman can be selected from among the members of the committee, but he or she should, by virtue of this position, then become a member of the executive committee.

In addition to symbolizing the importance of marketing, there are several other practical reasons for this. The marketing program will—or should—involve the commitment of substantial lawyer time and some amount of money. The executive committee should be kept regularly informed of what is being accomplished with this major allocation of firm resources. In addition, there will be times when the Marketing Committee will recommend certain courses of action or expenditures that must be approved by the management group. The process is much easier, and the chances of approval much greater, if the chairman is already a part of the executive committee rather than an "invited guest" making a special appearance before the group.

Regarding composition of the Marketing Committee, it is vital, not just desirable, that every department and office be represented. There will have to be department and office subcommittees, and unless they are represented on the firm's overall committee, inefficiencies and even chaos will result. Several senior associates must also be on the committee. Don't leave them (associates) off.

It is also extremely important that the firm management committee provide written and verbal support to the marketing program. Without this, the marketing effort in many large firms will appear to be merely the private project of a minority group within the firm.

INVOLVE OTHERS AS WELL

Because the size of the firm and the potential amount of marketing activity is much greater in comparison to the size of the Marketing Committee in a large firm, there is far greater opportunity to assign marketing-related projects to people not on the committee. Research of a target industry; development of a political activities program; development of a firm brochure; selection of target activities and organizations—all these and many others are the types of projects that can be given to people who are interested in helping the marketing program even though they are not part of the committee. The more of this that can be done, the more lawyers will be involved with the program and the better its chances of achieving, if not even exceeding, its objectives.

Don't spend a lot of time in meetings and don't get bogged down in paperwork, two dangers that can particularly befall the Marketing Committee in a large firm. To avoid these pitfalls requires a chairman who can make decisions and move things along. Get people active as quickly as possible. Good places to start are:

1. The client review program.
2. Development of target prospect lists.
3. Completion of personal marketing plans. This is one of the earliest tasks that must be done.
4. Identifying clients for cross-selling effort and then meeting with them.

As early as possible, begin publishing the internal marketing newsletter. Include new clients obtained; major new matters for existing clients; marketing activities of departments, offices, or individuals; seminars; articles written; talks given, etc. This will do a lot to raise the marketing awareness within the firm.

If a Marketing Coordinator was not appointed during development of the plan, appoint one now. He or she can save a great deal of lawyer time by handling many of the marketing support activities and services that do not require a lawyer. It will start requiring about 50 percent of that person's time. In some large firms the position soon grows into a full-time one. In terms of what a good marketing coordinator or administrator can accomplish, and also the lawyer time that can be saved, it is a wise investment.

It's a lot of work to launch a marketing program program in a large firm. But, like everything else, if it is launched properly, it will soon develop a momentum that will produce results exceeding all plans and aspirations.

And keep pushing. No marketing program runs itself.

Reports: The Marketing Information System

When it comes to the reports necessary to measure the results of the marketing program—the Marketing Information System—there is very little difference between the smaller firm and the large firm. The same reports are needed, although they may be generated by computer in the large firm while many of them may be done manually in the smaller firm. The important point is: *develop these reports and study them.* There is too much time and money involved in a comprehensive marketing program in the large law firm to leave the monitoring and evaluation up to impressions, hunches, and guesswork. Good reporting, both quantitative and qualitative, provides the basis for not only measuring results but also for keeping the keeping the program up-to-date and focused on current and future needs, not past ones.

There are one or two additional reports which I feel the large firms should have that the smaller one does not need. Here is the list of reports needed by a large firm:

Monthly
New clients and nature of work
New matters for current clients
Firm target prospects and status

Semiannually
New clients and their fees
Profitability by department
Summary of referrals in/out, by source

Annually
Fees by client, in descending order of magnitude
Fees by client, by area of law (or at least of the top 100 or 200 clients)
Fees by client by industry
Fees by client by geographic area (i.e., where the firm's contact point is)
Origination—new clients and fees, by attorney
Progress toward Strategic Marketing Objectives

Accomplishment of Tactical Objectives
—total firm
—by department
—by office
—by industry team
Accomplishment of each lawyer's Personal Marketing Plan

As discussed in the Reports section on smaller firms, most of these reports are quantitative. They should be prepared by the firm's administrative operation. The qualitative reports should be prepared by the Marketing Committee and summarized for both the executive committee and all the partners. It also helps to give the entire firm, associates and support staff as well, a summary report. After all, they are heavily involved in the program.

Monitoring and Evaluation

Monitoring the marketing program in a large law firm is a big job. But it must be done. And it can be done. The secret is staying on top of it constantly through committee and subcommittee meetings and the reports submitted at these meetings.

Most of the techniques applicable to a smaller firm also apply to a large firm, so go back and read the Monitoring and Evaluation section in Part III. Then, in addition to most of those points, let me add a few more.

Expect that certain departments or offices will not be as active or diligent as others. The larger the firm, the more this will be true. That is one of the reasons for having the internal marketing newsletter, in addition to committee meetings. It publicizes those people, departments, and offices that are doing something and accomplishing results. At the same time, it exerts some peer pressure on those who are lagging behind. In a large firm, where marketing nonperformers can often hide for a period of time, this is important.

In the large firm the Marketing Committee will have to receive a larger number of reports in order to monitor the program. This can get out of hand unless it is controlled. I know this may work against the grain of many lawyers, but I urge you to make every effort to have these reports submitted verbally, with a time limit, and supplemented with a one-page written report. Of course there will be times when this rule cannot be followed, but if it is adopted and the committee sticks to it, you will be delighted with how well it works.

Minutes of committee meetings should be kept by the Marketing Coordinator and drafted for the chairman immediately after the meeting. The chairman should, in turn, edit and approve them for distribution as quickly as possible to all members of the committee and anyone else involved. I do not favor sending copies of the minutes to every partner in the firm.

No less than once a year, the firm's Marketing Committee must report in writing to the executive committee or equivalent its evaluation of the program. This report will obviously be more than one page! Coupled with the recommended plan for the following year, it is an extremely important report. It must be done.

PART V
PERSONAL MARKETING
TECHNIQUES

Overview

The first four parts in this book have been devoted largely to what I call the *management* aspects of law firm marketing. For the most part, they have dealt with how to prepare, implement, administer, monitor, and evaluate a marketing program.

This is only a part of the story, however. The overall objectives of a marketing program are twofold:

1. To bring opportunities for increased business to the firm.
2. To enable the members of the firm to convert these opportunities into actual business.

Many lawyers have the fundamental misconception that a marketing program should generate new business without any personal involvement on their part. They think that an effective marketing program will, all by itself, bring in new business and new clients, and that they can then take over and do the work.

Unfortunately they are wrong.

A well-conceived and executed marketing plan merely identifies growth opportunities and presents an organized approach to utilizing the firm's resources to maximize these opportunities. Some aspects of the marketing program—such as advertising, a firm brochure, or some public relations programs—do not require much personal contact by the attorney. Most of them do, however. In fact, the successful marketing of legal services becomes ultimately a personal marketing activity.

To put it another way: *It takes a lawyer to sell legal services.* No one else can do it. The public relations firm, the ad agency, the graphics artist, even the marketing consultant can all make substantial contributions, but they can't do the actual selling. The lawyer has to make the plan work. The lawyer has to do the personal marketing.

Most lawyers need help in this regard. Few people are natural salespeople and the legal profession probably has an even smaller percentage than most. The good legal marketers have had to *learn* how to market their firms and themselves. The best-designed marketing plan will not be successful unless the members of the firm personally implement it and can deal with clients, prospects, and other contacts on a one-to-one basis.

If some of the professional staff are reluctant to do their share of the marketing effort, it is often because they don't know how to get started. They need training in personal marketing skills, which is a fancy but somehow more acceptable term for sales training. Work with them, train them in-house, or arrange for some practical outside training for them. Include marketing training in the CLE program (most state bar associations now recognize this and some even offer it). Educate the firm's people in what marketing really is and how they can be more effective in the role that each must play. This training is inexpensive in comparison to the results the marketing program should achieve.

This Part V addresses the subject of personal marketing. The material is drawn from our training seminars on how to develop personal marketing skills. Parts of the program were originally developed by Mike McCaffrey, an outstanding motivation specialist from Newport Beach, California.

The Basic Concepts

Practically everyone, it seems, has developed a sales training program that will turn wallflowers into whizbangs after only a few short sessions and many hundreds of dollars. Whether the programs are given in books, in seminars, on cassettes, or on video, they all seem to promise instant success. Many of them are general, supposedly directed to people in every walk of life who could sell anything. Others are aimed at highly specialized audiences such as Left-Handed Combustion Engineers in Peoria, Chief Financial Officers for Fertilizer Companies, and Reluctant Attorneys Who Don't Want to Be Selling in the First Place.

There are only three problems with these programs, both general and specialized. The first is that the majority of them don't work. The second is that they are usually based on some kind of "system" that requires so much concentration to follow it that the person forgets what he or she was selling. The third is that they are generally designed for people who spend all their time in sales work anyway.

No one, not even Robert Denney Associates, can turn the typical lawyer into a supersalesperson, not in one training session, ten, or even one hundred. What can be done, however, is to provide every attorney with some aids that will help him or her find their own personal comfort zone when it comes to personal selling. There are several kinds of selling situations that the lawyer encounters. He or she may feel at home in one of them. Some people are comfortable in formal presentations, others prefer to be one-on-one with clients. Some are champions at the cocktail party circuit and others detest the whole thing. There are a few basic concepts, however, that will help anyone to improve their level of personal sales ability by ten percent. And that's all that is needed in any law firm—to raise everyone's sales ability just ten percent.

Before we begin our discussions of the various types of sales situations and what to do in each, let's examine these few basic concepts which apply in every situation.

WORDS TO REMEMBER

You only need to remember four words—*opening, interview, response,* and *conclusion*—plus the name *Al.* That's all there is to it; no body language; no "Red Station, Blue Station"; no formulas to work out on the calculator. Here is what the words mean:

The Opening	This is the "attention getter," the statement that captures the other person's interest and makes him or her want to hear what you are going to say.
The Interview	This is just what it says. You literally interview the other person, just as a guest is interviewed on "Good Morning America" or "The Today Show."
The Response	This is the message you deliver in response to what you learned in the interview.

The Conclusion　　This is also just what it says. It is the last part of your meeting or contact.

Al　　In addition to being a person's name, Al stands for the two most important watchwords in personal marketing: "ask" and "listen."

There you are: "All you need to know in order to improve your personal marketing techniques." The only thing remaining is to practice the use of them and know how to apply them in the various types of sales situations a lawyer faces. Let's discuss each of these a little further.

THE "ATTENTION GETTER"

The *opening* is normally the opening statement you make at the start of a meeting or contact. You will see later on that there are some times when it isn't the actual opening statement. Therefore, think of the opening as the attention getter, the statement or point that you make which will focus the other person's attention on what you are going to say next. Some examples of attention getters that we all use from time to time are "I have some good news and some bad news; which do you want first?" "Your wife just called." "I think I know the answer to your problem." In the remaining sections in Part V we will discuss various kinds of opening statements that are appropriate for each type of sales situation.

The *interview* is really just getting the other person to talk about himself or herself and their interests. The way to do it is to ask questions. Depending on the situation, some typical interview questions might be: Where did you live before you moved here? What are some of the problems that have caused this situation? How did you first become interested in collecting alligators? Notice that these are all open-ended questions that cannot be answered with a single word. They elicit statements from the person to whom they are addressed. These are the kinds of questions an interviewer asks a guest. They are also the kind of questions you use in order to get the other person to tell you about himself or herself, their company, problems, and opinions. While the other person is answering, you must listen very carefully, because you will be using some of this information in order to make your sale. Don't listen like a lawyer preparing a rebuttal! Listen like a vacuum, taking everything in.

NOT A "SALES PITCH"

The *response* is your part of the conversation in which you pick up and comment on some of the points that the person raised during the interview. Some people would call this the sales message, but that is only partly correct. It is really the message you deliver in response to the points the other person raised. As you will see later on, when it comes to selling legal services, you cannot sell a person what he or she does not want to buy. Therefore, your "sales pitch" is more accurately your response to the stated needs and wants.

The *conclusion* is the note on which your meeting or contact ends. It could range anywhere from "Good. We will start working on your case tomorrow" to "May I call you next week to set up a meeting?" There are any number of conclusions, most of which can't be foreseen at the beginning. The important point about the conclusion is that, when it comes, you have made it happen in some way. More on this when we discuss some specific sales situations.

By now you do not need to be told the importance of *AI*—asking and listening. One of the greatest mistakes that lawyers, and many other people for that matter, make when they are trying to sell is that they think they have to do all the talking. This may be true for someone selling cars, insurance, or burglar alarm systems. But it is not true when you are selling services, and particularly legal services. Some of the most successful "rainmakers" are those who talk the least. They ask questions, the right kind of questions, and they listen carefully to the answers and also how the person gives the answers. A hesitant "I don't think anyone can answer that" means something far different than a firm, positive "I don't think anyone can answer that!" The effective marketer picks up these differences and learns what is behind them in order to make his or her response effective.

To repeat again: This is all there is to know and do in order to improve your personal marketing techniques ten percent.

Cross-Selling, Referrals, and Leads

In the first section of this book we discussed the fact that marketing begins with the client. It is no coincidence that the most frequent sales opportunities lawyers face are with clients. Therefore, this is the place to begin working on personal marketing techniques.

In this section we will not discuss the various aspects of providing service to clients. These points have been touched on at various points throughout this book. What we want to discuss here are the opportunities that arise with clients to obtain additional business with and through clients.

There are basically five kinds of opportunities to build sales through clients:

1. The client review program
2. Selling additional services to a client—"cross-selling"
3. Asking a client to serve as a reference
4. Asking a client for leads
5. Asking a client for help in landing a prospect

Each opportunity is somewhat different, and yet each follows a pattern. In addition, each makes use of the basic concepts we discussed in the last section—opening, interview, response, conclusion, and AI.

Let's set the stage for the client review program. The purpose of this meeting with the client is to provide him or her the opportunity to critique the firm's services. It is not to be construed by the attorney as an opportunity to sell additional services—although that opportunity may arise quite naturally out of the meeting. But don't go in with that idea in mind. The client will sense it, and the basic purpose of this opportunity will be destroyed before the meeting even starts. Prepare yourself, "psyche" yourself if necessary, to say, in effect, "Client, we want to know your thoughts on how we have served you."

Don't expect a litany of criticism in every case. You will be surprised at how many good things you learn about your firm and your people. By the same token, don't expect a whitewash from every client. One of the things you are trying to do with the client review program is to catch some dissatisfied clients before they change law firms. So be ready for both the good and the bad. Accept the good with modesty; don't be defensive about the bad.

YOU ARE ALSO SELLING

If you stop and think for a minute, you will realize that the client review program is also a very powerful sales tool with clients. The very fact that someone from the firm says, "We want your opinion on how we have served you," is extremely impressive to clients. It means more than all the platitudes about client service, etc., that the firm could write in its brochures. Other than accomplishing what the client wants, it is the most powerful sales technique a firm could employ to retain its clients. It is also an effective way to institutionalize the practice.

Remember that the client review is most effective when it is not conducted by the responsible attorney. This puts the client more at ease and enables him or her to be more open than they would probably be with the partner they deal with on a regular basis. It is human nature that most people find it far easier to compliment or to criticize a person to a third party than to the person himself. In some cases, the review will have to be conducted by a lawyer in the same area of law. It is very difficult, for example, for a divorce lawyer to review a corporate client.

Remember also that the client review is best conducted in a more relaxed setting than the usual business meeting. If possible, set it up for a breakfast, lunch, or at least a coffee discussion. (Never do it over a drink!) If this is not possible, conduct it in the client's office or where the client will be most comfortable. If it must be conducted in conjunction with a meeting on other matters, make a sharp break between the two discussions before you launch into the client review. Don't just treat it as another item on the agenda.

Now that we have set the stage, let's go into the meeting.

CONDUCTING THE REVIEW

The opening is where you remind the client of the purpose of your getting together. I say "remind" because the purpose of the meeting should have already been discussed with the client when it was originally set up. It is important to repeat this in person because it serves to further emphasize your sincerity and also to focus the client's attention on what you want him or her to be thinking about. The opening should run something like this:

> "We have a program with all our major (or key) clients. We sit down with them at the end of the matter (or at least once a year) to ask them how we have served them. You are one of our major (or key) clients. It is important for us to know your opinion of how our firm has served you. Please be frank and open."

Don't memorize that statement, just catch the spirit of it. It will capture the client's attention and lead you right into the next step.

The interview: This is where you interview the client to determine how the firm has performed. An outline of the points to cover is included in the earlier section on the client review program. Once again, don't memorize any questions. Each person should cover the essential points in his or her own particular style. Ask open-ended questions such as "What is your overall opinion of how our firm has served you?" rather than "Have we given you good service?" Listen attentively to the answers and also be alert to the manner in which they are given. Is it enthusiastic, angry, hesitant? This will give you the necessary clues as to whether to pursue a point or not. Don't hesitate to ask for clarification or to pick up on a hesitant or less-than-enthusiastic response. You won't offend the client, and you will also reinforce your sincerity and desire for honest answers.

The response in this situation is to acknowledge compliments, discuss complaints, and clarify doubtful points. Don't worry that you aren't trying to sell the client some additional legal services at this meeting. If you have handled the discussion properly up to this point, you have done a topflight selling job.

The conclusion, which must come out the way you want it to, may call for follow-up action on the firm's part, or merely a "thank you" to the client for the time and comments. Follow-up action may be required if there have been complaints or questions that the interviewer could not answer. (Remember, whenever possible the interviewer should not be the responsible attorney.) For example, you as the interviewer might say, "I will discuss these points with Lawyer X and have him get back to you." Another possible conclusion could be, "I will discuss your comments with our tax department and get back to you myself within a few days." However you conclude the meeting, you want to leave the client in a positive and even enthusiastic frame of mind about your firm.

TESTING THE ANSWERS

You may well wonder if the client is being honest with you, particularly when you are told everything is just wonderful. If the meeting has been generally favorable, you can confirm the sincerity of the client's remarks with an important question at the end: "May we list you as a client?" If the client says yes, you can bank on what was said. If the client hesitates or says no, go back and explore things further. There are some people and companies that do not like to be listed as clients and customers. This may be one of those cases. Most of the time, however, a hesitant or negative answer is a warning signal that there is something wrong that the client hasn't yet told you. Go back and try to dig it out. On the other hand, if the client says yes, stop there and get out. You've made your sale.

Be prepared in advance for the client review meeting. Be particularly prepared to tell clients what the firm has done for them. Many clients will not be aware of everything. This is all part of the response and may be the most important selling point you could make.

Also be ready for the client who asks your opinion of their personnel. This is a very delicate situation and yet one which does come up on occasion. The client may just be baiting you or may have already decided to fire someone and wants to use your firm as the scapegoat. Or he or she may be very serious and want your opinion. This is another reason I prefer that the responsible attorney not conduct these reviews. It either avoids the question on the part of the client or gives the interviewer the chance to note it and discuss it later with the appropriate lawyer. If you are meeting with your own client and are hit with this question, stop, breathe deeply, and be very careful how you answer. "Fools rush in, etc."

PLAN BEFORE YOU SELL

The proper person to initiate the cross-selling effort is the responsible attorney. But some preparation is needed before the effort is started. Remember the client profile? This can serve to identify other areas of potential need for additional legal services. If the responsible attorney is taking a real interest in the client—not just in the specific matter—he or she will have learned a lot more about the client than what the particular file involves. This all provides background for a successful cross-selling program at some point. Another helpful source is the Marketing Information System if client fees are recorded by department or area of the law. Look at this example.

	TOTAL FEES	LITIGATION	CORPORATE	LABOR	TAX	ESTATES
Client A	$87,000	$87,000	—	—	—	—
Client B	84,000	20,000	$46,000	—	$8,000	$10,000
Client C	80,000	—	80,000	—	—	—

A quick scan of this report indicates that Client A and Client C *may* be prospects for service by other departments in the firm. At least the subject merits investigation and even discussion with the client.

Once the responsible attorney has identified certain areas for possible additional service, it is often good to meet with lawyers from those particular areas and develop some background and even strategy for the responsible attorney to use. I stress this because I strongly recommend that the cross-selling be initiated by the lawyer who works most closely with the client before any other lawyers are brought to the client. That can look like "sandbagging."

CROSS-SELLING

There are few clients of any law firm who are using all of the firm's services that they could. To put it another way, a majority of the firm's clients are also prospects for cross-selling of other firm services. This does not mean that every client can use every service or, even more to the point, would want to use the firm for other services. For example, a company may have selected the firm or one of its lawyers to defend it in a major piece of litigation but still wants to retain its original firm as general counsel; or a person may use the firm to prepare an estate plan but, in the case of a subsequent divorce action, may prefer another firm that has a reputation in that field.

Nevertheless, *most of a firm's clients will not be aware of all the ser-*

vices the firm provides and, as a result, will often use other firms for matters that the first firm could have handled if the client only knew about them. This may shock a lot of lawyers but it shouldn't. It comes up time and time again in our interviews with firms' clients. "I really don't know what else the firm does" is a typical client comment.

The way to prevent this wherever possible—and also to obtain additional business—is cross-selling.

OPENING AND INTERVIEW

The opening can take one of several forms. If the client and the attorney have had some previous discussion about the subject, the opening should be along the lines of "Client, remember months ago you said that you wanted to review your estate plan?" or "You have told me several times about the problems you are having with waste water disposal. I'd like to talk about this problem." If the subject has not come up, a different approach is called for. For example: "We have several other clients in your industry. I discussed your company with the lawyers on our industry team and I have some suggestions for you." Or "There have been some zoning changes in the county in which you own that undeveloped property. I'd like to discuss them with you and determine what changes they may make in your plans."

Notice that the opening sets the stage and also serves to arouse the client's interest in what you are going to say. Then you swing into the interview. It may be very short or it may be extensive in order to give you necessary background as well as an indication whether the client is ready to discuss the subject—or has another law firm already working on it. The basic purpose of the interview here is to arouse or confirm the client's concern about a problem that your firm can solve or prevent.

THE CLIENT MUST CONCUR

The response will be the major part of this type of selling situation. This is where you will point out the client's problems, dangers, etc., that have not been handled and then go into a discussion of how your firm can help. Notice in this response that you must be addressing a need, problem, or missed opportunity that the client has *before* you can discuss what your firm can do. If the client doesn't acknowledge or agree with the need, problem, or missed opportunity, don't launch into your "sales pitch." Remember, this is a *response*. You can't sell someone what they don't want to buy. Or, to put it another way, a doctor can't treat a patient who won't admit that he is ill.

The conclusion of this meeting is the moment, ideally, when the client says, "Get to work on this." Often that will happen, but sometimes it will not. If the client is still in doubt about what to do next, go back and interview again. Ask enough questions to make the problem hurt. (We will discuss this technique in the section on selling to prospects.) If the client still is not interested after all your marvelous and concerned comments, ask him or her to keep an open mind and to observe the situation more closely from now on. Drop the subject, switch to another topic (probably nonbusiness), and follow up to the client some time later on (unless, of course, the client has called you in the meantime and said, "You were right. I need your help.")

In these situations you must be prepared with some idea of what the fee would be for the work you are discussing. After all, you brought the subject up. You cannot duck the question if the client asks it. That is equivalent to saying "I want to sell you something but I have no idea what it will cost you." Be prepared with some kind of estimate.

On the other hand, don't mention the subject of fees unless the client asks you. I realize that many lawyers will say that they know their clients well enough to know that the fee question had better be addressed right then and there. If you really feel that way, go ahead. But then play down the fee. Don't be apologetic or act as if it is a lot of money. If you give that impression, the client will certainly feel that way. Emphasize the need for the services, sell the benefits of the services, and don't mention the fee—or at least play it down. In either case, however, be ready to discuss it. (A more extensive discussion on how to handle the question of fees is contained in the next section on Selling to Prospects.)

SERVING AS A REFERENCE

The next sales opportunity is to obtain the client's permission to use their name as a reference. This is best done as part of the client review—but only if the client has expressed satisfaction with your firm. You don't want to ask a client for a reference only to have him or her turn you down and then tell you what a lousy job the firm has done. When you are ready to ask clients for permission to use them as a reference, go through an entire client review. If the client is important enough for you to want as a reference, he or she is important enough to do a client review on.

ASKING FOR LEADS

The next sales opportunity with a client is to ask for leads for new business. Some lawyers will not be comfortable doing this. That's fine; it is not for everyone. For those who are comfortable, however, it can be a most valuable source of new business.

The prerequisite to asking a client for leads is to be sure that you have a satisfied or delighted client. You don't want to assume that the client is so pleased with the firm that he or she will give you some leads and then find out, in the middle of your enthusiastic request, that he or she is considering firing your firm. Therefore, a client review should have first been conducted with the client. You want to be on firm ground before you ask.

In this case the opening is very simple. You say, "I have something very important to discuss with you." That's about all it should take to get your client's attention.

There should not be any interview unless you have reason to be uncertain about the client's feelings toward the firm. If this is the case (and, as stated above, you should know the situation before you ask), then the interview should consist of a few brief questions to confirm that the client is a real booster of the firm.

BUILDING THE BRIDGE

The response could be quite lengthy here or not, depending on your relationship with the client and the client's personality. The points that may be necessary to cover are these:

- The firm is growing (you never want to ask for leads out of desperation).
- The firm's reputation is growing.
- The firm has identified growth markets or types of businesses of

which the client's operation is one. The client will be flattered with this association.

- The firm believes it can help others in the same industry (same type of operation) as the client's so that these people can grow or the market or industry can grow.
- Current clients are the best source of new clients for the firm, and the firm much prefers new clients that have been introduced or referred by current clients.

This builds the bridge into the request you are going to make of the client. It sets the client up. Then go ahead, ask if they would provide you with some leads or introductions to others they know who might be interested in talking to you or someone else in the firm. You may have some specific people in mind that you know the client knows, or your request may be general.

At this point the client will take over and lead you to the conclusion. It will be either (1) an immediate discussion of whom they could introduce you to; (2) a promise to prepare a list of appropriate people; or (3) a turndown.

If it is the first conclusion, you have made your sale. Discuss with the client the best way to contact the people, such as client sets up a meeting, client makes a call or writes a letter. As quickly as possible, you swing over from a discussion of whether client will give you the leads, to how client will give you the leads. If it is the second conclusion, ask when you can follow up to find out who he or she has on the list. Then be sure to follow up. If it is the third conclusion, don't press the matter. Some clients may be very pleased with the firm but just do not want to commit themselves to introducing the firm to their friends and acquaintances. Don't take it as a danger sign; it probably isn't. Thank the client for listening and swing over to another subject.

When your client has given you leads, follow up on them and, after you have made contact, let the client know what happened. This is an important courtesy that many, many lawyers fall down on. Don't you be guilty of it. In cases where a particular lead may have brushed you off, your client may even want to talk to that lead on your behalf. But in any event, report back to your client.

Once again, the word of caution: Be sure you have a delighted client before you ask.

THE CALL FOR HELP

The most challenging or difficult sales opportunity with a client is to ask for help in landing a specific prospect. In these cases you are probably asking the client to write a letter, make a call, or in some way tell your prospect that they should choose your firm over any other they are considering. This is asking a lot, so you want to be sure about your client before you ask for help.

The opening is very brief, simple, and direct: "I need your help." This will certainly get your client's attention. There is no interview unless you want to confirm that the client knows the person. The main part of your contact is the response or, in this case, the request for the client's help or involvement in landing a new client for the firm. Before your client answers your request, you may have to provide a brief recap of why your firm would be the right choice for the person you want the client to speak to.

If you have chosen your client correctly, the conclusion will be an agreement to take some action on the firm's behalf. Try to find out what the client will do and when, but don't be "pushy." If time is of the essence, let the client know. If the client is hesitant, or turns you down, don't press the point, no matter how much you may need support. If the client isn't responsive to the idea almost immediately, he or she won't do an effective job for you anyway and may actually hurt your cause. Don't ask for other suggestions either. And evaluate very carefully whether you want to ask that client for help again in the future. If his or her reluctance or refusal was because of the particular person in question, you might try one more time in the future. But if the client didn't give you any particular reason, don't press. You are asking a lot of a client.

Selling to Prospects

As we stated in the first section of Part V, the initial objective of a marketing program is to bring opportunities for increased business to the firm. This means that the marketing program, if it is at all successful, will generate prospects. At this point we arrive at the second objective of the program: The members of the firm must talk to these prospects and convert them into clients.

Some attorneys still reject the idea of talking to any prospect other than one who comes in ready to retain the firm. The cold fact of legal practice today is that people and companies are interviewing and comparing law firms just as they have been doing with accounting firms for years. This also applies even if a particular lawyer is regarded as a superstar in an area of the law; in many cases the prospective client will still interview that lawyer, and perhaps several others, before selecting one. I know of one case in which a company was hit with a major law suit and the company president and general counsel literally flew around the country to interview six outstanding trial lawyers before selecting one of them to represent the company.

Many lawyers already realize this. As competition among lawyers and law firms increases (and it will), most lawyers will realize that they must, at some time in their careers, sell a prospect on retaining them and their firm over someone else.

What a frightening experience it is for some lawyers to have to talk to a prospect and "sell" him or her! Nevertheless, the time finally comes in the life of almost every lawyer when he or she must come face to face with a real, live prospect. And the more successful the firm's marketing program is, the more prospects there will be to face.

It really isn't as bad an experience as some people think it is. Prospects are human beings and therefore responsive to some of the same things that lawyers are. Equipped with the knowledge of the basic sales concepts and how to apply them, even the most hesitant attorney can often convince a prospect that his or her firm is the one to use. That is a very rewarding experience.

Stop for a minute and ask yourself why clients change law firms. We discussed, back in the first section of this book, what clients and prospects want from their legal counsel. Seventeen points were listed there. Not every "want" is going to exist with every client or prospect, but some of them will. When a client decides to change law firms, it means that the client's particular wants and needs are not, in his or her opinion, being fulfilled by the current firm. Therefore, when you are trying to land a prospect, the only thing you have to do is uncover what they are looking for and then convince them that you and your firm can and will fulfill their wants and needs.

It is no more complicated than that. Let's discuss how you go about it.

DO YOUR HOMEWORK

When you know you are going to be meeting with a prospect to discuss the possibility of their using you and the firm, you want to know as much as you can about that prospect. If this is a target prospect that you or the firm have been tracking and perhaps courting for some time, the chances are that you have a pretty good file. Review it. On the other hand, if this is a call out of the blue, drop everything and find out as much as you can before you meet with the prospect. The more you know about the prospect when you finally sit down with the prospect to talk business, the better your chances of landing a client.

In addition to this research, do some planning. If someone else will be with you, get together with that person first. These are some of the points you want to cover in your preparation.

1. Review all the information, data, and background you have on the prospect.
2. Determine what you do not know or would like to know.
3. Who is the "decision maker" on the prospect's side? Is that person attending this meeting? Who else is influential?
4. What is the object of the meeting? Is it a screening session, an elimination session, or a preliminary interview?
5. Select your team if you are not going to be alone.
   a. Determine who will cover which points, ask which questions, etc., and who will take notes.
   b. Who will be the "master of ceremonies" to take the lead and also hand the ball off to the others?
   c. Be sure everyone has a "speaking part." Don't take along anyone who would just sit there and not say a word.
6. Decide what materials you should take with you—firm brochure, newsletters, copies of talks, publicity, list of references, etc.
7. Prepare an outline.
   a. The questions you will ask

  b. Who will ask what
  c. The points you want to make
 8. Have some idea when you could begin the work if you were retained.
 9. Rehearse. Anticipate the prospect's questions.
 10. Prepare an opening statement—or several.

THE PROSPECT'S PLACE OR YOURS?

The question often arises whether to meet in the prospect's office or yours. For lawyers, I prefer that the first meeting be held at the firm's offices if at all possible. There are some obvious reasons for this. It takes less of the lawyer's or lawyers' time and it makes it easier to call other lawyers into the meeting if necessary. There are also some good marketing reasons. It enables the prospect to see what impressive and efficient quarters you have. It gives you the opportunity to show off your facilities and operations—the library, the word processing operation, the computer, the conference rooms. You can also introduce other lawyers in passing so that the prospect realizes this is a *firm,* with real depth, not just one person. Also introduce your secretary; explain that she might be able to handle a lot of routine questions if you are out or not available. It all adds up to making the most of the opportunity to market the firm in every way possible.

If the meeting is at the prospect's place of business, the next question that comes up is, when do you start selling? At the beginning of the meeting, after a few polite pleasantries, or after the prospect asks a question? The answer is: when you walk into the office.

When they walk into strange surroundings, lawyers often react in one of two ways. They either creep into the room, feeling and looking intimidated, having put the prospect up on some kind of throne. Or they strut in as if they know all the answers and the prospects is lucky to have them there. Of course both "entries" are wrong. The best way to enter the office is confident, relaxed, and at ease. Smile, introduce yourself, look around, notice things. Wait to sit down until the prospect indicates that you should do so and then sit where indicated. If you are a smoker, don't smoke unless and until the prospect does. If he or she doesn't smoke, don't ask if you can. (Note: I am a smoker. I still observe the above.)

What we are really talking about here is the first impression. Many people are sold, or unsold, on their first impression. So start selling when you walk in the room by acting as if you belong there and know just what you're doing there.

> The result of this deception
> Is very strange to tell
> For when I fool the people I find
> I fool myself as well.
> — "Whistle a Happy Tune"
> from *The King and I*

THE KICK-OFF

After everyone is introduced, polite comments made, and coffee orders taken, the stage is set for the meeting. Do you, as the polite salesperson, wait for the prospect to indicate they are ready to start the meeting? No. *You* start the meeting. You do it, easily and naturally, by making an opening statement (selecting from one of several you have prepared). Remember that the objective of the opening is to get the other person's attention and focus it on what you are going to say next. The most appropriate opening varies with the situation. It is to be hoped that your preparation will have provided you with some ideas. If not, have a few "stock" openings that could work fairly well in most circumstances. Here are a few examples:

"I have been looking forward to this meeting. Our firm and your company have a number of things in common."

"We have worked with a number of companies in your industry and have watched your company with great interest."

"You mentioned some of your problems on the phone. We have some thoughts on how to address them."

"(Name of reference) told me that you are looking for the same kind of help we gave them several years ago."

I do not pretend that these are the greatest examples. The exact circumstances always dictate the best openings. Notice, however, that each of the above statements is intended to grab the other person's interest and get him or her to say, "Tell me more." That is the other secret of a good opening statement. Grab their interest and make them want to hear what you are going to say next.

Now you have the prospect's attention. He or she is waiting to hear your comments or presentation. Instead, however, you start the interview. You begin the interview by "asking to ask." For example, "Would you mind if I asked you a few questions first?" "On the phone you said you had some tax problems. May I have some more information on that?" "Before I tell you about our firm, it would be helpful if I knew more about your company." Then launch into your questions.

ASKING IS CONTROLLING

Why do you so quickly put the ball in the prospect's court? To begin with, in order to take control of the meeting. The person asking the questions is the one who controls the situation. You want to be in control. Furthermore, the purpose of the interview portion is to get the prospect to tell you what they believe they want and need. There are several reasons for this. The first is to find out if you really want the prospect as a client. Perhaps, after hearing the story, you may decide you don't. You can then adapt your presentation later on. Or your firm may not be able to handle the matter and you will want to refer it to another firm or lawyer. The next reason is to have the prospect tell you what he or she wants you to sell him or her. Remember what I said in the section on selling additional services to clients: You can't sell someone what they don't want to buy. You must address the wants and needs the prospect thinks he or she has, not the services you want to sell.

For example, the prospect may be facing a union organization drive. You are head of the corporate deaprtment and would like to be general counsel to the prospect's company. Don't try to sell that; talk about the prospect's labor problems and what your firm could do to help. Since you can only sell a prospect what he or she wants to buy, you must interview the prospect to find out what they want to buy.

There is one more important reason for launching into the interview right away: If you ask intelligent questions, particularly if they reflect some knowledge of the prospect's operation, you establish your credibility with the prospect. That is a subtle but very important thing to accomplish. You also lay a foundation for future cross-selling *if* you land the prospect as a client.

Remember to ask open-ended questions, ones that will keep the person talking, such as "How do you feel about . . .?" "What happened after that?" As the meeting goes on, don't be afraid to make the prospect be specific. "I don't quite understand; do you mean . . .?" "Do I understand you to say that . . .?" In addition to making the prospect clarify the problem or need, you will also be impressive with your thoroughness and exactness.

SHOW EMPATHY

As the prospect is talking, practice empathy at appropriate times. Smile at the pleasant things, frown or look concerned at the bad ones. Showing empathy doesn't mean that you agree with the prospect; it does mean that you understand their feelings. This helps the prospect to elaborate on what they want and what you will be selling.

Can you educate a prospect? Can you tell them they have other problems that haven't been recognized? At first meeting it is usually difficult. The prospect generally knows what they want, or, don't want, before they meet with you. How can you possibly know what they need when you haven't examined the situation yet? The only way you can attempt to educate the prospect or direct his or her thinking to some other point is through questioning.

If the prospect picks up on this, keep on going. If they do not want to consider it, you can't push it. Don't press on issues the prospect is not interested in. You will appear "pushy" and aggressive, you will have ignored his or her comments, and you will be eliminated as a contender right away.

Should you take notes during such a meeting? Of course you should; you are going to need them to refer to when, or if, you are retained. Furthermore, it shows that you regard the prospect's statements as important. Think how you would feel about a doctor who didn't make a single note while you explained about all your pains, aches, and problems. So go ahead and make notes, but do it quickly and accurately.

Eventually you will have learned all the prospect can tell you, or wants to tell you, at this time. Now he or she wants to hear about what you will do to fill these needs. Now it is time for the response in which you specifically address what you and the prospect mutually agreed are the needs and wants. This is where you sell benefits, not features. For example, a feature is "We have a unique system of cost control," a benefit is "Our unique system of cost control will keep your fees as low as possible." A feature is "We have offices in every city in this state," a benefit is "Because we have an office everywhere you have a facility, we could handle your matters more efficiently."

PACKAGING THE FEE

At some point the question of estimated fees will come up. There are some important guidelines to follow in handling this. Never give a single figure, even if it is only a rough estimate. Always give a range such as "We estimate that this may cost somewhere between $8,000 and $11,000." Always "package" your answer; never just mention the fee by itself. When you package your answer by restating all that you are going to do for such-and-such a fee, you make the fee seem smaller in comparison to the services you are going to perform. This also provides you with the opportunity of "reestimating" the fee if it becomes necessary. Which leads me to a very important point.

Never cut a fee! Some prospects will try to bargain on any estimate you give them. Once you give in and cut your proposed fee, you have ruined yourself forever with that prospect. If they become a client they will always try to bargain with you about your fee from then on and you won't look very professional.

You may, however, "reestimate" your fee if you have packaged it along with all the services you will perform without itemizing what each service costs. Reestimating consists of reexamining the list of things you were going to do, eliminating one or several of them, and then quoting a new figure. On the surface, the prospect now has a lower proposed fee because you have eliminated several steps or services. The prospect does not know if you have actually cut your fee or not because you did not itemize the various fees for the individual steps and services. If you decided to take out $1,500 of work and drop the fee $2,200, they won't know it and you shouldn't tell them.

Yes, it's a game which you will have to play some of the time. If you use the above approach, however, you can win some of these games without developing the reputation of a firm that will cut its fee if the client or prospect only challenges them.

One of the important sales techniques that successful people use is to obtain concurrence as they proceed through the response. "Don't you agree that this problem should be addressed as part of this matter?" "This is important, isn't it?" This accomplishes two things. It gets the prospect agreeing with you as you go along. It also acts as a "safety check" so that you don't construct your entire response on some points the prospect doesn't agree with.

OBJECTIONS

Most prospects will have some objections. Don't take it personally; don't think all is lost because the prospect doesn't agree with everything you've said. It's part of the game. Even if they are 100 percent sold, most people don't want to admit it right away, so they try to find some things to pick at. Just be prepared to handle the objections as they come up.

First of all, keep your patience with the prospect. Some will even try to aggravate you, but don't let that happen. If you lose your patience, you lose the sale. Your initial reaction to the objection can be any one of the following:

- Save face for the client—"I apologize for not making that clear."
- Make an apparent concession—"That's a good point, but . . ."
- Say he's not alone—"A lot of people have that reaction; however, . . ."
- Restate the objection—"Let me be sure I understand . . ." This is a good technique to give you some time to answer or to make sure you don't answer the wrong objection.

Your subsequent response can flow from any of these approaches:

- Direct denial—"That is not correct." (Never tell the prospect, "You are wrong.")
- Indirect denial—"On the surface it might appear that way, but . . ."
- Explanation—"This is what that means."

- Compensating factors—"That is true, but this offsets that."
- Question—"Why do you say that?" Another good way to stall for time while you figure out an answer.
- Defer—"Let me come back to that in a minute."

No matter which approach you use, you ultimately should take the prospect back to the need or want they defined in the first place. Get concurrence on what they are looking for. Make the problem hurt a little more. "That may seem expensive, but didn't you tell me that this situation is costing you over $100,000 a year?

Finally you arrive at the conclusion. This you will want to control as best you can. Sometimes the conclusion will be "You've answered all our questions. When can you start to work?" Sometimes, however, the conclusion will be something else.

THE CLOSING

Many sales training experts teach all different kinds of closing techniques such as "May we start next week?" or "I'd like to put you on our schedule right now" or "Why don't we start tomorrow; you can always stop us at any time." I don't like any of them. They are too high-pressure and, in my opinion, more associated with insurance and magazine subscription sales. I believe the most effective conclusion is direct, simple, and professional: *Ask for the order!*

The only difference between most of the successful and unsuccessful salespeople in any field, including law, is that the successful salespeople ask for the order. An attorney can do this too, without being high-pressure, in a manner something like these:

"Are you ready to decide now?"

"Is there any more information you need in order to make your decision?"

"When do you expect to make your decision?"

"Would you like us to meet with anyone else to review our ideas?"

Always let the prospect know that you would like him or her as a client. Most lawyers forget to say it.

As the final point in the conclusion, you should have determined the timetable for follow-up action—the date by which a proposal is due, or a decision made, or another meeting held. Ask, don't just leave the meeting. If the prospect says, "We'll call you," ask when. Or, better still, ask if you can call. Don't go back to your office without knowing what the next step is, yours or the prospect's, and when it should be taken. If you want to follow up the prospect, set that up. "If I haven't heard from you by the fifth, may I call you then?"

If anyone from the firm attended with you, always hold a debriefing afterwards. Compare notes, review the questions and the answers, evaluate techniques, and be ready for the next meeting.

Turning Social Contacts into Business Opportunities

Some people in this world seem thoroughly at ease in any situation. Whether it is a business or social occasion, they are able to meet complete strangers, converse with them, put them at ease, and be natural and relaxed in the whole process.

Other people do all right as long as someone or something gets them started. They are not the type of people to introduce themselves to strangers or start a conversation with someone they don't know, but they are capable of pleasant and even warm interaction if the other person starts the ball rolling.

Then there are those people who are scared stiff whenever they are among strangers. Even if someone else shows a sincere interest in them, they are unable to respond to the overture, as much as they might want to.

People in the second and third categories, particularly the third, need not give up and resign themselves to living like hermits. For one thing, they are not alone. Even some famous people have the same problem. Here's a story to prove the point.

A TRUE STORY

A women and her husband were invited to a museum party by a friend of hers who was a member. The woman's husband could not attend, so her friend would be the only person there that she knew. When the woman arrived at the party, she desperately looked around for her friend but learned she had not yet arrived. The woman was scared stiff. After getting a drink she went over to a corner and looked around. She didn't see a single person she knew.

Finally she saw another woman by herself, a rather large blonde woman who also looked very lonesome. Mustering all her courage, she went over and started a conversation. The stranger seemed as happy to see her as she was to talk to the stranger.

After they had talked for about fifteen minutes, the woman's friend showed up. The woman excused herself, but, as she was turning away, she realized she had never introduced herself. She turned back and did so. The stranger responded, "It's nice to know you. I'm Shelley Winters."

Moral: There are a lot of wonderful relationships, potential new friends, and even some excellent business opportunities waiting out there if you just "reach out, reach out and touch someone." There is no magic or mystery to it. The same basic concepts that we have discussed in the last two sections give us all we need to know in order to do it.

The format is slightly different from that used in personal selling to clients and prospects. The opening, the "attention getter," is not the opening. That comes later on in the initial conversation or in the relationship. You start off with the interview. It also constitutes most of the contact, at least the initial contact. At some point later on, the "attention getter" is used. The conclusion follows that. There is no response in a social situation.

The setting could be anywhere outside your own home or office where you are in the company of strangers—one person, as on an airplane with someone sitting next to you, or many, as at a committee meeting, party, or convention. Many of these strangers are potential clients for a lawyer. But you may never know, or never have the chance to land them, unless you find out.

It is important, however, to understand that the object in this game of turning social contacts into business opportunities is not to make a "sale" then and there. The object is to find out who might be a prospect, arouse their interest, plant the seed that you and your firm might be able to help them at some time, and finally set up a business meeting with them.

The following example could occur entirely at a single initial meeting or it could develop over a number of meetings and conversations. It is the technique that is important, not the time frame.

FOCUS ON THE OTHER PERSON

The reason you start with the interview rather than the opening is, first, that you don't really know anything to make an opening statement about, and second, that your interest should be on the other person and learning about him or her.

You begin the conversation (and perhaps the relationship) by focusing on the other person and making it easy for them to discuss themselves, their life, interests, and, eventually, business. Ask general, open-ended questions that will lead to the identification of potential business interests and concerns. Listen, show interest, keep the conversation going. Don't talk about yourself yet; you will have the chance later on.

What we are really talking about is the art of purposeful small talk, or how to start and continue a conversation with a stranger. Each person really has to develop his or her own technique in this regard but, to start you off, here are some ideas:

On an airplane: "Are you just starting a trip or are you on your way back home?"

"Is this a business or pleasure trip for you—or both?"

"This flight crew is really working hard. How do you rate this airline compared to the others you fly?"

At a party: "How do you know (the host and/or hostess)?"

"(Host) tells me you're in (line of business). How did you get into that?"

"Are you from around here or are you visiting?"

At a business luncheon: "What prompts you to attend this meeting?"

"What have you gotten out of these meetings (speakers, conferences) so far?"

"Are each of these luncheons as well-attended as this one?"

At a committee meeting: "How did you get involved with this group?"

"Which subcommittee are you on?"

"I saw you talking to _____. Are you in the same business he is?"

These types of openings may not lead to great intellectual discussions, but they are intended to be "door openers" to start the conversational ball rolling.

Many people wonder whether they should start out by introducing themselves. At a private party, a good rule of thumb to follow is to begin by introducing yourself. At other types of parties, receptions, etc., if this seems a little awkward, just launch into a question. (But never start out by saying, "I'm John Jones. I'm an attorney.")

KEEP THE BALL ROLLING

Now, having started the interview, you must keep it going. Show interest, respond, show empathy, ask further questions. Comment briefly, then toss the ball back to the other person. Here are examples of conversational techniques that continue the momentum of the discussion:

"That's interesting. Would you elaborate on that?"
"I've never heard of that. Tell me more."
"Oh? How did that happen?"
"Don't stop there, go on!"

The idea behind this little technique, and the reason it works most of the time, is this: Most people like to talk about themselves if given the chance or encouraged to do so. All they need is someone to show an interest in them and to be a good listener. There are some great stone faces around, but some of them can be made to open up, too, Here's a story about one:

My grandmother loved to give small dinner parties long ago before it was even fashionable. She would have six or eight people, many of whom were strangers to each other. By the end of the evening, however, everyone had gotten to know everyone else and they always seemed to have a good time.

There was one man, a bachelor, whom she often invited even though he hardly ever said a word to anyone. Finally, one night she seated him next to a widow. An amazing thing happened. He started talking to the woman and never stopped the whole night long! The next day my grandmother couldn't wait to call the widow and find out how she got this great stone face to talk.

"It was easy," she said. "I did have to introduce myself first. Then I asked him what he did. He said he was in the leather business. I said, 'How interesting. Tell me about the leather business.' That did it. I hardly had the chance to say another word the rest of the evening."

This story led to an expression in our family: "If you want me to talk, touch me on leather." The same thing goes for strangers. Touch them on leather.

Note: No, I do not know what, if anything, ever happened between the bachelor and the widow after that evening.

BE READY FOR THE OPENING

Now that you have the interview rolling, you will sooner or later be able to lead the conversation into business interests. This may occur at this meeting or it may be at another time. At this point you learn if this person is also a prospect. If so, you want to be alert, on this occasion or a subsequent one, for the opportunity to make your opening statement (the attention getter) which informs the prospect of your potential ability to aid their business or help solve their problems. Sometimes the prospect will give you the opportunity by asking, "What's your business?" If they don't give you the opening, make the opportunity for yourself.

Your opening should be directed to what the prospect has been saying about his or her business or himself/herself. Here are a few examples:

"That is a problem; our firm has handled a lot of those situations."

"It might be helpful for you to have another perspective."

"Although that entire area is new, we have just finished working on a similar case."

"I'm not certain, but I believe we could shed some light on this."

From this "attention getter" you want to go right into your conclusion, which should establish the future action or follow-up:

"That's something we should talk about further. Could we have lunch together next week?"

"I'd like to hear more about that. Could we talk again after next month's meeting?"

"You might be interested in some of our recent experiences in this area. Would you like to sit down and discuss it when you get back?"

"One of my partners has handled a number of those. Why don't the three of us get together and talk about it?"

After their response to this, don't continue on with the heavy business discussion. Save it for the business appointment, whenever that comes.

Remember, the object in the social situation is to plant the seed that you or your firm might be able to help the person. If you plant that seed and keep watering it over the course of time (a few minutes, several weeks, months, or even years), you are preparing your prospect. When you get that prospect to agree to meet with you in a business environment and talk further, you have "closed" that part of the sale and turned the social contact into a business opportunity.

BUSINESS CARDS

There are some other techniques in connection with this social contacts game that should be discussed, such as business cards. Should you carry them? Should you ask someone for theirs? If so, how do you do it?

First of all, you should always carry business cards (clean cards, not dog-eared or dirty) if the situation is appropriate. That does not mean that you should carry them in a holster on your hip, ready to whip out at the slightest provocation. Whenever you would be carrying a wallet (or briefcase) is an appropriate situation. The tennis court, a sailboat, or the middle of the golf course would not normally be the appropriate situation to produce a business card; you might appear a little too eager!

If you have been discussing the person's business, it is entirely appropriate to ask, "May I have your card?" particularly if they have asked you to contact them or follow up in some way. When they give you a card, it is very easy to say, "Let me give you mine."

Generally you should not take notes in front of the person in a social situation. The only notes you should take are their address or phone number if they do not have a business card. To take any other notes in a social situation puts too much of a business emphasis on it. If you want to make some quick notes to yourself for future reference and follow-up, excuse yourself, go to the restroom or anyplace out of sight, and jot the notes down quickly.

There is another little technique that can be extremely effective, not only for letting the prospect now what you do, but also for testing the image and reputation of your firm. When the prospect asks, "What's your business?" or "Whom do you work for?" answer by saying, "I'm with Jones, Smith and Loggins." If they recognize your firm, that is generally a good sign. It may also indicate that your marketing program is building recognition for the firm. If a prospect doesn't recognize the name, they might feel that they should. You can then inform the prospect that "We are attorneys who specialize in patents and trademarks" or "We are the largest law firm in this area" or "We are a regional, full-service law firm."

Never just say, "I'm a lawyer." If you do, you have missed the opportunity to spread the name of your firm, and, even more important, you have just dumped yourself in that great big category that includes every other lawyer in the world. If you can't bring yourself to pop out your firm's name, say you're a lawyer who specializes in computer law or that you are a tax attorney. That, at least, has a little more ring to it and positions you a little better than just saying you are a lawyer.

IF ALL ELSE FAILS

The techniques discussed here will not work immediately with every prospect you meet. Some contacts must be nurtured and developed for some time in the social arena before they can be worked over into a business relationship as well. There are some lawyers who are very successful and effective with the interview and even the "attention getter" but who cannot quite bring themselves to the conclusion, that is, suggesting a business meeting. In these cases, there is another technique. It is called the "war story."

Some attorneys are masters at this. They never suggest that the prospect should sit down with them and talk business. They keep the entire relationship purely social. But every once in a while they drop a little story about how they, in their law practice, were able to help someone. They are obviously very excited about it, and, strangely enough, the "war story" always has some relationship to the prospect's business or a problem they had mentioned. Over the course of time the storyteller weaves a beautiful picture of how he or she (or the firm) has been very successful, particularly in dealing with the same type of operation or problem that the prospect is involved in. If the storyteller does this with just the right amount of quiet satisfaction (without boasting), the prospect generally develops the feeling, often without realizing it, that here is a lawyer or firm that appears to be much better at what they do than others. At some point the prospect will finally say to the storyteller, "I'd like to talk to you about something."

Not everyone can be a star in the game of turning social contacts into business opportunities. But just about everyone can improve their social techniques. If you follow the approach given in this section, you will, at the very least, meet some new and interesting people. You may also make some new friends. And every once in a while you will even land a new client!

So touch them on leather—and see where it leads you.

Sourcing

In this Part V we have discussed how to build sales through clients, how to sell to prospects, and how to turn social contacts into business opportunities. Each situation is handled differently, yet each makes use of the same basic concepts. Another important type of personal selling situation is turning your contacts with potential sources of business into actual business. Here again the situation is handled somewhat differently from the others, but the concepts you employ are the same: opening, interview, response, conclusion, and AI.

The first step in the process is to identify the people and operations that could help bring you new business. The specific ones will vary to a slight degree with the nature of the practice, but that is just a matter of individual selection. Some areas that you should explore include:

- Banks, particularly trust, loan, and work-out officers
- Lawyers and law firms, particularly those not having the same special expertise as your firm

- Commercial real estate firms
- Life insurance agencies
- Management consultants, particularly general business and financial management
- Local industrial development authorities
- Securities firms
- Corporate finance specialists
- Trade association specialists
- Trade association executives
- Accountants

In addition to a categorical list, consider those people who have contacts or clients in common with you. For example, if you have an up-to-date profile on each of your clients, you can easily determine who their accounting firms are and who their banks are. Assembling this list may even prove that your firm and certain banks or accounting firms have a number of clients in common. This forms an excellent basis for sitting down with these people and discussing how your respective operations could help each other do more business in the future. The final place to check for sources is your own list of personal contacts.

PERSONAL CONTACTS BEST

The most effective sources are generally those with whom you have had prior contact. If a potential source does not know you or at least about you, it may take a while for that person or group to feel that they know you and what you can do well enough to be giving you leads and referrals. On the other hand, we know of many cases where an intelligent, effective presentation to a brand new source began leading to new business opportunities almost immediately. As with anything involving personal selling, a lot depends on the people and the chemistry between them.

After you have prepared your initial list of potential source contacts, you must do some research on them before you make contact. Learn as much as you can about the state of their business or practice, what they do, who their customers or clients are, etc. Also try to determine if any of them work with or know any of your clients, contacts, or friends. This will not only provide an opening when you make contact, if you do not already know the source, but also provide some indications as to what the source might do for you, and what you in turn might do for the source.

If you have identified an organization that you feel should be a good potential source but do not know anyone there, start at the top. If it is an accounting firm, contact the managing partner; if it's a bank, contact the heads of the appropriate departments. Presidents of banks are not usually good initial sources unless they are also personal contacts; department heads are much closer to the "firing line," i.e., the specific kinds of opportunities you are seeking.

As we discussed in Part II on Marketing Activities, some of the sources may also be prospective clients. Don't confuse the relationship, however, and try to work on both objectives simultaneously. Treat them primarily as sources and you will, in the process, have also done the proper marketing job toward them as prospects.

The objectives in selling to sources are several:

1. To help each other out in business.
2. To learn about:
   a. Them.
   b. Their clients and customers and the needs of the clients and customers that you and your firm could fulfill.
   c. Who are the other people in their operation that should be contacted.
3. To educate them about what you and your firm do, and specifically what you could do that would help them.
4. Perhaps to have the source as a client.

IT MUST BE MUTUAL

The main point that you want to examine with each and every source is how you can help each other out in business. This is not a subcontractor relationship you are discussing but a mutual-referral relationship that could prove beneficial to both parties. This is the key of most good source relationships, identifying what you can do to help your source as well as what the source can do to help you. Sometimes these mutual benefits are very direct, such as referrals, introductions, and joint ventures. In other cases they may be very indirect or subtle. We know a number of source relationships where it appears that there is very little the law firm can do for the source. In many of these cases, the return benefit the source receives is from the people they introduce the law firm to; the law firm is the vehicle through which the source can establish mutually beneficial relationships with other people. In these three-cornered (or more) relationships, everyone benefits: the law firm, the source, and its contacts.

And so it goes. This is why marketing to sources can be such an extremely important part of a firm's overall marketing program and why it must be done well. As with the other types of personal selling that we have discussed, the secret that ultimately makes the sale is the personal marketing skill of the attorney.

LEARN EVERYTHING

Part of the "selling job" entails getting the prospective source to tell you about themselves, their firm or operation, their clients and customers, and what the needs of their clients or customers are. You should record all this information in a file on that source. You also want to learn who else in the source's organization should be contacted and developed. In most accounting firms, for example, it is not enough to make contact with just one accountant, even if he or she is the managing partner. The word just doesn't get around the firm. In banks, as another example, it is generally not enough to meet with the head of the commercial lending department. You should also get to know some of the important lending officers. Source relationships generally start out as one-on-one relationships, but the personal contacts should be expanded to include all the individuals in an operation who might be helpful.

One way to institutionalize the source relationship to some degree is to involve a group of people in the source's operation with a group of lawyers from your firm. More on this a little later.

The next part of the selling job to sources is to educate them on the full capabilities of you and your firm. You must emphasize the particular areas where you can be of help to them. Finally, you may want to indicate, without stressing the point, that you would also be happy to have the source as a client—if it is appropriate or realistic. If, for example, you are developing a senior lending officer as a source, it probably is not appropriate to also indicate to that person that you would welcome the bank as a client. He or she is not in a position to do anything about it. Besides, they might feel this is the real reason for your contacting them. Or, if you are a tax attorney working with a securities firm, it would not be realistic to think that you would be retained as general counsel.

In preparation for your first serious contact with a potential source:

- Try to anticipate what you can do for them.
- Try to determine what it is you want them to do for you.
- Have some examples or case histories ready to relate.
- Have some ideas of how you want to follow up on the contact if the source is interested in working with you.

Now to the meeting, the actual personal selling situation with the source.

THE OPENING

You begin with the opening, the attention getter that will focus the person's thinking on the idea that you can help them (the first thing you want to put in their mind) and that they probably can help you (the second thing you want to put in their mind). An extremely successful consultant friend of mine calls this the "mutuality of interest." In this opening you are really establishing the tone not just of that meeting but of the entire relationship you hope to develop with that source. Therefore, you must give at least equal weight to determine what you can do for them as you do to what they can do for you.

The opening with a potential source is really quite simple. Don't beat around the bush, don't try to be subtle or indirect. This is a business discussion. Dive right in and set the stage with an opening statement that goes something like this:

"I want to explore with you how your operation and mine could help each other obtain more business. I have some ideas on the subject and I'd like to hear yours."

An opening along those lines almost always grabs the source's attention. But now, just as when you are selling to prospects, you stop. Don't give your ideas yet and don't tell about your operation. You need to know something more about the source's operation, so start the interview.

Unlike the other selling situations, the interview with a source is a mixture of both open-ended and direct questions. You want to learn everything you can about the source personally, the nature of their business, their operation and what it does. You are trying to spot opportunities where you and your firm can work with them. This usually calls for a great variety of questions. Don't conduct the interview like a trial lawyer cross-examining someone on the witness stand. If you listen attentively, show interest, and keep the discussion rolling, your questioning will have the right effect on the source.

You should probably be taking notes, even if you are talking over lunch or dinner. At least make a few summary notes so that the source realizes that you are treating the discussion and their remarks seriously.

At some point in the meeting the interview portion will come to a close, either because you have asked all the questions you can think of or because the source wants to learn some things about you. Now you are into the response.

DON'T TAILOR—EMPHASIZE

The response in this situation is not the same as in the other selling situations where you tailor your selling message to the points that were developed during the interview. In this case you want to tell the source everything that you and your firm do, even if some of it does not relate to what the source has just told you. Emphasize, however, the particular areas that do fit with what you've learned, and even refer back to the source's remarks during the interview. Be ready with examples that illustrate your points; they offer proof and support your presentation.

The question of fees may come up; the source will want to know how and what you charge. I feel it is best to avoid being too specific. Certainly you must give the source an idea of what your services cost. You want to avoid, however, giving the impression that your services are too expensive or that you have a preprinted price list. So give the source some idea, but make the point clear that the cost depends on each particular case. Lawyers, for obvious reasons, generally understand that better than anyone else—including management consultants!

When you are selling to sources, unlike when you are selling to prospects and social contacts, you should sell your entire firm and everything you do, not just what they define as their needs or wants. In a manufacturing sense, you are "selling from inventory" rather than "making to order." You want the source to know everything that your firm can do because some of your remarks may trigger other ideas they had not mentioned during your interview.

Now you are up to the conclusion, which in this case means "Where do we go from here?" Some of the possible conclusions are:

- You and the source agree on where you can help each other and how you can work together.
- The source wants to immediately introduce you and perhaps some of the attorneys in your firm to other people.
- The source wants you to meet other people in that operation in order to get the ball rolling.
- The source wants to think about it, which means they either don't know what you can do together or they are not interested.
- The source has all kinds of ideas on what you can do for them but none on what they can do for you.

TRY FOR CONTROL

The important point here, as in all other personal marking situations, is that you want to control the conclusion and, if at all possible, the next step. If the source wants to "think about it," try out a couple of ideas right then and there. Refer back to some of the points made during the interview, just as you would do with a prospect who was raising objections. If this doesn't develop into anything, ask if you can follow up to the source in a little while after they have had a chance to ponder your meeting. Make one follow-up attempt. If the source hasn't come up with any ideas or you can't interest them in any of yours, drop the effort and concentrate on other sources.

If the source has some ideas on things you can do for them but no thoughts on what they could do for you, consider whether you want to do anything or not. By now you will have developed a feeling about the person. You may conclude that this is the kind of person who will only take from you and never give anything in return; in other words, he or she won't be a source of new business, just a source of irritation. If you feel that way, do the "I want to think about it" routine yourself and see if they follow up to you. The chances are they won't. On the other hand, you may feel that the person has excellent potential as a source but wants to see how you or your firm perform before he or she commits to helping. If you feel that way, agree to do something. Then later on get together again and see what the person's attitude is. Some of the most effective sources do not jump at your first approach; they want to see what you can do. After you convince them that you have a lot to offer, they often become better sources of new business than those people that you "sold" right off the bat.

In cases where you and the source agree that there is potential in the relationship, you want to map out some course of action as part of the conclusion. Don't leave the matter up in the air; such things have a way of cooling off or getting lost very quickly. Discuss the next step that could be taken or things that each of you could explore. Some of the possibilities are:

- Arranging for you to meet potential prospects the source wants to introduce you to.
- Arranging for you to meet other people in the source's operation.
- Arranging for some of their people and your people to get together in a meeting.
- Joint projects that could be undertaken such as seminars, articles, working as a team with one of your clients or theirs.
- A social function that would bring the people in your respective operations together.
- A presentation you could prepare for their people on what you can do to help them.
- Clients of yours that you want to introduce to them.

You will see that many of the possibilities are joint activities. In the case of larger organizations, this is often the best means of "spreading the word." Two people can have a mutually beneficial relationship, but the benefits are multiplied many times over if that relationship can be institutionalized. This takes additional time, effort, and patience, but when it can be accomplished, it is a powerful source of new business.

DON'T DROP THE BALL

Whatever is concluded, the most important point in developing a good source relationship is to follow up on it, just as you would with a hot prospect. Don't depend on a one-shot get-together. Stay in touch, keep at it, even if nothing develops at first. After a while, evaluate whether the effort has been worth it. It may not be. But also remember that some of the best sources, particularly the institutional ones, take time to develop.

One other aspect of the follow-up to be considered is this: It may not be appropriate for one or both of you to continue the contact. Perhaps you are both heads of your own firms and the most effective development of the new relationship would be done by other people on that side and yours. Or your role may have been to make the initial contact, but now that the door is opened, someone above you or even below you in your firm would be more suitable to develop the relationship from there. In these cases you must designate, order, persuade, or cajole someone to pick up the ball and continue running with it. That is perfectly all right and very appropriate in some cases. Just one suggestion, however: Monitor what the results are, particularly in the early stages, to make sure that the relationship you initiated continues to develop.

As a consolation to those lawyers who are not comfortable selling to prospects—some of you can still be excellent developers of good sources. It's a different kind of personal marketing.

Using the Telephone Effectively in Business

Complaining about the telephone is as common a habit for many people as complaining about the weather. About the only people who don't complain about the phone are those who make a living by using it, such as telephone salespeople and stockbrokers. Yet think where your practice would be if you didn't have the telephone. You may not make your living by using the phone, but you certainly depend on the phone to help you practice law.

What is probably amounts to is that we consider the phone an annoyance when it interrupts us but we never give a second thought to using it ourselves and possibly interrupting others.

Either because so many people complain about the phone or because most of them simply take it for granted, few people learn to use the phone effectively in business. This results in a great number of missed opportunities, errors, misunderstandings, and even lost business. Yet none of this need be.

Using the telephone effectively is an important part of the personal marketing skills an attorney needs. It is essential, not only to market the practice but to conduct it as well. Because of this, we added a section on telephone etiquette and techniques to our personal marketing skills seminar several years ago. Many attendees wonder why we include that section until after we complete it; then they understand and appreciate it. The material in this section has been adapted from that seminar program.

In order to use the telephone effectively in business, there are only three things to remember: voice, inflection, and words.

YOUR TOOLS ARE LIMITED

Most people do not stop and think that, when they use the telephone, the communications tools available to them are very limited. The person you are communicating with cannot see you. They cannot read the expression on your face. If they don't understand what you are saying, they can't try to watch your lips. You can't gesture, you can't touch. You can't see the person's reaction to what you are saying. You can't write out something or draw a diagram if they don't understand your point. You have only three communications tools at your disposal: your voice, your inflection, and your words. While this makes the communication process more difficult, it also means you only have three things to remember. Therefore, you must make the best of it, which really isn't that hard to do.

Voice: Speak *into* the mouthpiece, not over or around it. If you do this, people can hear you and understand you much more easily. It also means that you can speak in your normal conversational voice. Have you ever noticed how on a long-distance call some people automatically raise their voices and some even shout into the phone? We're not talking about when the connection is bad; most of the time this is just human nature. You don't have to do this if you just speak into the mouthpiece. The phone is a marvelous device, designed to carry your normal speaking voice almost anywhere in the world; so let it do its work.

Inflection: Some people freeze up on the telephone. They speak unnaturally, without any inflection. They talk *at* the phone. When they do, the party on the other end often misses much of what they say as well as the way in which they intend it to be taken. Relax. Instead of speaking into the instrument, forget you have it in your hand. Picture the person you are talking to as sitting right in front of you. Speak to the person, gesture, stand, sit, pace. Be as natural as if you were carrying on the conversation in person. Your voice will then have the right inflection and will convey all the unspoken messages you want it to carry.

Words: Speak distinctly, and perhaps just a little slower than you would if you were talking to the other party in person. Try to use the shortest and simplest words you can.

To the above three points we should add another that you should follow whenever you are talking to anyone, in person or on the phone: concentrate. Concentrate both on what you want to say and on what the other person is saying to you. This is even more important on the phone than in person.

If you keep the above points in mind—and that means you should continually practice and work at it—you will find that you are getting more benefit out of your time on the phone. And the people you are talking to will feel the same way.

If, in addition to that, you master certain telephone techniques and etiquette, you will find that the telephone has become an effective aid to your practice rather than an annoying interruption.

PREPARE FOR EVERY CALL

Before you place a call, stop and think what the purpose of the call is. What are the points you want to cover? If you are calling for one particular reason, are there other things you should remember to cover in the same call? Whom do you want to talk to, or will you have to ask for the person who handles such-and-such?

If there is more than one point you want to cover, make a few notes and have them in front of you. If you have a lot of things to cover, make an outline. In any case, be ready to take notes. Many a contract or business deal was saved because someone kept good notes of an important phone conversation and even dated them as well.

If you are placing the call yourself, ask for the party you want as soon as the phone is answered. If you are calling long distance, either direct dial or on one of the phone services, immediately say, "I'm calling long distance for _____." Operators, secretaries, and most other people treat a long distance call with considerably more urgency than they do a local call. Unless it's a person-to-person call, they won't know you're calling long distance unless you tell them.

(If you want to have some fun testing this idea, call back someone locally whom you were just unable to reach because he was "tied up in a meeting." Say you are calling long distance. Many times you will get through to the person without being told he's "tied up in a meeting.")

Identify yourself, don't wait to be asked. There are some exceptions to this, particularly if you are trying to reach someone who you know doesn't want to talk to you. But we are talking about the greatest percentage of calls. When you identify yourself immediately in a clear, strong voice, you convey a sense of authority and conviction that generally causes the person on the other end to give more attention to your call. If you feel it is necessary or helpful, also give your firm name.

If you are calling someone you don't know on the reference of someone they do know, also give that information at the start. "Ms. Smith may not recognize my name. I am calling at the suggestion of _____." This often saves time and sometimes gets you through to people the first time, particualrly if your reference is important to the person you are calling.

WHEN YOU CAN'T REACH THE PARTY

If you cannot reach the party you want, you have a number of things to consider. The first is to find out if the party is away, out for a while, or just tied up. Then you should decide:

- If you should speak to anyone else.
- If you want to leave a message.
- If you will call back.
- If you want to have the party call you back.

If the person will be able to call you back when you will either be out or tied up, tell the person taking the message. It borders on rudeness when you are told that the person will call you back in a few minutes and you know you will not be able to take the call. Tell the message-taker your schedule, such as, "I will be out until this afternoon. Will you ask her to call me back after three?" Your message, along with your obvious respect for the other person's times, will be conveyed and will earn you and your future phone calls the respect they deserve.

When you are calling a prospect or a person who does not know you, I strongly believe it is better if you leave word that you called and that you will call back, rather than expecting the person to call you back. When you are calling a prospect, you are really the "salesperson." Experienced and successful salespeople will tell you it is poor technique to expect the prospect to spend their time and money to call you back so you can try to sell them something. When it comes to leaving a call-back message for someone you do not know, think of how you react when the same thing happens to you. Most of us have enough call-backs we have to make to people we do know (some of whom we may not want to talk to), and that is generally annoying enough. When you receive a message to call back someone you don't know, unless it is a famous or important person you'd like to know, you are probably even more annoyed. The chances are you put that message at the bottom of the pile—and may not get around to returning the call at all.

If you are going to call the party back, try to find out when they will be available. If you can call then, say so. In other words, make an appointment to call back. It will save your time. It will also convey to the person taking the message both your efficiency and the importance of your call.

One more point: Always *ask* to have the person call you back, don't tell them to call you back.

DON'T WASTE TIME

When you reach the party you want, identify yourself again unless the person addresses you by name. Assuming that this is primarily or totally a business call, state the purpose of your call as quickly and clearly as you can. Don't waste a person's time, particularly when you are calling at their office, with irrelevant comments or conversation before coming to the point. This, of course, can vary depending on your relationship with the person you are calling. The best bet, however, is to come to the point before they get annoyed and wonder why you are calling.

Once you have said why you are calling, listen and concentrate on what the other person is saying. Close your eyes if necessary. If there are distractions at your end of the line, try to stop them. Take notes—fast, brief, but complete enough so you can understand them. Redo them right after the call if necessary. Try not to interrupt the person. Show courtesy and you will generally receive it in return. And remember: voice, inflection, words.

When you are calling a prospect to set up a meeting, don't try to interview the prospect over the phone. There are, however, certainly things you do want to do on this call. Clarify the objective of the meeting. The best way to do this is to "ask to ask" so that you can be prepared for the meeting and also to bring other people with you if appropriate. Obtain the names and positions of other people who might be attending the meeting with the prospect. Establish the time, place, and expected length of the meeting. If it is for lunch or dinner, establish who will make the reservations. (In most cases you should unless the prospect is insistent on handling it. After all, he or she is the prospect and you are the salesperson.) At the end of the call, repeat the date, time, and place of the meeting. It is amazing how often in these circumstances you say one thing and the party on the other end hears another. Make every effort not to have that happen.

If the meeting was set up some time in advance, it is a good idea to call the day before and confirm things.

If you are calling a prospect to discuss something you want to discuss, stop and think if the prospect will be interested—or if you can make them interested. If not, maybe you shouldn't call. If you are calling to follow up on something, remind the person immediately what it is. Not only does this focus attention on what you want to discuss, it also reminds the person that you follow up on things. This indicates that you and your firm would do the same if they were a client.

Finally, if you are calling a prospect "just to keep in touch"—don't call. You may think you are showing your interest and furthering your sales effort with the prospect. The chances are, however, that the prospect may be annoyed and will probably think you have nothing else to do. *Always have a reason when you call a prospect,* preferably one that will interest the prospect too.

Being Busy

In this Part V on Personal Marketing Techniques, we began by stating the two basic objectives in any firm's marketing program:

1. To increase the opportunities *for* additional business.
2. To convert these opportunities *into* additional business.

The real purpose of all the brochures, newsletters, seminars, articles, PR programs, advertising, community activities, contributions, and everything else is to get more clients and prospects interested in talking to the law firm about representing them. The lawyers in the firm must then capitalize on these opportunities and convince the clients to use more of the firm's services and convince prospects to select the firm in the first place.

The accomplishment of the first objective depends to a greater or lesser degree on personal marketing by the attorney. The accomplishment of the second objective depends *entirely* on personal marketing by the attorney.

Many people continually say how busy they are. This seems to be particularly true of lawyers. More than any other group of professionals or business people, they seem to be always talking about how much work they have to do. It sometimes seems as if they enjoy being overworked or at least enjoy giving the impression that they are overworked.

But as Shakespeare put it, "Aye, there's the rub."

DEFEATING YOURSELF

The "rub" is that many times the "overworked" attorney, who may indeed be working very hard at marketing his or her practice, is at the same time keeping new business away. By constantly giving the impression of being overworked, they discourage people from approaching them to take on their work because they feel the attorney wouldn't have the time to handle it. By their own words they destroy the effectiveness of their own marketing program. Ah, you say, that's the Catch-22 of being a lawyer. And it is; there's no doubt about it. No professional, particularly a sole practitioner, can afford to look as if he or she has spare time on his or her hands. People will interpret this as meaning they aren't as successful, and therefore probably aren't as good, as other lawyers who appear to be a lot busier. On the other hand, if the sole practitioner looks as if he or she can't even handle all the work already on hand, people who might want to use them won't even bring the subject up because they feel the lawyer just couldn't handle any more.

This is a book on marketing, not on time management. We are not going to discuss whether or not the attorney is using time efficiently. From a marketing viewpoint, however, we must discuss whether or not the attorney gives the impression of using time efficiently.

It is a fine line the professional must walk, particularly the lawyer and the accountant. He or she must let the world know that they are busy because they have a lot of work from a lot of clients. Most people will therefore assume that such a person must be good because they are so busy. On the other hand, a lawyer cannot afford to give the impression—even if it is true—that he or she couldn't take on any more clients. Prospective new clients will then never approach them or the firm.

The marketing message that attorneys must somehow convey is that they and the firm are very busy, and by implication therefore very good, but never too busy to handle one more client. If you only remember one point out of this part of the book, let it be that one.

PART VI
COMPENSATION

"The System"

I have worked with enough law firms over the years to know that "The System" works against the marketing program—unless "The System" is changed.

By "The System" I mean the fact that the name of the game is billable hours. Much of the firm's fee income is based on billable hours; associate promotions to partner are based in part on billable hours, and partner income is largely determined by the billable hours and fees generated by the partner. It doesn't take the new associate very long to realize that, no matter how much the partners may talk about the importance of marketing, billable hours are what count. Marketing doesn't *really* count because it cuts into the number of billable hours a person can carry. Of course some partners, particularly the "old guard," will say that marketing must be done on your time. To some degree this is still true. However, the marketing of legal services has changed so much in recent years that it is no longer realistic to say that *all* marketing must be done on a lawyer's own time.

Years ago, marketing, or business development, generally meant being active in a number of outside organizations and little else. Most of the time required was spent after working hours. Billable time was affected little, if at all. In fact, about the only time you could do any marketing—by this definition—was on your own time (nights and weekends) because that was when most of the things that were considered marketing activities took place.

The world has changed. Much of the marketing activity a law firm must conduct these days cannot be done at night and on weekends. Even if talks and seminars were prepared on a lawyer's own time, they must be given during the business day. Most client reviews can't be held after business hours because the clients don't want to give up their own time. Attendance at trade shows and conventions, involvement with certain business groups, many PR activities and other marketing activities must generally be done during the business day—in addition to, perhaps, some nights and weekends. Furthermore, the marketing load in a firm today can no longer be carried by just a few partners as it could in years past. Everyone in the firm can and must do something. Therefore, the total number of hours a firm must devote to marketing today is far larger than it used to be.

ACTIONS SPEAK LOUDER THAN WORDS

In order to have a successful marketing program and therefore to keep on growing, a firm must *act* as if marketing is important, not just *say* it is. A firm that still maintains the old-fashioned attitude that "marketing must be done on your own time" is out of touch with the times because:

1. As discussed above, much of the marketing cannot be done on the person's own time.
2. The firm still has not realized that marketing time is just as important as billable time.

What this all means is that a firm must recognize that an effective marketing program *may* reduce individual billable hours although it will *increase* the firm's total billable hours and, therefore, its fee income and its profitability. To expect all attorneys, partners, and managers to carry a heavy load of billable time and also devote worthwhile time to effective marketing is to live in a dream world. Firms that are in step with the times, firms that understand that time must be devoted to marketing and management as well as to clients, live in the real world. They have modernized their thinking on what it takes to build and manage their practices today.

They have also adjusted "The System" in their firms to conform to the realities of legal practice today. The firms that are in step with the times realize that billable hours are no longer the only thing a firm must give attention to. They realize that billable hours are no longer the only measure of an attorney's productivity and value to the firm. And they also realize that a traditional compensation system based almost entirely on billable hours is actually working to the disadvantage of the firm and its people.

This means that "The System" must be adjusted so that it supports the marketing program instead of working against it.

Forms of Compensation

The simple fact of life in a law firm is this: most of the attorneys will not take marketing seriously until it is given recognition in their compensation. All the meetings, memos, training programs, and everything else that is done to urge people to get out and market will not have nearly the effect they should have if the people aren't compensated for doing it.

There are several forms of compensation:

Recognition
Promotion
Money

In a law firm, as in almost any business, all three are necessary; none can be omitted.

RECOGNITION

Recognition is often overlooked, particularly when it comes to marketing. The partner or partners who brought in a large new client may receive a congratulatory handshake from some of the people in the firm but that is about it. Word will spread around the firm, sometimes quickly and sometimes not too quickly, that the firm has a big new client; not too often will the word also spread on who was instrumental in bringing this important piece of new business into the firm. Likewise, the person who works closely with a small client and helps it grow into a much larger operation is rarely recognized. And the attorney who takes a litigation client and subsequently sells him or her on using the firm as general counsel is almost never saluted as a good business developer.

The lawyer who spends his or her own time writing articles for publication; the people who develop and give seminars that spread the firm's expertise and reputation to nonclients; the person who writes and edits the firm's newsletters—few of these people ever receive the recognition that their time and efforts, as well as the results, deserve.

The tradition in most firms has been to not provide recognition for marketing efforts or even marketing successes. It is somehow considered unprofessional or perhaps unimportant. Maybe it is just overlooked. If the marketing program is going to be successful, however, recognition must be given to those who participate meaningfully in it.

One of the best ways to provide this recognition is by giving firm-wide publicity to people and their marketing activities. Internal marketing memos or the internal marketing bulletin discussed in the section on organization, administration, and communications are an extremely effective way to publicize the people and their marketing activities throughout the firm. Talks that lawyers have given, articles and books that have been published, organizations and groups that attorneys are active in (not just members of), ideas that people have come up with—all these and more should be publicized in some way around the firm. When a new client is obtained, whether large or small, word should be put out along with recognition of who was responsible for bringing the client in. If a large new client is obtained, a special memo to everyone in the firm, lawyers and support staff as well, would give the event and the people responsible the recognition they deserve.

Another form of recognition is to give people responsibility and then publicize it. If two associates are appointed to the firm's marketing committee, this should be noted. When a marketing coordinator is named, this should be announced. If a young partner is given the responsibility for publicity and press relations, this should be known by everyone. If another partner has been given the responsibility to market the firm's expertise in a specific industry, this should be publicized as well. Giving responsibility to various people spreads the marketing workload around. Publicizing this lets the rest of the firm know that the people who devote time and effort to marketing are recognized for it.

There are other forms of recognition that could be considered, depending on the personality and style of the firm. Whatever is done, the effect should be to show that marketing is a serious matter and that the people who are active in the marketing program are singled out for recognition.

CONSIDER IN PROMOTIONS

Participation in the marketing program should be included in the factors that are considered for election to partners. Associates must also be aware that this is considered. Doing this accomplishes two things.

First, it again emphasizes the importance of marketing in the firm. Second, it helps the associates become more well-rounded rather than one-dimensional as they move up in the firm. Law firms can no longer afford to hire and develop people who are only technocrats. Today's business environment requires that lawyers be well-rounded people with at least adequate if not superior technical skills, the ability to communicate in writing as well as in person, good interpersonal skills, and at least some management ability.

Marketing activities certainly cannot be considered for the promotion of lower-level associates. There is little they can do to aid the marketing program other than to develop peer relations within client organizations and to keep on the alert for possible business opportunities. Nor should they be thinking much about marketing at this time. Their first priorities should be adjusting to the firm and learning how to practice law. As an associate moves up, however, increasing weight should be placed on marketing activity. By the time an associate is a candidate for partner, marketing should have as much importance as any other factor.

Recognition and promotion are basically qualitative forms of compensation. Now let's address the quantitative form: money.

Money

My old skipper in the Navy used to say, "The most sensitive nerve in the body of the human male is on the left hip," meaning where the wallet is. I have never heard anyone express that more colorfully—or accurately. Money is still the single most important form of compensation. Recognition and promotion are also important; they cannot be ignored. After a certain point, however, cold hard cash is the thing that counts the most.

If marketing is really important to a law firm, its compensation program should recognize that, not ignore it or work against it. The problem with the traditional forms of compensation is that they are based almost entirely on billable hours. What then is the answer?

I do not pretend to have the perfect answer to a compensation formula that will meet the needs of every law firm of any size anywhere in the country. If I did, I would have been out marketing it long before this. I don't think there is any perfect formula. I do, however, have some thoughts on the subject which may help each firm work out the formula that is best for it.

As you have probably gathered by now, I believe that any law firm that is going to survive and grow from now on must excel in three areas: technical, marketing, and management. The size of the firm is not so important in my opinion, even though there are experts who claim that a firm must achieve a certain "critical mass" or it cannot survive. That may be true, although I do not agree. Even if it is true, however, that still does not address the need for legal marketing, and management ability in a firm.

If all three areas are essential to a firm, its people should be paid accordingly. A compensation system that only recognizes billable hours and total fees generated is hastening that firm down the road to extinction. A firm should pay its people, starting with partners, for both effort and accomplishment in all three areas, not just one. In other words, the people in the firm, particularly the partners, should have the opportunity to earn as much money as possible regardless of which area or areas they concentrate on.

RECOGNIZE EACH PERSON'S STRENGTHS

There are very few people in law (or in any other field) who can excel in every functional area—in this case, legal work, marketing, and management. Each person, however, will eventually develop particular ability in one and perhaps two areas. Since a law firm needs people with particular abilities in all three areas, the attorneys should be encouraged to develop in the area or areas they are most qualified in—and they should be compensated accordingly. If a person has good marketing skills and is successful at marketing, their earnings should not be penalized just because they are not also carrying 1,700 chargeable hours a year. If another person has the ability to manage an office or even the firm, he or she should not be penalized because they are not carrying the same client responsibilities other partners may have. By the same token, the partners who want to spend all their time serving clients and excelling in the practice of law should not suffer because they are not bringing in new business or managing the firm's total operations.

To sum this up, as long as an attorney is performing well in an area that the firm needs, that attorney should have the opportunity to make as much money as someone who is performing equally well in another area.

Let me hasten to say that I fully realize that the main business of a law firm is to practice law, not marketing or management. That means that most of the people should spend most of their time doing that. While not at all perfect, billable hours has been the accepted measure of productivity for most kinds of legal work as well as the basis, in most cases, of charging for the firm's services. I am not advocating a change in that, at least not in this book. But since the firm's internal needs require excellence in other areas as well, these factors should be included in determining how much its people earn.

EVALUATING MARKETING PERFORMANCE

Whenever you address the subject of compensation, you must also address the question of productivity or performance evaluation. How do you do this in terms of marketing?

In a law firm, a person's marketing productivity or performance must be measured with the following factors in mind:

Effort or participation
Responsibility
Accomplishment

Accomplishment should be further analyzed in terms of:

New business brought in
Additional business developed
Firm image or projection

At the medium associate level (we have already agreed that the lower levels have very little personal involvement in marketing) the emphasis must be on effort or participation. A one-year associate has little opportunity to assume responsibility for any part of the marketing program, to bring in new business, to spread the firm's reputation, or to develop additional business with clients. Therefore, effort is about the only thing that can be measured. What ideas have they come up with? What client needs have they spotted that have led to the client making more use of the firm's services? What outside activities, professional or community, have they become involved in that could be of benefit to the firm?

After a person has been an associate for a while, he or she should be measured by additional criteria, including a higher level of effort or participation in the marketing areas. Has the associate assumed responsibility for some part of the marketing program, written any articles, given any talks, or developed or participated in any seminars? Has the associate convinced any of the clients he or she is working with that they have need for additional firm services? Has the associate even brought in any new business, alone or in conjunction with others?

EVALUATING THE PARTNERS

Finally, at the partner level, all three factors must be equally included in the marketing performance evaluation: participation, responsibility, and accomplishment. New business generation is the easiest to measure, although the origination credit for a new client may often be shared with several other attorneys. Sometimes, the larger the new client, the more people involved in landing it. Additional business developed with current clients is sometimes harder to measure, either because it is not recorded or because it may just be the result of the client's own growth or initiative.

Accomplishments in raising the firm's image, spreading its reputation, or increasing its visibility in its market areas requires a great degree of qualitative judgment because they cannot be measured precisely. A partner who devotes hundreds of hours a year to civic and charitable activities, thereby raising the firm's image and visibility, may be extremely important to the firm's marketing program even if he or she never personally brings in one new client. Or a partner who is recognized as a leading authority in a particular industry and is responsible for developing the firm's reputation in that industry may have accomplished as much as a partner who brings in several new clients a year. These are difficult accomplishments to measure and to rank. Just because they are difficult, however, does not mean that evaluation should not be attempted. Even an imprecise evaluation is better than totally disregarding them as being of no importance to the firm.

FOUR AREAS TO MEASURE

Because of the many factors involved as well as the qualitative judgments that must be made, I favor a compensation program that evaluates a person in all four areas: legal ability (including quality of work), billable hours (you can't eliminate them), marketing performance, and management ability. Whatever method is used to "score" the evaluations, I believe each of the areas should have equal weight. No one should be penalized because he or she scores low in one or two areas as long as he or she scores high in other areas. Most attorneys will have a billable hours goal for the year. The exceptions would generally be partners who were given other full-time responsibilities such as being managing partner. In setting these billable hours goals, however, the firm must recognize and allow for the particular strengths of each individual and the firm's objectives for the year. If some partners are extremely successful marketers and only adequate as practicing lawyers, they should be given a lower billable hours goal and a higher marketing hours goal than someone whose greatest strengths lie in client service or practice management. The important point is to set these goals for each person at the partner and associate level rather than categorically assign all partners or all associates the same number of hours.

BONUSES

Some firms, particularly when they are starting out, pay bonuses to the lawyers who bring in new business. Some even go so far as to pay a small bonus for each article written and published, each talk given or seminar participated in, and so on.

While many of these firms claim this system is successful, I do not favor it. For one thing, I think it is unprofessional. The quality of a new client should be as important as the amount of fees it will produce. A firm must have the right and the responsibility to refuse a client that does not meet its criteria and objectives. Law is not the same kind of business as selling cars or shoes or insurance. In those fields and in hundreds of others, bonuses and commissions have proven the best forms of compensation for salespeople. The law is very different. Its business is not just sales. A firm must have as its first priority quality work in both the technical and the marketing sense and quality clients—not pure "tonnage." A bonus program for new business goes against this.

Second, I think it is an unwise policy to put a price tag, in effect, on each possible marketing activity. These activities should have some intrinsic personal value to the attorney as well as to the firm. Furthermore, determining what will be paid for each activity gets ridiculous. Is a talk to twenty CEOs worth more money than a talk to thirty house counsels? Is a four-page article worth twice as much as a two-page article? Is a committee chairmanship worth more in the local bar association than in an industry trade association? There is just no way to "price out" marketing activities intelligently and no reason for doing so.

Those are my thoughts on compensation. While they may disappoint those people who are looking for a magic formula, I believe they address all the issues that should be involved and provide sound guidelines for each firm to develop its own program. The concept behind them is to adjust "The System" to support a firm's needs in marketing and management, not oppose them.

PART VII
THE SECRETS OF
SUCCESSFUL MARKETING

Every author must hold the reader until the end. In a well-written murder mystery that is fairly easy: don't reveal who the murderer is until the last page. In a book of this kind, however, it is more of a challenge.

For this reason, as well as my feeling that they do not fit in appropriately any earlier, I have saved the Secrets of Successful Marketing until the end.

We have already discussed everything that I believe is involved in marketing legal services, from a definition of what marketing is all the way to an approach to compensation that encourages marketing activity. The two essential ingredients, the secrets if you will, that make marketing successful have flowed throughout this book, just beneath the surface. Now they should be identified. They are:

Attitude
Commitment

Marketing is really an attitude that all the people in the firm, attorneys and support staff, adopt toward their practice. It involves placing the client—and the client's needs and wants—first and managing the firm's entire practice with the idea of serving the client. Once this attitude has been understood and adopted, commitment must follow. When a firm makes a real commitment to being successful in its marketing, all the many steps and procedures we have discussed begin to fall into place. No firm can be successful in marketing its practice without first having the right attitude and a definite commitment.

The best example I know of the attitude and commitment needed for successful marketing is in the last paragraph of a memo to all the lawyers in one of our client firms from the chairman of the firm:

We have collectively come to the realization that practice development is critical to our future success. It is as important to us as the legal services we provide our clients and it should be done with the same care, sophistication and professional responsibility we accord our clients.

On that thought, I rest my case.

INDEX